WEB SITE MANAGEMENT

WEB SITE MANAGEMENT

Excellence

Linda G. Brigman

WEB SITE MANAGEMENT EXCELLENCE

Library of Congress Catalog No.: 96-69967

ISBN 0-7897-0911-2

98 97 96   4 3 2 1

Interpretation of the printing code: The rightmost double-digit number is the year of the book's printing; the rightmost single-digit number, the number of the book's printing. For example, a printing code of 96-1 shows that the first printing of the book occurred in 1996.

Composed in *Bergamo* and *MCPDigital* by Que Corporation

CREDITS

PRESIDENT
Roland Elgey

PUBLISHER
Joseph B. Wikert

EDITORIAL SERVICES DIRECTOR
Elizabeth Keaffaber

MANAGING EDITOR
Sandra Doell

MARKETING DIRECTOR
Lynn E. Zingraf

PUBLISHING MANAGER
Jim Minatel

EDITOR
Robin Drake

PRODUCT MARKETING MANAGER
Kim Margolius

REVIEWER
Ed Fang

ACQUISITIONS COORDINATOR
Jane Brownlow

BOOK DESIGNERS
Ruth Harvey
Barb Kordesh

COVER DESIGNER
Dan Armstrong

PRODUCTION TEAM
Marcia Brizendine
Brian Grossman
Jason Hand
Daniel Harris
Daryl Kessler
Michelle Lee
Ryan Oldfather
Laura Robbins
Bobbi Satterfield
Donna Wright

INDEXER
Craig Small

For Roy Schonberg, Liese Tajiri, and Eileen Gordy, who have helped me maintain my sanity through the challenges, the frustrations, and the rants.

ACKNOWLEDGMENTS

I couldn't have written this book without the help and encouragement of a lot of good people. Thanks to Robin Drake, my editor, for all her help and suggestions, and for kindly undangling my participles; and to Jim Minatel, publishing manager, for his interest in the subject matter and for guiding the project through from beginning to end.

My special thanks to those who've read and offered suggestions as I prepared the text: June Maxwell at the University of NC (from whom I stole a few paragraphs); and Clare Durst at Brown University, Monica Reynolds at Labrador Internet Consulting, and Jim Wright at RTI for their suggestions in matters technical. They attempted to steer me in the right directions. If I missed a turn here and there, it's my own fault and none of theirs.

To my family, Helen, Debbie, and Charlene Brigman, and my coworkers, Bruce Young and James Brown, thanks for your patience and for picking up the slack while I worked on this project.

Many, many thanks to those who have encouraged me to write over the past few years: Dave Jacobson at Brandeis (it's not exactly a "beach" book, Dave, but it will have to do); my very special e-mail support and grouse group (who offered to write my biography in some wonderfully creative ways); and Mac Parks at the University of Washington. I'd never have had the courage to do this without you.

Last, and far from least, my sincere thanks and love to Marcus Speh at Andersen Consulting in London—a good friend and the very best of mentors from my earliest days on the Web. You convinced me that even an old dog could learn new tricks, and the Web has certainly taught me a whole host of new tricks. Now, Marcus, dear—if you would send me your special formula for untangling myself from the Web for a few days, I'd be ever so grateful.

About the Author

Linda G. Brigman lives in Durham, NC. Her résumé includes (when she has the nerve to go back that far) personnel placement, advertising sales and design, meeting and convention management, and management of a non-profit state association. After a $1\frac{1}{2}$-year adventure into the world of survey research at Research Triangle Institute (RTI), where she served on a national study sponsored by the CDC, in 1989 she transferred into the world of networking at RTI and acquired her very own tool bag—complete with all the requisite screwdrivers, cable testers, and a magic wand. Network logistics and monitoring the LAN and WAN for RTI (with 16 buildings and 7 off-site offices) consumed her time until 1994, when she assumed her role as Webmaster simply because she had had the uncommon good fortune to meet some of the brightest and the best of the Web in her personal wanderings on the Internet in 1992.

Her credits on the Web include assisting with the Globewide Network Academy Web site, which won the 1994 "Best of the Web" award for its (completely virtual) campus, and providing HTML coding and support for GNA's first C++ course text. She presently administers RTI's external Web server and intranet with the welcome addition of three staff members who have become as entangled in the Web as she is.

While resigned to the title *Webmaster*, she much prefers her very unofficial title of *WebVixen*.

At present, she's not particularly creative or interesting, and is a very tired person. Prior to writing this book, she was the antithesis of the above, and she dearly hopes to regain those qualities once the blessed thing is published. As do her friends, relatives, cats, and ailing PC, who have all suffered through the exercise. She is planning her next authoring project (yeah, right): an instructional manual entitled "How to Get a Life on Your Coffee Break Without Pointing and Clicking."

CONTENTS

TABLE OF CONTENTS

Contents

Contents

Contents

Contents

Contents

FOREWORD

In 1994, when businesses first began to consider the possibilities of the Web, it wasn't unusual for some (generally technical) department's employees within a business to build a Web site—usually small, and seldom what a Marketing department would have wanted if the people in Marketing had even heard of the Web, and most hadn't. Those businesses had a year or so to quietly—almost invisibly—learn the workings of the Web, Web servers, and the culture of what audience there was on the Web then, and it wasn't a particularly large one. The Web browsers that were available were, for the most part, limited to viewing text only. Mosaic, the first graphical browser, was still an infant; while the brightest minds among the Internet literati were already predicting an amazing future for the Web, that future seemed a long way away.

Two years later—not so long chronologically, but an eternity in the fast-paced market that is now the Web—things have changed dramatically. The media found the Web and fell in love. The public followed right behind and was captivated. The halcyon days are well and truly over for businesses on the Web. There's no more time to start slow and learn at a leisurely pace. Business has found the Web and it's time to do business on it.

If you're considering building a Web site, you simply don't have the luxury of near-obscurity to learn what you'll need to learn for the Web market. You need to do some quick studying and have a production Web site that hits the ground running. It's going to require an investment of time and money, and you'll have to justify that expenditure to senior management or a Board of Directors, or to yourself if you happen to be the ultimate decision-making authority.

You'll also need to know what's in store for you—how many people are going to be involved in the Web project, how much time it will take to accomplish if you *do* decide your future is on the Web, and what work will need to be done once you bring that Web site up and sit back to study it. And you need to sort out the hype from the reality.

None of those things are easy to do. The Web is so completely hyped by the media and by those who love it (and we are many), and so completely new and exciting, that it's all too easy to be pushed into adopting technologies and strategies that not only won't work for your business, but could do it harm rather than good. You need practical advice and common sense methods for approaching a Web site project. I attempt to give you some of that here.

Some people will read this book and assume that I'm not at all enamored of the technologies. They would be very, very wrong. They not only fascinate and draw me, but if I could use every single one of them on our Web pages I would be the happiest Webmaster on the planet. This book is conservative because I'm conservative in my approach to a Web site.

Business is still business—it moves many times more slowly than most of us would like, even those of us who are firmly grounded in its principles. But the Web demands that we move a bit more quickly than other media we've experienced. It also demands that we learn new tricks and a new audience.

It's worth the effort. Trust me on that small point. I'm not the only Webmaster I know who has spent many years in business and finds herself positively *captured* by this new medium—one that requires creativity, organizational skills of the highest level, and a sense of real connection with the audience that is the Web.

I've survived the entrance of the marketing folks and the designers who followed the media into the Web and were entranced—and appalled—but who didn't understand the culture of the Web or how to design for it. We've all learned. We had the luxury of learning a bit more slowly than you will. We're still learning, just as you will continue to learn.

Foreword

This book is designed to guide you through the planning and implementation of a Web site. That's nothing new in this market. There are a wealth of technical books that can assist you in that process. This one goes a bit further—and it doesn't even *attempt* to give you more than the most basic of the technical details that you'll have to learn to accomplish your Web site. You and your Web development staff can easily find those details—on the Web and on the shelves of your local bookseller.

In this book, you'll find the truth as I know it about the business of building a Web site, and what you can expect in the process. Conservative—yes, my approach to Web site management is conservative. A Web site is a business project that requires time, care, and consideration. You can't accomplish a good Web site without all of those if you intend to stay the course. I do hope you will. It's frustrating, annoying, and great fun.

I don't advocate technology for technology's sake. I do, however, advocate technology for the sake of expanding your business and for displacing (moving) some of that business from traditional places to this new one. A call that your technical support staff doesn't have to take is a call that can save you money. A product description that your sales staff doesn't have to mail is a product description that can save you money. A person you can teach about your business, who would never have learned about it otherwise, is a person who may produce business for you. Yes—a conservative approach. No hype. No promises of wealth and success—the facts, and just the facts, as I've learned them.

These lessons have been hard-learned and sometimes not learned pleasantly. I think I've avoided most shouting matches, though I've been sorely tempted to join the fray from time to time. You will be, too. I carry a pager. I use it (see Chapter 7). It's the nature of the beast. The Web is about learning and growing, and those of us who are in this business are forced to learn and grow with it.

Your Web site, if you choose to accept this rather hazardous (or, at the least, crazy-making) duty, will require you to use every diplomatic skill you've ever learned, and every ounce of common sense you ever thought you had (and will question from time to time). You'll question yourself a million times a day. That's good. It's healthy. Stress is inherent in this business, but it's inherent in every business. Nothing new. Nothing different. The Web is just a new medium and a very exciting one. I invite you to join those of us who are already there. Most of us are far from perfect. You're welcome to eclipse us. You'll give us a new challenge.

It's the Web. It's just never, ever dull.

◄ 1 ►

To Web or Not to Web—
That Is the Question

Do you have good reasons for
building a Web site?

◆

What's involved in creating
and maintaining a site?

◆

Do you know all the
pros and cons?

◆

Would it be safe to wait for a
while to get on the Web?

◆

How do you make
the decision?

It's all just too much! Suddenly it seems as though every company's ad carries a URL (Uniform Resource Locator), its location on the World Wide Web. You knew Time Warner was on the Web. That made perfect sense—big multimedia company with a world of resources—but Ed's Repair shop down the street? He's listed parts and labor prices and… what is *this*? a number you can call if your car happens to die and you're stranded with your cell phone and modem? Sure, Ed's got a pretty successful business, but you didn't know he was doing so well that he could join the ranks of such companies as Time Warner. Maybe you should look into this whole idea a little more, give some serious thought to putting your business on the Web? Maybe.

You're not a technoprimitive, exactly, but you're not a programmer either. You don't want to know all the technical things about how Web servers work, and you definitely don't want to learn how to code Web pages. You just want to know how you should go about deciding whether or not to build a Web site. These are the pertinent questions for which you need some hard answers:

- How complicated is it to build a Web site?
- What will a Web server do for my marketing efforts?
- What other benefits are there?
- Are there reasons not to have Web pages?
- What if we decide to wait for six months or a year before we have a Web site?

The purpose of this book is to provide some answers to these questions. And many more questions. Setting up and maintaining a Web site for your business isn't a one-time commitment. It's ongoing, and continued expenditures of time, effort, and money will be required to make the initial investment pay off for you. Is this really what you want to do? What you need to do? This book attempts to give you that information in as straightforward a manner as possible, with a minimum of technical or management jargon. The technical is unavoidable to an extent (and most of it isn't terribly difficult to understand). If you're seriously in need of infusions of paradigms, strawmen, and TQM, you'll have to take them in that one big gulp I just gave you, because you won't see those words again in this book. No doubt they'll be used in discussions of Web sites in your future, but for now the Web is new and it's developing its own language. If you decide to serve pages on the Web, that language may be yours; and this book may help you decide whether, when, and how to adopt the *lingua franca* of the Web. It can at least give you an idea of what will be expected of you as a manager, if you're adventurous enough to start your own Web site.

"BECAUSE IT'S COOL" ISN'T GOOD ENOUGH

The Web is cool. It's hip. You can't pick up a newspaper or magazine or turn on the TV without finding an article about the Internet or a piece about the Web. Entire magazines are devoted to surfing the Web and building better Web sites. The computer section at your local bookstore is overflowing with books about the Web. What was once a tool for educators, scientists, and students is suddenly a way for individuals and businesses to publish their ideas and plans to the world—with the advent of browsers like Netscape, Mosaic, Internet Explorer, and the many others that are widely available to take the mystery out of it all.

Putting your company on the Web is just, as the kids say, "way cool," but so is a swim in an icy pond—and it's possible that the latter might be more beneficial at this point. Before you tell Human Resources to place ads for a qualified Webmaster (the person who will direct and coordinate your efforts at Web spinning) or begin writing the Request for Proposals for consultants or Internet service providers, you need a reason to be on the Web. This is a business decision, not a lark. Ed's Repair Shop may buy a limo to ferry his customers and their laptops and cell modems around, but that doesn't necessarily mean you need to do the same. First you need to understand how it all works and what it can do for you.

The Facts (Minus Gory Details and Media Hype)

Let's first get what little you really should know about this technology out of the way. It isn't rocket science—though there are those who, for their own financial purposes, would have you believe that it is.

What Exactly Is the World Wide Web?

The World Wide Web is software. It runs on the Internet on hundreds of thousands of computers. Ten years ago, if you wanted to access information on the Internet, you needed to have some basic knowledge of a lot of different types of software to be able to locate and read or download the information. In 1989, Tim Berners-Lee recognized the need for some easier way to share the information that was then accessible only if you understood those many (and in many instances, arcane) protocols. His immediate goal was to make specific information available for researchers in the particle physics community. What he ultimately made, with a little help from his friends, was history. (This isn't information that you absolutely must know before you set up a Web site, but it really impresses people at cocktail parties if they haven't seriously considered setting up a Web site themselves.)

What Do You Need to Build a Web Site?

At a minimum, to serve documents to the World Wide Web, you (or the Internet service provider you hire) will need:

- **A reasonably powerful computer.** As in all things computerized, the more powerful the better—but you don't have to have a high-end,

8

super-fast computer to operate a Web site. You can initially get away with something as small as a 486/40 PC with 8MB of RAM. It won't be terribly fast, but it will get the job done.

- **Web server software.**
- **Internet access.**

You may eventually need much more, but that will depend on what, exactly, you want your site to do and how you decide to implement your plan. (For more details, read on—and then consult Chapter 2.)

BASICS OF WEB SERVER SOFTWARE

A Web server runs what is called a *hypertext transfer protocol daemon* (abbreviated *HTTPD*). Not to worry about the dangerous sound of such an animal (most people pronounce it *demon*, after all); it's just software. It's generally no more difficult to install on a computer than any other application software you are already running in your business.

You can get Web server software free on the Web, or you can purchase it. The software is available for every major operating system, so you don't need to purchase special equipment to operate a Web server. The server software, once installed, sits quietly on your computer waiting to (you guessed it) serve up Web pages that someone's browser requests. The server couldn't care less whether that file is straight text, a coded Web page, a sound file, or a movie. It's the browser's job to figure out what to do with it. Web servers don't yet have a union, but they've got one very well-defined job description—serve documents.

INTERFACING WITH THE USER'S BROWSER

The *browser*, on the other hand, has a long list of jobs to do. It has to display the text from the Web page and interpret any other types of files that may be resident on a page, whether those files are graphics or sound or programs that are coded to be called from the page. The original browsers could read text pages only. They couldn't interpret other types of files. As with all things on the Web, though, that situation changed very quickly. Now browsers run all sorts of *helper applications* to interpret a wide range of file types. Because the browser runs from your customer's desktop, you don't have to concern yourself with how that works.

It's true that Web pages must be coded to make them attractive for the browsers to display. *Hypertext Markup Language (HTML)* is what you use to accomplish that purpose. It's not rocket science either. If most people took a look at the source code for pages and took a few days to study the basics, Web service providers would have to start modifying their price lists downward. HTML is terribly simple to add to a document. You don't need any special software. Software is available that's helpful, but most people who do HTML coding don't trust that software yet. It tends to produce unpredictable results when exposed to various browsers (and a good Webmaster will test pages with more than one), and the coding is generally so simple that, well, 10-year olds are doing it. You can prepare the coded documents in any word processor or text editor. Hardly rocket science.

That's it. Painless technical stuff complete. You don't absolutely *need* to know more than that unless you're going to do the server installation and HTML coding yourself. Serving Web pages can be as simple or as complicated as your resources allow. The Web is simply the Internet with a twist or two (graphics, sound, etc.) and a lot fewer twists (protocols), too.

WHAT'S YOUR PLAN?

As with any other business venture, if you don't have a good plan for designing and implementing a Web site, don't build one. You and everyone associated with the project will be completely frustrated and eventually angry because it doesn't work. Of course, the fact that you didn't have a plan will be the reason it doesn't work, but no one will remember that little tidbit. You absolutely must have some basic plan for what you want your Web site to do for you. It may be one completely focused reason like marketing a specific product, or it may be less specific if you have multiple departments or divisions with multiple purposes and goals, but there must be some overall guiding purpose and plan that will not only make your site a cohesive whole but add to your other, more traditional efforts.

YOUR WEB SITE IS PART OF YOUR MARKETING STRATEGY

Your business may be located in 10 different cities or countries, but it probably bears the same name in all of them. The letterhead from one to the other of the divisions remains very much the same. The logo is standardized. Your mission statement doesn't vary from one place to another. A Web site needs the same kind of standardization (in a less formal way), but it represents you to the world as much as your logo and your letterhead. In many ways, it represents you more than those things. It's quite likely that more people will see your Web pages in a day than will see your letterhead in your lifetime. Those pages need to represent you in the best possible way.

Your letterhead was designed to be visually appealing, and the text that you produce on your stationery is articulate and professional; like those, a Web page requires care in crafting. It reflects your professionalism and attention to detail. Your Web audience is unlikely to take you seriously if your pages are littered with typographical and grammatical errors. And a minor error can make a huge difference. Consider: "Read on to see how our customers assess our service." Now omit the final s from assess. Minor error? Hardly, in the context of a worldwide audience.

The Web community doesn't necessarily know or care whether your company is multinational or you run it out of your home office and you are the single employee. What they will decide about you from your site is whether you're professional, and whether they're interested in doing business with you. If you attempt to enter the world of the Web without a plan, at best they'll ignore you; at worst you'll join the ranks of Mirsky's Worst of the Web (**http://mirsky.turnpike.net/wow/Worst.html**) and they'll laugh at you. While it's generally not considered a bad thing to produce a laugh for someone on the Web, you should do that on purpose, rather than by mistake. It's more than okay to have a plan that includes some good humor; it's not okay to be hysterically funny by accident.

In truth, the majority of people who will visit your Web site are likely to be unaware of or unconcerned with Mirsky or those like him. It's actually a greater sin to be uninteresting than funny. Indeed, good humor is valued on the Web, and those who accomplish it with flair are admired.

You will actually be in good corporate company if you happen to attract Mirsky's attention. He's panned 3Com, Pirelli, and Wendy's, not to mention a number of federal government agencies and quite a few other businesses. The problem with making Mirsky's list is that you just never know who else will be featured that day. It's probably not too amusing to find your corporate site featured with the sites on his list—some of which can give all new meaning to the word *worst*. CEOs tend to be a bit humor-impaired about that sort of thing, unless it's their competitor's page.

BUILDING YOUR PLAN

To avoid generating the kinds of mistakes that make CEOs and Boards of Directors cringe, you need a solid business plan. The plan may change as you learn how your site is being used and who is accessing it, but you still must have an initial plan that answers these basic questions:

◆ What do you want the site to do for your business? That may be anything from delivery of information internally to saving money on order processing to selling products. As a start, pick one or two specific goals and develop your plan around them.

- Who is your audience? Is it your present client base or prospective customers? Is it your own employees?
- How do you currently approach that market? How do you think you can use the Web to improve your approach to that market?

Be realistic—and, to a certain extent, brutal. Look carefully at your approach, your audience, and your purpose. Do the pieces fit together? Do you honestly think it will work? If you don't really buy into this whole idea, your eventual Web site will lack direction and purpose—and that will be obvious to people who visit.

▶ **TIP** As you brainstorm new and even more creative uses and goals for your site, always remember your intended audience. They're your primary reason for considering a Web site in the first place. Why not ask your present clients or customers what they'd want from your Web site? Send them a survey in your next regular mailing. And don't just give them a list of the things you think they'd want—give them an opportunity to suggest specific things that would be of interest or help to them. ◀

Before you jump into the tantalizing world of high tech, decide what you want to accomplish with your Web site. The following sections provide some ideas to help you begin brainstorming the ways you may benefit from the Web.

▶ **NOTE** Lest you think that the Web is just trendy, not useful, consider this: SunSoft Press, a division of Sun Microsystems, has been marketing their books on the Web since 1994. They offer each one for sale before publication. According to their own white paper (**http://www.sun.com/960101/ index.html**), their Web catalog "is directly responsible for *1,000 to 3,500 pre- sales* before the book's publication" (emphasis added). ◀

THE PROS—MARKETING YOUR PRODUCTS OR SERVICES ON THE WEB

As a soft marketing tool, the Web is just about the best thing to happen to business since paper clips. No other medium offers you the ability to personalize your business to millions of people. There are no geographical boundaries. It's called the World Wide Web for good reason. Your prospective customer base becomes every person or business who owns a computer and has Internet access *anywhere in the world*. Got a client in Ghana who needs access to a project report in a hurry? Post it on the Web. Got an 800 number for technical support that's overwhelmed answering the same questions day after day for one of your products? Post those questions and answers on the Web, and they're available 24 hours a day, 7 days a week. Would you benefit if your products and pricing were available to a worldwide audience? Do you offer a service you'd like to promote widely? Do you have special knowledge you can share? Maybe just educating people about your business would be helpful?

EDUCATE YOUR AUDIENCE

The Internet has been used for educational purposes for many years. Researchers exchanged papers and ideas, collaborated on journal articles, and at times published the results of research long before it could be printed by normal channels. It is the rare business manager who has not said at least once in a lifetime, "If only we could explain to people exactly how this works." Now you can. A carpet manufacturer may want to explain how many strands per foot are in a piece of carpet and why that's important to the quality (and price) of the carpet. On the Web, not only can you explain it to your customers—you can show them. A teachers' association may want to show that test scores, while supposedly lower today than they were 20 years ago, reflect a much larger number of students tested. On the Web, you can put up all the charts and graphs and bells and whistles you'd like.

14

To Web or Not or Web—That is the Question

Consider creative ways to present your educational offerings:

◆ Take questions presented from the Web and have your resident experts answer them. Then post the questions and answers on the Web.

◆ Set up a "Careers" section where you not only list your current openings but explain what you look for in prospective employees.

◆ Have pages of interviews with people from your staff and let them explain how they chose to pursue their areas of expertise. Teachers may very well appreciate that type of information for their classes, and students would appreciate the insights your employees could bring to their career decisions.

In the process of educating, you can learn. You can request feedback from people who visit your site, asking them precisely what they think of the facts and figures you've provided. From that feedback, you can tailor your educational efforts (or marketing) for the people who are visiting your site. They'll tell you about themselves, whether simply through their writing styles or through forms that you ask them to complete.

After all, marketing is, in its best form, education. People who don't understand what you do or why you do it aren't likely to be your customers or clients. On the other hand, people who once thought that they would never consider being your customers or clients may very well be persuaded to at least try what you offer, if you can persuade them that you have something they need. Whether you run a recruiting office or a professional association or a car dealership, you still must sell your prospect on your service or business or brand. On the Web, it doesn't cost much to attempt the sale—and your prospects come to you. Whether they visited your site originally because they really were interested in what you offer or because they just wondered "what those crackpots are doing," you have an opportunity to sell them (or at least to educate them).

▶ **TIP**   Your sales staff can help you focus your Web marketing. They know the questions and the concerns that potential customers are likely to have, and they know successful ways to answer those questions and concerns. Their direct contact with your customers can be of invaluable help to you, especially since the Web is very much about talking with each of your visitors as individuals. ◀

ADD THE WEB TO YOUR MARKETING TOOLBOX

The Web is different in many ways from your traditional marketing tool. While it's true that you are essentially communicating to many people (the one-to-many approach), you are communicating with each individual on what they consider to be a very personal basis. They have invited you into their home or office by visiting your site. You aren't making a cold call. They have sought you out and you must now engage them in some personal way. How you decide to do that will depend on your understanding of the clients you want to address with your Web pages. Take one step back from your business when you think about your reasons for having a Web site; consider not only what you want them to know about you, but how you will appear to them, what you have to offer them—don't think in that old one-to-many way. Put a face on that person and talk with him or her, one-on-one.

ONE-TO-ONE COMMUNICATION

The first mistake that corporate sites typically make when they begin serving Web pages is to start with the one-to-many approach. Most don't step back and view the pages from the perspective of the client. It isn't always an easy thing to do.

Think of it in terms of giving a prospective client a site visit. You'd make sure that she was greeted by a friendly, knowledgeable staff person. You'd want her to meet those people in your business who can accomplish the work she

16

wants done. You'd take her to lunch and chat about things totally unrelated to your business so that you could develop a rapport with her. Your Web site can do those same things, to some degree. It will never replace face-to-face contact with a client, or a firm handshake; but if you work at it, it can be friendly and inviting.

CREATIVE ISN'T NECESSARILY EXPENSIVE

Think of all the ways you may have wanted to market your product in other media and weren't able. Your newspaper or magazine advertisements can't give your prospective clients a sound clip of your hot new CD—but your Web site can. You can't really show them your manufacturing process in an advertisement because it's just too involved and would be too expensive. You can do it on the Web—and you won't have to float a stock option to do it.

When you think of marketing on the Web, think creatively. It won't cost you your firstborn to implement some of those ideas. Some of them will be expensive, but many of them won't. When you think about marketing on the Web, toss traditional thinking out the window. You don't want to go too far to the extreme, but you don't have to think in terms of sound bites or ½-page newspaper ads either. Super Bowl ads are terrifically expensive because the Super Bowl draws a huge audience. People look forward to those ads because they're fun and creative. Your Web site will have a huge audience; think about being fun and creative.

TIME IS MONEY

The immediacy of the Web is powerful. Millions of people are monitoring the news not on TV but over the Web. News headlines, sports scores, and stock quotes are becoming as ubiquitous on desktop computers as those flying toasters once were. Having a special sale on fishhooks or RVs? You don't have to wait for your ads to be printed and circulated, or redubbed. Put the information on the Web now. Did one of your employees win the Nobel Peace Prize? No need to wait for tomorrow's newspaper to, quite literally, tell the world.

SELL YOUR PRODUCT OR SERVICE

If you want to sell specific products and services, you would probably be wise to list those items and their prices in your Web pages. It isn't at all uncommon now for an administrative assistant to go "shopping" for his boss' airline tickets, rental cars, hotel rooms, and conference registrations on the Web. In the same way, a person who wants to buy a computer or a piece of jewelry, or even chocolates, can shop at one of the many malls or storefronts that are springing up every day on the Web. Those people may or may not actually make their purchases on the Web, but their decisions to buy a particular item may very well hang on how well the Web vendor has presented his product and engaged the shopper.

INSTANT GRATIFICATION SELLS

As with shopping by catalog, shopping on the Web has tremendous appeal. Only a masochist could actually look forward to fighting holiday crowds to find a sweater for Great Aunt Margaret. It's three days before Christmas and the last gift absolutely must be purchased. If you can offer him the sweater he needs and delivery on time, you've just made a friend for life.

The fact that Lands' End (**http://www.landsend.com**) is on the Web and may have a similar item is not a disadvantage to you. There's a much-repeated phrase among people who frequent the online world: "On the Internet, no one knows you're a dog." Conversely, on the Web, your business can compete head-to-head with others that have far more or far fewer resources. Quality counts more than the amount of dollars you spend. You can have as much presence on the Web as Lands' End if you're willing to spend the time and devote the effort required to have a good Web site, or if you're willing to pay for that presence. In most respects, what counts on the Web is what counts to your business whether you advertise in print or on TV or radio—your ability to deliver what you promise. If you tell your customer that you'll have an item delivered to her within three working days and you don't deliver for two weeks, the odds are that you've lost any future business from that customer (unless you have some really compelling reason that you can convince her to accept).

Apply the same common sense reasoning to selling (or marketing) on the Web that you apply anywhere else. Understand that people have the perception that the Web is a "fast" way to do business. The truth is that it is and it isn't; but the perception is what's important to the customer, and just as important to you. That's one of the reasons that the Federal Express Web site (**http://www.fedex.com**) is one of the most successful—instant gratification. Customers can track their own packages and determine exactly where they are. That's empowerment—and it's fast! If you accept orders for your products (whether those are orders placed online or by traditional methods), issue the customer a number so that he can determine the status of his order. Even if you've clearly stated in your Web pages that orders are shipped only on Tuesday and Thursday every other week, give the customer a chance to check in at your Web site to determine whether his order got shipped early. If it was, you look great; if it wasn't, you've at least given him some information, and that's what he wants.

CAN YOU REALLY MAKE MONEY THIS WAY?

The answer is a resounding "maybe." You can certainly offer your products for sale on the Web. The real beauty of advertising your products or services on the Web is that you're free to

- ◆ Describe them at length
- ◆ Offer pictures, specifications, and prices

◆ Include information that you could never afford to include in a catalog or a radio or TV advertisement. The technology exists, for instance, to allow you to offer an animated, step-by-step guide for how to assemble a product. Other media may allow it, but the costs would be prohibitive.

At this point, quite truthfully, most of the people making money on the Web are Internet and Web service providers, those who sell Web browsers and Web servers, those who were out there early with a good idea for a way to make navigating the Web easier, and probably (though no real facts exist to prove it) some businesses that had limited clientele and were able to extend their customer base to the wider audience of the Web—artisans, mail order firms, and similar concerns. Oh, and con artists.

If the first item on your list of reasons to launch a Web site is to double your profits, you need a reality check. You've been taking the media hype entirely too seriously and probably should take at least a long weekend off at the shore or the mountains. It's true that you may have just the perfect product and the perfect approach and precisely the right mechanisms to make the Web add to your bottom line, but don't count on it. Approach the Web as a marketing tool with a great deal of potential and flexibility, and you're less likely to be disappointed.

Do put your products and prices on the Web, though. If you're a good businessperson (and the assumption is that you are, as you're doing your homework now before you invest time and energy in a Web site), you'll find a way to sell that product to a larger audience than you may have ever dreamed before the Web was developed. At minimum, you may attract a customer simply because he remembers your name. At least one company (and probably more) has experienced increased on-premises sales because of its Web site.

Selling a Service

If you offer a service rather than a product, the Web can be just as beneficial to you. Obviously, it's not possible to pet-sit or clean someone's house via the Web, but it's possible to schedule appointments to do either of those things (and many other things like them). The fact that your audience is outside your geographical area isn't particularly important. Simply state your terms and geographical boundaries in your Web marketing. The Web is world-wide, but that doesn't prevent it from working quite well locally.

Some people who attempt to engage your services will be completely out of your area. It may be a joke or a misunderstanding—or a new opportunity for you. If enough of those requests come in, you may just be offering a service that's needed and that may be worth franchising. At the very least, you may learn a great deal about the demand for your service when you market it on the Web.

Thinking about setting up a service but just not sure what the market is? Test the idea with a Web page. You lose little if the idea doesn't work. You may gain a lot in the process. You can take a chance without quitting your job or mortgaging your home to support yourself while you wait for customers to find you. If the market exists on the Web, and if you can deliver what you promise, you may just be on your way to much bigger and better things.

Go for an Image Makeover

You may simply want to create a slightly different, more modern image for your company. A Web site enables you to reinvent yourself in interesting and creative ways. Used well, a Web site can give your clients a view of you as forward-thinking and in touch with the future. The Internal Revenue

Service (**http://www.irs.ustreas.gov/**) actually made some friends this year. People pointed and clicked their way to just the right tax forms and information to help them make that April 15th deadline. The IRS was praised by taxpayers. In public. Now there's something to think about. If the IRS can improve its image, anyone can.

Test Your New Ideas

Because you can do things on the Web quickly, you can try new approaches to your marketing and sales efforts with minimal disruption. Your Webmaster is likely to break out in hives every time she sees you coming her way, but you can and should use your Web pages to supplement and improve your traditional marketing. You don't need to spend hundreds or thousands of dollars designing and testing a new approach before you launch it. Put it on the Web and ask people what they think of it. People will be willing to register at your site and give you demographic information about themselves to be part of a regular focus group for your campaigns.

You may not want to make those campaigns available to the wider Web audience. Technically, it's not very difficult to password-protect documents so that they're available only to your demographically selected focus group. Send them e-mail (based on their registration information) that announces your prospective campaign, and ask them to take a look at your latest idea and comment on it.

▶ **CAUTION**   Don't use those e-mail addresses to send people the electronic equivalent of junk mail. While it's unusual for people to scream and shout about junk mail they receive by way of the U.S. Postal Service, you can expect them to scream and shout on the Internet. Your mail can cost them real money, because many users pay for their Internet access by the hour. If enough people on the Web are screaming and shouting, they can effectively close down your site. It has been done. You might save money over a bulk mailing, but if you do that at the expense of your Web site the savings may not be quite so measurable. Learn the rules of the Web before you venture very far into it. ◄

Web surfers are generally a well-educated, literate group, and many of them love nothing better than to tell you exactly what they think. More than a few are going to tell you what they think whether you ask them or not, so you may as well put them to work for you.

You have at your disposal one *very large* focus group. You lose nothing but some time and effort if your approach doesn't work. Trash the pages and start over. If your Webmaster is particularly flexible, she may not even suffer a nervous breakdown at hearing "I've got this great idea" for the fifteenth time.

INTERNAL AND EXTERNAL COMMUNICATIONS ON THE WEB

You may decide that marketing won't be the primary purpose of your Web site; it will instead be a communications tool. Some companies, or divisions within companies, are actively using their Web sites not for marketing to prospective clients but rather to communicate with their present client base—to offer product support or technical information. It's much easier to point and click to get a copy of the specifications for a piece of equipment than it is to sit on the phone for 10 minutes pressing 1, 4, 3, 6, 7, 5, and 2—only to discover that where you are now isn't where you wanted to be and you've got to start all over.

Generally, a quick glance at a Web page will reveal whether or not it's useful to you, and you aren't forced to listen to Muzak in the process. Your client still may spend 10 minutes trying to find just the right information (though, if the site is well-designed, that shouldn't be necessary), but you can save him some time by simply adding an e-mail link so that he can communicate with a real person. He won't get disgusted listening to "All representatives are busy.

Your call is important to us. Please hold and it will be answered by the next available representative." He can go about his business while he waits for a response by e-mail. It's decidedly more efficient for both you and him.

TECHNICAL SUPPORT ON THE WEB

Cisco, a manufacturer and distributor of communications equipment, lists on their Web site what appears to be virtually every product specification they offer. Network managers love their site for those things, but they also love the pages of technical support information that Cisco publishes on their site. Cisco doesn't have the slickest site on the Web by any means, but they have one very functional site that makes their customers very happy. Technical support is an area that costs many companies a great deal of money. If yours happens to be one of those companies, you may save yourself (or your technical support staff) a lot of headaches by putting information on the Web.

BUZZWORD OF THE YEAR—INTRANET

You may simply want to make internal communications more efficient. Instead of issuing the two-page change to the Policy and Procedures manual in print form, put the entire manual on the Web and change just those parts that need changing. This type of Web server has become the basis for what are now called *intranets*. Intranets are Web servers located in companies, but not accessible to the outside world.

You can use an intranet to make information widely available in your company, or you may restrict access to certain individuals or groups. Perhaps you have a project that involves people in several departments but that shouldn't be available to other people in those same or other departments. It can be done. You may want to make certain information available to executives but unavailable to other staff members. You can do it (or, more precisely, your Webmaster can do it).

24

To Web or Not or Web—That is the Question

Intranets make a great deal of sense for businesses large and small. Because Web servers are available for most major operating systems, and because browsers don't distinguish between the various systems, the Policy and Procedures manual can be served transparently from a Macintosh in Human Resources to a Silicon Graphics workstation in Engineering. Depending on the size and complexity of your business, you may have one computer that functions as the Web server for your intranet, or you may have many.

This setup is similar to the older centralized computing concept wherein all documents were housed on one or more large computers, but it's also very different. Human Resources doesn't have to physically run its own server, and yet the H.R. staff can maintain control over updates and changes to that Policy and Procedures manual on the Web server, no matter where it is in your company. Effecting those changes on the Web server and making them instantly available to staff is far more efficient than changing the documents, printing copies (from five to tens of thousands, depending on the size of your company), and then sending the changes by interoffice mail to employees who have copies of the manual, where someone must replace the old pages with the new and send the old to the recycling bin.

You can announce new plans and projects to your staff easily and efficiently. Those remote offices no longer will feel quite so remote, because they can have available to them the same information at the same time as your local staff. Staff who travel can be kept up to date on changes in production schedules or delivery times. Your sales staff in the field can fill out order forms and inform you of special instructions for those orders, using Web-based forms.

Time spent training new employees can be reduced, because accessing the information you want them to have won't involve learning several different software applications. People love Web browsers. They're simple to use and they're easy to learn. Put your new employee orientation information on your intranet and let the employee print the parts she's actually interested in keeping, rather than handing her that daunting packet of information (which is as likely to go into the recycling bin as it is to be read).

If your company has a sports program, you're likely aware of the amount of time that gets eaten away while teams are formed and reformed and schedules made and changed. Allow the participants access to do it all on the Web server. They can sign up for teams, arrange their schedules, and post delays or cancellations—rather than making many phone calls and running from one office to another to discuss changes, or printing out the latest iteration of the schedule, making dozens of copies, and sending them by interoffice mail. (Post scores on your intranet, too.)

What works for the sports program can also work for meetings. Arrange meetings and schedule the necessary conference rooms and audiovisual equipment for those meetings through your intranet. (Maybe posting meeting scores wouldn't be a bad idea, either. Consider a scoring system of 1 to 10 for actual productivity versus person hours charged to the project or overhead for it. A few less meetings couldn't hurt.) It simply doesn't matter how large or how small your company is; the efficient use of time and tools is important. An intranet can be one of your most efficient tools.

Now before you rush right out to invest in this fabulous technology, it does have its inefficiencies as well. Those are discussed a bit later in this chapter. You'll want the full picture before you make your decision.

Conferences and Forums

Some companies are using Web-based forums in the same way that they once used electronic mail for extended conferences and conversations to exchange ideas and information. This is especially useful for businesses or projects that are widely distributed geographically. E-mail sometimes goes astray or arrives out of order, so that it's difficult to reconstruct the ongoing thread of the communication. Web forums can be posted in order and immediately, making them much easier to follow. They also provide people who are new to the project with a history of what has gone before. That not-so-bright idea that was offered and hashed out six months ago doesn't have to become the focus of another round of mail messages.

26

Web forums are an efficient means of communication both in-house and outside your company. You can use them to gather information about how people view your products, your services, and your Web site. Remember that although the Web is a new medium, it's no different from the old ones in one very important respect—if you're going to make a sale, whether of a product or an idea, you must make some kind of connection with your client. You must engage him in some way. Forums on your Web site can give you clues to how to do that. Ask visitors to your site what you're doing right and wrong, and what you might do to serve them more effectively.

FIND A FEW GOOD PEOPLE

In addition to marketing and communications, the Web is a good way to attract employees. More and more companies are posting their job listings on the Web. That paper résumé is quickly becoming a dinosaur. You've got an opening and your prospective employee can find you fast, send you a résumé, and set up an interview by electronic mail. No phone tag. You've done her a service by telling her about your business. You've given her a sense of who you are and what you do. Unless you have the hottest new product or the coolest site on the Web, the odds are good that the majority of inquiries you receive as a direct result of your pages will be from people who are looking for a job. These prospective employees have at least one skill that's valuable in today's market: They're computer-literate. Of course, the fact that they had the good sense to seek out your company says a lot for them, too.

The people who are Internet- and Web-literate may surprise you. They're not all 22 years old and enamored of this new technology. Yes, a lot of them are, but many of them are 30 or 40 or 50 or older. Stop in and play a hand of Bridge, or one of the other games, at the Internet Gaming Zone. (First you'll have to wander over to their Web site at **http://www.zone.com** to pick up the software to interface with the Zone, but you'll learn something in the process.) Your partner is as likely to be 50 as 20.

You'll find software engineers, salespeople, social workers, anthropologists, chemists, particle physicists, teachers, and students on the Web. Could your employee pool use some extremely knowledgeable people? You might wind up hiring a physicist to head up your Web project. Stranger things have happened on the Web.

THE CONS—THE WEB IS A TIME SINK EXTRAORDINAIRE

Broaden your potential customer base with a worldwide audience. Market your products and services. Test your new ideas and strategies. Attract a few good people. All in all, a Web site sounds like it might be a really good idea, but there's a down side, right? Right. All isn't sweetness and light when you add a Web project to your already busy life.

Whether you decide to install a Web server internally simply to share information within the company or with the world at large, you'll want your own people to review your pages. You install Web browsers for them to use. You don't really think they're only looking at your pages, do you? Really? Well, if you only installed an internal server and you either don't have Internet access or are behind a firewall that blocks outgoing traffic, you're probably right. Otherwise, you can bet that your employees' bookmarks to sites aren't exclusively devoted to your company's Web pages. They may tell you they just happened to find the Playboy site while researching the effects of human exposure to extreme elements. You'll have to be the judge of their sincerity.

The Web is a black hole for hours of useless surfing. The best-intentioned staff person will begin looking for specific information on a specific topic and spend two hours being sidetracked by interesting or funny or foolish information that has little or nothing to do with the task at hand. After the first week or so, most people will recognize that the work they're being paid to do isn't getting done thanks to this snazzy new toy called the Web, and they'll settle back into the more occasional break for some serious Web surfing. Some will take every spare moment to check out all the cool sites of the day (and there are a lot of them). Some will never recover their sanity.

Yes, it gets worse. Now that everyone who is anyone at all in the software industry is integrating Internet capabilities into their products, it's even easier for your employees to surf the Web to no good purpose. Joe over in Accounting takes a break to surf, finds a great new site that is just wonderfully funny, fires up the mail package attached to his browser, and sends the URL to 17 of his closest friends—14 of whom are his coworkers, who click the highlighted URL to jump immediately to Joe's favorite site. As long as they're there, they might as well see where those other links go, no? Yes, for the most part. It'll take only a minute.

▶ **TIP**   Do yourself a favor and go Web surfing. Plan to do it for 10 minutes and 10 minutes only. Check the clock when you start and again when you finish. Did you manage to stop in less than an hour? If you had an appointment 10 minutes from the time you started and had your secretary buzz you, it doesn't count. ◀

Few of the magazines, articles, books, or media pieces about the Web admit the stark truth that the Web isn't always a particularly productive tool. Those magazines, articles, books, and media pieces are in many instances written by reporters who are simply delighted that someone is paying them to surf the Web. Many others are written by Web service providers or programmers, who have a very real vested interest in convincing you that the Web is "the future." The truth is that the Web isn't much different from other tools on desktops. Some employees make personal phone calls all day long, on company time and money, while others seldom do. Unless you removed that Solitaire game from every computer, there's probably one person on staff who spends hours every day playing cards. The Web may cut down on some of the personal calls or lessen the hours spent playing Solitaire, but it won't turn a bad employee into a good one or vice versa. It's very likely that the Web is the future, but you should know what the future holds, rather than taking the hype at face value.

The Time/People Investment

In addition to the time and resources that will be wasted on surfing the Web, setting up a Web site and maintaining it will require staff time and effort, whether you do it yourself or outsource it.

Updating and Improving Your Site

Web pages must be written and coded, revised and re-coded. Regular revisions must be put into effect. A static Web site is worthless, so if you plan to just put some pages up there and leave them, you may as well avoid the process entirely. Unless the site changes and people have a reason to come back, they won't. That process of change is a way of engaging your customer. If you've asked them for ideas and suggestions for ways to improve your site and you don't respond in some way to their suggestions, they won't experience any personal involvement with its growth or changes. You may not like the changes some of them suggest, but you should respond to them anyway, whether through personal e-mail or by addressing the suggestions on one of your Web pages.

Handling Incoming E-Mail

At the very least, someone is going to have to deal with the inquiries that will come about just because your pages exist. You won't know whether that mail message is from a prospective customer, a competitor, or a college student, when it arrives addressed to **webmaster@yourcompany.com**. It won't matter. It's the equivalent of a ringing phone, and should be answered cheerfully and promptly. It may pay off in a major contract or it may be a prank,

30

but you must assume the former rather than the latter. A good Webmaster answers e-mail at night and on weekends as well as during regular working hours, because the Web works on a 24x7 basis and because, as your front office receptionist knows, you get only one chance to make a good first impression. That's truly the very *least* investment of time and people you can make for a Web site.

OUTSOURCING

Realistically, you'll want to have someone in-house who can at least code your pages so that you don't have to pay someone outside the company to do it. There are good financial and practical reasons for this setup. If you're dependent on someone else to do the coding, every revision, no matter how small, is probably going to cost you money. In addition, you're going to be dependent on someone else to implement those changes, and that can take time—that outside person probably isn't working just for you, and your priority may not be a priority for him or her.

You may want that news release on the Web tomorrow, but the person doing the coding may have a client (who has already contracted for more money than you're spending) with a large project that's much more sexy (which, in this instance, may mean only that it's technologically more challenging and fun than your news release) and pays very well. Your news release may very well be the one that announces that one of your employees won the Nobel Peace Prize. But the independent contractor may be having a lot more fun programming a few bouncing heads on someone's Web page (go surfing... you'll get the picture) than turning your news release, however exciting to you, into HTML code.

▶ **NOTE**   It will be abundantly clear as you read that I strongly advocate doing the preponderance of your Web site in-house. In the long run, I think that the benefits of having staff trained in this medium and able to effect

continues

continued

changes, additions, and revisions are enormous. As with any medium, though, there are certainly times when it makes good business sense to hire expert assistance outside your company. There are excellent Internet service providers available if you simply don't have sufficient talent within your company to design and build the Web site that you think you need. Your choice should be guided by your site requirements and your evaluation of how much time, talent, and effort will be necessary to put that site together and maintain it. ◄

DO YOU NEED A NEW DEPARTMENT?

How many people is this really going to take? Many factors come into play, most of which are addressed later in this book. It's possible, even for a relatively large site, to accomplish the task with one person—who may not even be devoted full-time to the effort. It won't be easy, but it can be done—if you have someone who's crazy enough to want to do it.

Unless you have a most unusual staff, you'll probably have more volunteers for the job than you know what to do with. Your volunteers will be laboring under the delusion that being a Webmaster is easy and fun. In fact, being a Webmaster can be great fun, and parts of the job can be easy. The trick is to choose the person who combines delusion with an almost limitless amount of curiosity, patience, good humor, and common sense. This is not a good time to tell her about the incredibly long hours or the frustrations she's going to have when the entire site (by now populated with 100, 200, or more documents) gets redesigned by a committee. Be sure you judge the patience and good-humor quotients very carefully when you make your decision.

A HINT ABOUT COSTS

People and time—a Web site requires an investment of both, and we all know that translates to money. Whatever you originally budget for a Web site probably will double within the year. It will become a project that's all-but-impossible to kill. It will have its proponents and opponents, and both sides will be sure that theirs is the only true religion. The proponents will push for more and better. Even the opponents will push for more and better. They'll hate the site "because it doesn't do anything." They'll offer ideas for things it should do and in the end push you to improve it, all the while claiming it's useless—a total waste of time and money. They'll be the first to complain when their new business cards don't have the proper URL, too.

THE MAYBES— IT'S A SUPERHIGHWAY, RIGHT? FAST AND EFFICIENT?

The media continue to refer to the Internet and the Web as the Information Superhighway. That sounds good, but it's no superhighway—not yet, at least. Oh yes, most of the roads are in place and, amazingly enough, most of them work most of the time.

After all, the Internet was originally designed by the military, with an eye toward the computers on the network being smart enough to reroute information if some installation along the way became inoperable. It accomplishes that quite well in most cases. It would be exceedingly difficult at this stage of the game to completely disrupt the traffic on it—individual sites and installations may be unreachable at times but traffic still flows around them.

The roads are definitely in place in most parts of the world. They just don't all happen to have been paved or widened to superhighway status. Think of it in terms of driving. If you're driving from Los Angeles to San Francisco, you'll encounter some very good freeways. If you're driving from Los Angeles to Minot, ND, however, the roads may not be quite so good. The types of cabling and equipment that carry information range from very old telephone lines to the most up-to-date and fastest satellites. The speed of the Internet and the Web is directly affected by those lines. If that project report really must be delivered over the Web to your client in Ghana, it's probably going to be a slow process, simply because the lines between your site and his are likely to cover the gamut from the worst to the best. For all its slowness at times, though, it's still faster than many other ways of communicating large amounts of information in a timely manner.

As more and more companies add information and computers to those roads and the traffic becomes heavier and heavier, everything slows down. The Web can be very fast, but it can also be very slow and annoying. It'll get worse before it gets better, as more and more traffic is added. But more lines will be upgraded to superhighway status. Manufacturers of modems and other communications equipment will find ways to make that equipment move information faster over existing lines. The demand is certainly in place. Supply will follow.

Realistically, however, you can't plan your Web site completely around real-time video or crystal-clear sound. Neither the technology nor the roads are in place for that quite yet. They'll get there, but not as quickly or as painlessly as some would have you believe. A Web site isn't a fantasy project, though some pieces of it may be. It's a business investment. Don't let the hype guide your plans (and those who spout it can be wonderfully convincing, because most of them honestly want it all to be true right now). Set your plans firmly in the reality of what the Web is now, not what it will be at some nebulous future date.

THE DEMOGRAPHICS OF THE WEB

Studies are being done constantly on Web demographics. Experts are making claims daily about how many people have access, their ages, incomes, and gender. You should know at least a little something about those demographics while you're making your plans to build a site on the Web.

To Web or Not or Web—That is the Question

The Graphics, Visualization, & Usability (GVU) Center of Georgia Tech has been conducting surveys on the Web since January of 1994. It's the oldest and the largest of the studies. The results of the first four studies are available on the Web at **http://www.cc.gatech.edu/gvu/user_surveys/**. Magazines appear with new survey results regularly. Study them. What you'll learn from all of them are these two things:

◆ Millions of people all over the world access the Web.

◆ Most of those people are male.

Other facts you will be asked to believe are:

◆ The average age of those people is 25-50.

◆ The average income of those people is $25,000 to $60,000.

You may or may not want to take those last two "facts" very seriously. Respondents for surveys about Web usage are generally self-selected. They have chosen to answer questions about themselves, and in most cases have done that on the Web.

In addition, people lie about themselves on the Web. Anonymity is cherished among the Internet and Web communities. Men may profess to be women. Women may take on male personas. Students can claim to be 35-year-old corporate executives making $90,000 a year. How can researchers know? They can't, really. Of course, they report their results as accurately as possible, but even the researchers acknowledge that it's virtually impossible to extend the results of their studies to the Web population as a whole.

Count on the first two real facts. Millions of people do visit the Web daily. How many millions isn't something that could be easily determined. Most of those people are male, but the number of women is growing. The Web has something to offer them, and they're beginning to give it a look. How should these facts affect your Web site? If you happen to be a distributor of automobile parts to mechanics, it may be precisely the market you need. Not that there aren't female mechanics, but the percentage of them is probably fairly accurately reflected among the Web population. Depending on which survey results you prefer, women account for anywhere from 15 to 30 percent of the Web population.

KEEP YOUR VIRTUAL
NEIGHBORHOOD CLEAN AND FRIENDLY

The Internet, and by extension the Web, has a certain reputation among women. It's thought by many to be a rather rough-and-rowdy place where people tend to scream and shout at one another for fun. That reputation isn't totally inaccurate. Some places on the Internet and the Web could certainly be considered rough and rowdy. Those virtual neighbors are the equivalent of city neighborhoods where most of us wouldn't choose to walk alone after dark. The advantage of the virtual neighborhoods is that you can leave them quickly and safely. There are no guns or knives, only words. However, you don't want to build a site where women will feel uncomfortable, if you expect them to do business with you.

Web forums can be the equivalent of a virtual neighborhood. If you're going to implement forums as part of your plan for your Web site, seriously consider moderating or at least policing those forums. Plenty of people on the Web and the Internet can hold their own in any exchange of verbal abuse, but, while it's true that controversy can sometimes be good for business, is that your aim for your Web site?

IS NOW THE TIME?

Certainly, if you don't have good reasons for building and a good plan for using your Web site, you lose nothing by waiting. The businesses that are on the Web now are working hard at learning how to make their Web sites pay off—whether in increased sales, decreased overhead, or client goodwill. They're taking a chance on this new technology. Their reasons for being there are as varied as the products and services they offer, but they have one thing in common—they want their customers, clients, and yes, their competitors to be aware that they're on the forefront of what appears to be the future of global communications. They're innovative to the extent that they're willing to test new ideas and new strategies for the world to see. The Web is quite literally under construction, and they have a stake in the design.

How Long Can You Afford to Wait?

The Web is being driven by peer pressure. If your competition is online, you'll do well to at least consider being there too. The competition is already investing resources in a Web site, and you really shouldn't be spending too much time doing research and thinking about it, when you know you need to get on the Web immediately. Your time will be better spent working on your plan and design.

If your competition isn't online, they will be. Are you really willing to allow them to get a jump on a market as large as the World Wide Web? Being first isn't always easy, but it sure beats coming in second. Because you know your business better than anyone else, you must make the determination. Can you afford to pass up a business opportunity because it requires access to a Web site? Can you disregard those customers who simply don't have the patience to navigate your voice mail system but will spend hours pointing-and-clicking on Web pages? Are your clients the type who simply expect you to be on the Web?

If your business happens to be telecommunications or computers, this is a moot point. You don't have time to wait. Your competition is out there and your clients expect you to be.

▶ **NOTE**   I received e-mail addressed to me in my alias as Webmaster one Saturday morning from a U.S. citizen in the U.K. who was trying to determine whether a local (to me) electronics company had an e-mail address. The requester had searched for a Web site to no avail. I attempted to call the company, but they were closed for the weekend, so I replied to the request by telling him that I would contact them on Monday morning. I did. They had no e-mail access, and I forwarded that information along to the potential customer. He replied with thanks and said, "Just wait until I *fax* them… an electronics firm… without e-mail!!"

That company was lucky. The customer was persistent, and he wanted to do business with that company specifically. Another customer might have just gone to the competition, which had a Web site for easy access. ◀

Other types of businesses may be able to avoid making the transition to the Web for six months or a year, or in some cases maybe even longer, but the longer you wait the fewer mistakes you'll be able to make with your Web site. The perfect Web site has yet to be designed or built. The businesses that are on the Web now are allowed to make mistakes because everyone does in one way or another. Those of us who entered the Web early made horrendous mistakes and had relatively crude sites. A company that offers information as crudely now as we did then will take a beating from their clients and their competitors. There's less room for mistakes now, and there will be even less room for mistakes in a year. The sooner you begin planning and building your Web site, the better.

Building a Web site now is harder than it will be in six months or a year, because the tools that are available are still a bit primitive. They're getting better and more user-friendly by the day, and they're getting cheaper, too. If you decide to wait for the easy-to-use tools and the cheaper hardware and software, however, you're going to be forced to have one very spiffy Web site when you bring your business online.

The competition will be much stiffer, too. Businesses that are on the Web now are already learning how to make their sites work and how to attract the people they want. Whether you jump in now or later, you're still going to have to learn those same lessons. No one can really do that for you. Your business is the same in some ways as others like yours, but it's different, too. You're going to have to adjust and rework your Web site to work for your company, no matter when you decide to get into this whole business of the Web. Those redesigns and adjustments take time. The longer you wait to begin, the longer it will be before your site becomes the productive tool you need.

How Much Competition Is Already Out There?

The growth of the Web since April of 1994 is one of the most startling statistics and one most open to speculation (see the figure on the next page). No one really knows how big the Web is. The most conservative estimates are probably far too low and the most wildly optimistic are probably exactly that.

It's simply impossible now—and it probably will remain impossible for at least two to five years—to have any kind of accurate assessment of the number of Web servers operating on the Web at any given moment.

What About Money Transfers on the Web?

Predictions about when there will really be a secure system in place for safe transfers of money on the Web fall under the same heading as suggested numbers of Web servers. It may be next week. It may be another year. A year ago, most of us who had been in this business for a year (the oldtimers) fully expected that a secure system, one that had been tested, would be in place by now. The standard is not yet in place (as of publication) and we're still waiting. Computer professionals likely will be the last people on the planet to entrust their credit cards to the Web, just as they tended to be the last to entrust their payroll deposits to electronics. That should tell you something about how much you can trust the hype about secure transactions.

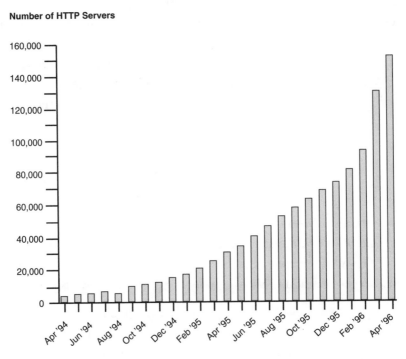

Number of HTTP Servers

Estimated growth of the numbers of computers serving documents to the Web since 1994.

It will happen eventually. There's little doubt about that. The more optimistic computer professionals tend to believe it will be very soon; the less optimistic tend to believe it will be some time later, but none of them really doubt that it will happen. The technology is moving quickly in many ways and slowly in many others but the technology will take us there, sooner or later. The question you must answer is whether you want to take a chance on the technology in *any* way right now.

▶ **NOTE**   I am admittedly conservative in my approach to financial transactions on the Web. The odds are good that you would never experience a problem with them. People don't hesitate to give their credit card numbers over the phone or to waitstaff in restaurants, who promptly disappear, taking that card with them. Risks abound in the real world just as they do in the virtual one. In truth, because there's so much concentration of interest in this particular area, security on the Web is likely to become much more reliable than in any other medium. ◀

THE BOTTOM LINE

The World Wide Web isn't going to go away. It's already too big and too functional to disappear. It's working well to deliver information and support for many companies. Lawyers, dentists, real estate agents, research firms, and auto manufacturers, to name only a few, are using it to promote their products and services. The numbers of businesses that have decided to tap the potential of the Web are growing exponentially.

You won't be stepping into totally uncharted territory, and you'll find that practically everything you need to know about how to build your own little piece of Web real estate is freely available to you on the Web. You'll find programmers who have already developed Web server applications that you can use without any charge. You'll find graphic artists who have designed buttons, bars, and backgrounds that you can use freely on your site. There are advertising and design firms that are willing to share the lessons they've learned so that you can improve your Web site. All you need to get their advice is a browser and the desire to learn.

Take advantage of that attitude of sharing now. No one really knows how the Web will evolve but, as more and more companies stake their claims, it may not continue to be quite the same sharing place it is now. Learn from those who are willing to teach now, and then give something back to the Web, based on your experiences. Tim Berners-Lee and his friends at CERN built the original Web, but they didn't make any money for that. They shared it with the world. That's an attitude that should guide at least some portion of your own piece of the Web. If your Web site is nothing more than a self-serving promotion, it's likely to be reviewed by various Web pundits as simply that. Word travels fast on the Web. Include giving something back to the Web community in your plan. You won't regret it.

When you have your plan and you're ready to build a Web site you'll be proud for people to visit, you'll still have a few other decisions to make. Your work is only beginning and it may never be finished. A Web site can seem to take on a life of its own. You're going to need to make decisions about where to build it, who will build it, and your budget for now and for the future. You're going to have a wonderful time learning about the care and feeding of Webmasters—yes, you really do have to let them out into the fresh air once every six months or so, or they'll turn on you.

Take a look at Web sites of companies that are similar to yours. Pick two or three that have sites you especially like and send e-mail to their Webmasters. Webmasters dearly love to talk about their work, and they like nothing better in the world than to have someone comment favorably about their sites. Ask how much time it takes to maintain, how many people are involved in the building and maintenance, and what their experience is with regard to increased sales or customer satisfaction with their site.

What you'll probably learn is that it's an exciting time to be in the business of Web site building and management and that the Web is a fascinating, often challenging, frustrating—but never boring—place to be. You'll put hours of time and work into designing and planning your site. You'll spend more time and effort refining it. Then you'll turn around and redesign the whole thing, but you won't be bored. As soon as you're sure you have it all under control, the next latest, greatest, niftiest new technology will come along and make everything you've done up to now obsolete—and you'll go back to the drawing board. And during the whole process, you'll face challenges, learn new ways to think about old ideas, put skills you don't even know you have to work, and learn something new every single solitary day.

Operating a Web site is a daily challenge, but it can breathe new life into your business—from the youngest staff members, who are enthralled with the technology, to the oldest, who are fascinated to learn more about this medium that they've read and seen so much about. It can bring about friendships and wonderful working relationships across departmental and generational lines that will surprise you.

◄ 2 ►

Now What?

What equipment and what
type of access to the Internet
do you really need?

◆

How do you go about hiring
a service provider?

◆

How much of the work can
you do without help?

◆

What's all this
really going to cost?

◆

How can you justify
the investment?

N o matter how good your reasons for building a Web site, or how focused your plan, you can't make it happen without the right combination of technical and managerial support. The site will require a financial investment, however minimal. You must know how much of an investment, and you may need to convince senior management to commit to that investment.

MORE THAN YOU'D REALLY LIKE TO KNOW ABOUT TECHNICAL ISSUES

You already know that you must have a computer, Web server software, and adequate Internet access to serve pages on the World Wide Web. You're also going to want to consider domain name registration. If you happen to have all of those things, you can skip this discussion entirely (lucky you). Otherwise, drag up a chair and let's get this out of the way as quickly as possible.

FIRST THINGS FIRST—THE COMPUTER

This part is a no-brainer. When talking about computers, faster is better. Admittedly, you can serve pages—at least in the initial stages—from a 486/40 with 8MB of RAM. And you don't need huge amounts of hard disk space right away (unless you've already got a thousand documents that you just know you absolutely, positively must have up and running on day one).

SPEED IS EVERYTHING

Your goal is to serve pages as quickly as possible. People who surf the Web have terribly short attention spans when it comes to waiting on documents to show up on their browsers. If you just happen to be recycling an old 486/40 because Mary over in Accounting got a snappy new Pentium and is delighted to say goodbye to that old, slow computer, and your budget won't allow anything else, by all means consider using it as a Web server. Don't plan on using it for long, though. It wouldn't be realistic on your part. Your own staff is likely to be first among those to criticize the speed and moan about how long it takes to load the pages.

You may be first, actually.

Your best possible plan is to use or buy the fastest machine you can get and to use it only to serve Web pages. Simply concentrate on having as fast a processor and as much RAM in that computer as you can afford—4MB of RAM will do the job slowly; 8MB is better; 16MB is better still, and on and on. No, you don't actually have to know what RAM is or how it works. You can ask your local computer nerds what they think and then try not to look completely bored as they extol the virtues of fast processors and gigs of free hard drive space. Your budget is your bottom line. You can spend $1,500 or tens of thousands. You're a business person. You know that the best choice is probably higher than $1,500 and considerably lower than tens of thousands. Engage common sense.

It's not absolutely essential that the computer be dedicated to serving only your Web pages, but that's the optimal plan. In fact, you can run other processes on the same machine; however, each one you add slows the overall processing speed. In all likelihood, you're going to be adding software to the computer to do specialized functions on your Web site. You're likely to add programs to do customized searches on your site. You may need to integrate existing databases, but the programs that make the databases available will run in conjunction with your server software. You're likely as not to want people to be able to download files from your site, so you'll need an FTP application to do that. You may need a mail program, too. There are endless software pieces you can use and may need. The more space and the more processing power you have available specifically for your Web-related applications, the better.

You want a computer that is reliable as well as fast. The Web is a 24x7 operation (24 hours a day, 7 days a week). You can't afford for it to be unavailable.

It's important to consider a regular schedule for service and backups. You may want to have a second computer that's equipped with the same software (and your eventual Web pages) so that one can be off-line while the other is still taking care of Web business. There will be times when software will need to be upgraded, and you may need to have one machine unavailable for some amount of time. For that, a backup server is a good idea.

KEEPING UP

Whatever equipment you purchase (or lease) will be out-of-date the day it's put into service. So what else is new? The first desktop computer that was installed in someone's office almost 20 years ago was out-of-date the day it arrived, and so it will go for the foreseeable future. You didn't really expect to find that computing had reached the end of its evolution, did you? We're dealing with reality.

FREE WEB SERVER SOFTWARE, OR COMMERCIAL?

Next on your list of must-haves is Web server software. This item ties right into the computer you're going to use or buy. Remember that the software for serving Web pages is available for all major operating systems. Don't choose your computer platform because someone once told you that XYZ server software is the best and it only runs on an operating system you've never heard of. If XYZ really is the best, but no one in your company knows anything about the operating system it requires, you've got a major headache in your immediate future. Your Web site isn't the place to be learning an operating system. You, your marketing gurus, your graphics designers, your editors, and your computing staff (especially if all of those are the same person) will have plenty of other things to learn as your Web site develops. Pick the platform that you (or they) are most familiar with now and use it. Your goal is to make this transition to the Web as painless as possible. It's not going to be the easiest thing you've ever done, so don't complicate matters.

48

▶ **NOTE**   You may find, as we did, that you'll change your mind about your choice of platform based on any number of considerations—familiarity with the product, software that offers more functionality, a need for quicker and more reliable connections. Our Web site was initially served from a UNIX platform, moved to a DEC VMS platform, and now runs on Windows NT. You can use the platform with which you are most familiar while you (or your technical staff) learn the ropes of Web site building and management, but you may need to be prepared to move to another platform. If you have technical staff that's well-versed in one of the major platforms (UNIX and NT are probably the most commonly used on the Web right now), you would probably be wise to consider housing your Web site on one of those platforms. ◀

If you're not going to run your own server, your service provider will determine what platform and server software you'll use. Some offer the full range of platforms and a choice of software products. Others may offer only one platform and one type of software. If the platform or the server software is a concern for you, be sure that you know what the provider offers.

You can use the free software that's available on the Web, or you can choose one of the available commercial products. Free software is great; if you have good technical staff, it may be perfect for you. The commercial products vary in price from $120 to $3,000, depending on the features supported. The most expensive server software generally includes security and other features that less expensive packages don't have. Whether you pay nothing or a lot, each package has its quirks and oddities, as in all software.

▶ **CAUTION**   If your documents are on a machine on the Internet, they are not secure. Period. If you can't risk someone getting their hands on that information, don't put it on a Web server or any other computer connected to the Internet. It's all but impossible to completely guard information from a determined, malicious hacker.

continues

continued

At the same time, being overly cautious is a sure way to keep your business in the dark ages. Your network staff should be responsible for ensuring that data is protected as necessary. A Web server can certainly be set up completely separately from any other computers on your network and pose no threat at all to data on other computers. ◀

FREEWARE AND SHAREWARE

Of course, the advantage of the freely-available software is its price (or lack thereof). The disadvantages are that it may have little (or unclear) documentation, no official technical support, and no scheduled upgrades. The fine folks who are generously offering their skills and know-how to give you the software probably don't have time to write the documentation. They're certainly not getting paid to answer your questions. They'll upgrade the product when and if they find the time. You could complain, but it won't do you any good, and you certainly would have no right. You can—and likely will be asked to—report bugs that you find to the folks who wrote the code. They sincerely are trying to make Web servers available to the largest number of people. They want your input; if you're taking advantage of their generosity, please do them the courtesy of complimenting what works and reporting, as pleasantly as possible, what doesn't.

COMMERCIAL SOFTWARE

Commercial software, no matter the cost, includes documentation and at least a minimal level of technical support. It's generally scheduled for regular upgrades, and the more common bugs will be patched in a timely manner. Unless you have good technical staff members who are whizzes with virtually all manner of software, you're probably better off paying for your software. At the least, you'll be able to get to a real person, either by phone or by e-mail, to answer your questions when something breaks—and it *will* break (or at least it won't work the way you think it should).

WHERE TO START SHOPPING

Take advantage of the information on the Web to start your comparison shopping. One of the best references is at Webcompare's Server Features Comparison Web site, at **http://www.webcompare.com/server-main.html**. They list virtually every piece of server software available for every platform, along with its features and costs. They also provide links to the various companies that offer the products. Many of those companies offer free downloads so that you can evaluate their products before you purchase them. For a lesson in just how easy it can be to install and run Web server software, take up one or two of the companies on their offers. Some of these products can be up and running in minutes, quite literally. Others take a bit longer and a bit more study, but most are relatively easy to use, especially if you plan to serve pages for only your own company.

▶ **NOTE**   A *domain name* is the designation for a specific company and machine on the Internet. In the URL **http://www.yourcompany.com**, for example, **www** would be the equivalent of the computer supplying your Web pages and **yourcompany.com** would be the domain name registered for your company. Some software (such as Apache, or WebSite by O'Reilly & Associates—and there probably are others) makes it very simple to serve pages for more than one domain name—you might even serve pages for **www.yourcompany.com**, **www.anothercompany.com**, and **www.yetanother.com**. ◀

You may have a more difficult time if you are planning to serve pages for more than one distinct domain name. At least one fairly expensive server program on the market now requires more RAM to be allocated for each domain that is served (which translates to buying more RAM for the computer). At the same time, at least one of the free server programs handles additional domain names very efficiently.

▶ **TIP**   Consider sending e-mail to Webmasters. Most who have been in the business any length of time have tried at least two or three packages on an evaluation basis if not in production. Some are running two or three in production. The people who are already doing this work are your best possible resource for information about what works and what doesn't. ◀

WIRES AND PLIERS— CONNECTING TO THE INTERNET

The next critical piece of your Web site puzzle is your Internet access. This is the part where you're going to fall asleep, even if you didn't while listening to the computer nerds explain about RAM. You need Internet access 24 hours a day, 7 days a week. Granted, there will always be the occasional interruption in service, but it shouldn't happen often or for long. The Web doesn't sleep. Your Web server shouldn't, either.

Internet access isn't magic. It's cabling and equipment in various shapes and sizes. You can hook the biggest, fastest computer in the world to a slow modem and phone line and waste a lot of processing power. The speed at which your Web site runs will depend on the speed of the equipment and the Internet connection to which it's attached.

TYPES OF CONNECTIONS

The most simple and the least expensive setup is access using a computer, a phone line, and a 28,800 modem. This is the "gravel road" access model. It isn't the best model for a business endeavor. If you're incredibly lucky, and your customers are incredibly patient, you might take a chance on it. You're going to need luck because you're going to need a very fast modem, a very clean telephone line, and a computer attached to those two, and all of them must be in perfect working order at all times. This is the shoestring budget plan for Web sites. It will work, but not as reliably as you'd like, and not quickly enough to suit anyone for long.

Now What?

If you now have an Internet connection from your home, this is probably the type of access you use. There are days when it works perfectly. Then there are days when no combination of patience, redialing, and offerings to deities will result in a reliable connection—and you don't stay connected all the time, do you?

Other possible levels of access, in order of their speed, price, and complexity of installation and maintenance (*kbps* stands for *kilobits per second* and *mbps* stands for *megabits per second*):

- **56 kbps lines.** Available in most places and reasonably easy to install and maintain.

- **ISDN (128 kbps).** Available in some areas and becoming more widely available quickly; installation and maintenance is rumored to be getting better. Charges vary widely.

- **T1 (1.544 mbps).** Very fast and probably more than sufficient for all but the most heavily accessed sites; pricey to install and maintain without good technical staff either on-site or contracted to come on-site quickly. Fractional T1 is also available and can be upgraded as your need for bandwidth grows.

- **T3 (45 mbps—the equivalent of 28 T1 lines).** Very, very fast, and expensive; a must for sites like Microsoft and Netscape and the other major players in this industry that count their "hits" in millions each day.

Prices for the various connections differ from place to place and company to company. The faster the access, the more expensive the service (T1 access, for instance, could be as expensive as $3,000/month, and a T3 as much as $20,000). Less expensive options are available, though. A Fractional T1 is also a fractional price of a T1. Some providers also lease lines, based on bandwidth usage. There are a myriad of pricing options (almost as many as there are providers). It will definitely require some shopping around on your part to find the most economical and practical solution for your business.

If you happen to be in Canada, you may also have the option of using cable access. There are plans for cable access in the U.S., and new areas are announcing test sites, but at this time it's simply unavailable in most areas. (By the time you read this, it may not be.) Depending on how the service is priced for business, it may be a good choice. Lots of factors will come into play when it comes to speed for cable access, including the amount of traffic on the cables. It will certainly be faster than ISDN and 56 kbps connections.

Other methods of access are already in the planning stages and may very well be stocked on store shelves by the time you read this. Intel Corporation and BroadBand Technologies recently announced that they are combining forces to produce cards that can be installed in PCs to offer quick access (quicker, they say, than cable modems) from homes and businesses, using fiber-to-curb networks that are being tested by phone companies. Each piece of new technology that appears on the market to make access faster and more convenient and less costly is good news for you. Keeping abreast of all the new technologies that are on the horizon, however, is guaranteed to make you dizzy.

What Do You Really Need?

Consider your audience when you make your decision about the type of line you need. If the majority of your audience is small businesses or individuals who are likely to be connecting to your site over dial-up connections, their access speeds will be dependent on their own lines and modems as well as yours. If your audience is companies or individuals in companies who have T1 or T3 access, they're going to expect reasonably quick access to your site. Unless you already have T1 or T3 access, or you honestly anticipate that your company's Web site will have a tremendous amount of traffic from the outset, a 56 kbps line will probably be sufficient. It's fast enough to serve pages easily to both the home user and the corporate client without doing unreasonable damage to your budget.

At the same time, if you install 56 kbps or ISDN and find that you need a higher level of connection, you're likely to have to pay another setup fee (all these connections require *some* initial setup fee—usually about the equivalent of one month's lease). Your budget is going to dictate, of course, but you can be sure that bandwidth requirements, whatever you judge them to be now, will increase.

It's possible that the worst thing that could happen when you debut your Web site is that you'll be entirely too popular. The speed of your connection and your computer, and the capabilities of the Web server software that you install, will determine the number of connections that you can serve to your Web audience. If users are unable to access your site for long periods of time because it's very busy, they're as likely as not to quit trying. Even the most savvy of technical operations can fall victim to the "we never thought so many people would be interested" syndrome, so don't conserve on the hardware and software that connects you to the Internet.

GETTING—AND STAYING—CONNECTED

Just where would you go about looking for one of these wires to connect to your business? Your local and long distance telephone carriers provide them and generally have lease arrangements for the equipment necessary to run them. Or you can lease the line and buy the equipment if you have the staff to maintain it. Make sure that your staff knows what they're doing with that equipment, though, if you choose to buy. Count on this to be true: If you call the carrier because your line isn't working, the carrier will steadfastly maintain that it's the fault of your equipment, not their line, and it won't be easy to convince them otherwise.

Connecting through your ISP. Most Internet service providers will offer you the connections through their company. Some of the providers are forming mergers and alliances with the phone carriers, which should help to reduce the cost for both services. (The jury is still out on this one at the moment—*should* is not the equivalent of *will*.)

A service provider has a sliver of an edge on you in the area of getting quick response from the carrier, because you won't be the only customer they're servicing. If their site suffers a disconnect from the Internet, they're going to have multiple angry customers beating on them, and they're pretty good at beating on the phone company in turn. If you happen to be the only customer who's unable to connect (or be connected to), you can trust that it's either their equipment or the phone line between you and them (you did verify that the computer is turned on and the Web server software is running, right?). They don't want it to be their equipment, so they'll do the troubleshooting and contact the phone company with all the technical particulars. The phone company wants to keep the service provider reasonably happy, because the phone company is making a good chunk of change on the lines the service provider is leasing.

The other side of that coin is more confusing and requires an understanding of how your service provider is connected to the Internet. If you lease a T1 from your business to your service provider, for instance, but your service provider's access to the Internet is 56 kbps, your data will zip right along from your business to theirs but then necessarily be slowed by the provider's connection. On the other hand, your provider may have a T1 connection. Your data will go from your T1 to their T1 quite quickly, but if 50 T1s are feeding into their site, traffic may slow down considerably as it queues up to access its share of that T1.

Worse, your provider may not have a direct Internet connection, but be buying their connection from yet another provider. In that case, you've extended your distance to the Internet, and it becomes increasingly difficult to know what speed lines are between you and the provider who has direct access. Unless your budget absolutely will not allow for a connection to a provider with direct Internet access, don't sublet from a sublet.

▶ **NOTE**   Providers that connect to the Internet backbone have direct access. Yes, it's all terribly confusing, but it's important for you to know where you fit into the big picture of the Internet. If your provider leases a connection from one of the direct access providers, your connection may or may not be slow, depending on their connection, but the further away you are from that backbone the slower your connection is likely to be. ◀

Leasing computer space from your ISP. If those options don't seem quite like perfect solutions, you can lease your computer space from the Internet service provider. In that case, the computer that serves your Web pages will be on their site. That's not at all a bad solution if you don't already have the technical staff to take care of the equipment yourself. Alternatively, you can purchase the computer and house it at the provider's site. That's likely to prove more economical than hiring a systems administrator for your staff. In either case, make sure that you have easy access to their site, preferably with a local telephone call, so that you can make minor changes and corrections to your pages. If you're forced to pay for every correction or change that you make, you're going to eventually break your budget or abandon your Web site.

What Does the Connection Cost?

Whatever combination of technical know-how and access you want is available for a price. That price is going to vary from city to city and telephone carrier to telephone carrier. It's also going to vary, in some cases, depending upon the type of company you have. If your company is a not-for-profit or an educational institution, you may be able to find a service provider that will offer you a reduced rate for both the access and the equipment necessary to install it. If your organization is a professional or technical society, you may have a company or a service provider in your area that's willing to serve your pages for you at little or no charge, if you'll maintain the pages.

Consider combining forces with another business or two in your area. There are no rules that say you can't use one computer and Internet connection to operate a Web site for you and your business associates. That's essentially what the service providers are doing; you'd simply be doing the same thing as a business partnership and sharing the costs for equipment and maintenance. Shop around. A way exists for you to set up a Web site that will fit your budget; you just need to find the right set of circumstances to work for you.

▶ **CAUTION**   If you decide to join forces with other companies, make sure that your Internet access provider allows it. Some don't. Others charge a higher rate for those who are basically reselling their service. ◀

If you don't like to shop, or your eyes glaze over when technical terms start flying through the air like so many buzzing bees, delegate! That was your original plan anyway, wasn't it? Good thinking.

Now, About Your Name

Your company already has a perfectly good name. The question is whether your company name will appear in your URL. Most Web surfers learn the fine art of URL-guessing quickly. A URL is, quite simply, a domain name followed by a path. The *path* is nothing more than directions to directories and files on the computer serving the Web pages. The path is almost always impossible to guess, but the domain name isn't. If you want to locate a specific company on the Web, your best bet is to type the following URL: **http://www.*companyname*.com**. More often than not, you'll find exactly the company you want.

If you don't have your own domain name, your URL is going to be the domain name of your service provider (**www.*your-isp*.net**, for instance) followed by the directory information the service provider chooses. You may get lucky and have an address like **http://www.*your-isp*.net/*your-company*/** or

58

you may instead end up with something like **http://www.*your-isp*.net/ customers/retailers/clothes/children/*your-company*/**. And it could be worse than that.

You've lost most chances of someone guessing your URL in either instance. Worse, if you lease your access lines and don't register your domain name, you'll be stuck with numbers rather than a name. You don't really *want* to be **179.254.254.254**, do you?

You may at some point change providers, too. Your domain name can go with you if it's registered. If it's not, you're going to have to scramble to publicize your site again, probably not something you'd really like to do. Registration fees are a very small price to pay for your own address that won't change, and URLs that won't either.

No, you can't just set up your Web site and decide to be **www.*your-company*.com**. It's a bit more complicated than that. Not a lot, but some. You have to register your domain name with *Internic* (the central domain-name registration repository), a non-profit agency associated with Network Solutions, Inc. Specific rules govern what type of domain you're allowed to register. Everything you never thought you'd need to know about domain names and how to register them is available at **http://www.internic.net** (but you'd already guessed that, right?). Internic registers second-level domain names—that's the ***your-company*.com** part of the name—for organizations that fall into five broad top-level domains:

- **edu**—Educational institutions
- **com**—Commercial businesses
- **org**—Not-for-profit organizations
- **net**—Network providers
- **gov**—U.S. government agencies

Most businesses will be registered under the **.com** domain. Check the specific guidelines at Internic to determine the most likely domain for your company. The current cost of registering your domain name with Internic is $100 for two years. After the initial two-year period, you'll be billed annually at the rate of $50. The process for most domain registrations is automated and takes very little time (sometimes less than two days, even for those domains that aren't set up for automatic processing—**net** and **org** aren't, at this time). Internic's response time is astonishing when you consider that, at the end of 1995, it was estimated that more than 20,000 domain names per month were being registered, up from around 400 per month in the spring of 1993.

Believe it or not, someone may already have registered your name. Internic isn't in the business of verifying that your company name is unique unto it-self, only that it's unique to the Internet when it's registered. If your desired name is already registered with Internic, you have only a couple of options. You can contact the party who registered your name and try to purchase the registered domain name from them, or request that they change their name (an extremely unlikely scenario), or you can choose another name. If your name is already a registered trademark, however, you may have legal avenues that you can pursue, if you choose to do so.

▶ **CAUTION**   Some completely unscrupulous people have registered do-main names that they hope to be able to sell. Lists of domain names have been sent by e-mail to various places, offering domain names at auction. If your name is important to you, register it. The sooner, the better. ◀

You need a minimal amount of technical information to register your domain name. Your access provider can give you that information. Most providers will register the name for you; they may charge a fee for the service in addi-tion to the charges by Internic.

Miserable technical stuff out of the way, let's move gratefully along. You folks who already have Internet access and a domain name can rejoin us for the rest of this discussion.

SHOULD YOU OUTSOURCE THIS WEB PROJECT?

Whatever your resources, you can turn the entire Web site project over to one of the Internet or Web service providers in your area—or even in some other area. If your business is like most today, you don't exactly have people sitting on their hands waiting for work to do. Devoting people to your Web project may not be an option. Unless you're in the deepest reaches of the least-populated rural areas, there are probably three new service providers opening their doors in your vicinity today. Three others are closing. This market is volatile as well as exciting, and highly competitive.

WHAT DO THE PROVIDERS OFFER?

If you don't already have Internet access, consider contracting with a provider now as a trial run. Make sure that the provider you choose offers Web service, but use only their standard services for a while—e-mail, file transfers, and Web access (for surfing and studying).

Use the service regularly yourself. If you have problems, call their help desk. Is their technical support staff knowledgeable and courteous? If there's some general problem on the network (and there will be, at one time or another), do they notify their customers about it and offer helpful workarounds—or at least an estimate of when it will be fixed—before a general riot? Your provider should be as professional about their business as you are about yours.

VISIT THE ELECTRONIC SITES

Before you sit down to write a request for proposals or quotes from specific providers, visit their Web sites and their clients' Web sites. There are service providers at every level of competence from abysmal to expert. If their pages are unappealing to you or seem to take a very long time to download to your browser, do you really want them setting up your site? You may dearly love those glitzy graphics they've got, but one word of caution: Content—not graphics or sound—rules the information superhighway. If the provider's pages aren't well-written, they don't understand the most basic of the rules of the Web.

At this stage of the game, and probably for some time to come, you're looking for function over form. Your pages need to work for you, not just be wonderfully cool.

Visit the Physical Sites

After you've looked at their pages and decided on several to consider as prospective providers for your company, meet with their representatives. If you decide to outsource this project, you're going to be working closely with these people for some time to come. You might buy a car from a truly obnoxious sales person just because he offered you the best price, but you're probably not going to have to deal with him regularly in the future (you hope). A service provider is another story entirely. You need to be sure that you can develop a reasonably comfortable relationship with them.

Scratch off your list of prospects anyone who seems to imply that coding and designing Web pages is rocket science and something well beyond the ken of mere mortals. They only want your money, and they want lots of it. Also scratch off your list anyone who shows you only a canned presentation over a snappy laptop they "just happened to bring along." You want to see pages working over the Web. A good laptop can serve up huge graphics in short order; the Web can't. That form that looks so very good when shown locally on the laptop has to *work*, not just look good, which means that it has to have some programming attached to it, and you want to make sure that the programming works.

Now that your original list is likely a bit shorter, a visit to their office won't hurt a thing and may shorten your list considerably. If you don't understand (or don't want to understand) the technical part of this process, take someone along with you who does. You're going to be looking at several things in the process, and not all of them are technical: You want a general feel for the provider's staff. You're going to be working with these people, remember.

◆ Do they have enough staff to service the accounts that they already have?

◆ Does everyone look sufficiently harried but still smiling? (Good sign, that!)

◆ You may feel as though you've wandered into the twilight zone. Don't expect suits and a quiet, reserved atmosphere. Expect jeans and T-shirts (crawling around in wires and equipment isn't easy in a suit).

◆ Expect telephones ringing constantly and tech support staff sporting nose rings. These people were hired for their technical knowledge (or at least they should have been), not their wardrobes or looks.

You also want to see their technical operation. You don't have to understand *how* it works to get a feel for *whether* it works:

◆ A well organized, functioning site will hardly look like a surgical operating theater, but it should be navigable. There are likely to be cables and wires by the ton, but they should be marginally contained at the least.

◆ Someone should be able to give you a non-technical explanation of what the equipment does and how it all works. Otherwise, your technically-minded partner should ask technical questions.

◆ If something is broken and the tech staff is busy fixing it, ask how long it's been broken. Ask how long before it will be fixed.

◆ You want to know their schedules for backing up your files. Will they do it daily, weekly, whenever they feel like it? Never??

◆ What about general maintenance? If the computer that serves your documents takes a nose dive at 3 a.m. on a Sunday, will someone know about it and begin to repair the damage before Monday at 7 a.m., when the first bleary-eyed person shows up for work? And when they do fix it, how quickly are they going to be able to restore your documents from their backups?

It's possible for you to contract with a service provider who's completely outside of your area, of course. You could operate your business in New Jersey and have a service provider in California. In that case, the site visit may not be an option. If you're sure you're dealing with an established, reputable company, and you have reasonable local access, a service provider across the continent may be a very workable solution. It will simply take some adjustments and some additional planning. You wouldn't be well-advised, however, to have your service provider in Europe or Australia—unless that's where your clients are.

Accessing sites outside of the U.S. can be very slow. There are some very long lines between you and those places, and data has to travel over them. The farther your customer is from your Web site, the longer it will take for her to see your pages. If you have a client base in the U.S. and another in France, you'd be wise to consider having a Web server located in both countries; some service providers can do that for you.

REQUESTING QUOTES FROM PROVIDERS

Now that your list of prospective providers is down to a manageable few, you can ask for quotes for the services you need. Even if you know that you aren't going to place your business with a service provider, you should still write the specification for what you expect from your Web site. It can serve as your basic plan to guide your staff in the implementation stages.

TYPE OF SERVICE

After doing your original homework and talking with the representatives of the providers, you should have a better idea of the type of service that will be best for your business. You want to specify the type of access you require, from none to top-of-the-line T3.

Now What?

Depending on the size of your company (and your budget), you may decide to share space on a computer with other companies, or you may feel that you need a computer dedicated to the task of serving your pages. You need to specify the level of service that you think will best meet your needs. If you're unsure, consider sharing space, at least in the beginning. As your site grows, and as the number of people who visit your site grows, the provider will certainly be willing to sell you more space; there's no reason to purchase more than you really need initially.

▶ **CAUTION** A company that advertises or presents their service as having "full" T1 or T3 access may very well have exactly that, but they also may have only one T1/T3 line that serves their entire site, rather than one T1 dedicated to your company. If you really need full T1 or full T3 service *for your company alone*, be sure to specify it. ◀

EQUIPMENT AND SOFTWARE

Make sure that your specification itemizes hardware (the wires and pliers of Internet access and the computer specifications) separately from software and customized services. Each piece of your specification should be relatively easy to separate from the rest of the pieces. You want to know exactly how much each piece will cost.

DOCUMENTS AND GRAPHICS

Since you've got that well-thought-out plan for your site, you should have a good idea of the number of documents that you want to serve initially. Detail how you will deliver those documents. If what you have isn't in electronic format, or is in a format that isn't easy to translate to the provider's platform, it will need to be translated or re-keyed. That, too, will affect the pricing structure you're offered. If you aren't going to deliver prepared documents, but want your site to be designed entirely by the provider, specify that. (The price just went up again.)

Do you want custom-designed graphics? Will you or your graphics designer provide them? In what format? If you provide them in electronic format, you won't need to pay to have printed graphics scanned into the provider's system. If you don't have them and expect them to be designed, you must include that fact in your specification, and you need to determine how many you absolutely require in the initial design phase.

▶ **CAUTION**   Remember that your browser is the part of this equation that interprets the pages you see. Web pages may look very different from one browser to another. That is *not* the fault of the designer or the provider. It's a fact of life on the Web. ◀

You also need to specify whether you will own the artwork or the programs that make the forms functional, if the provider does the design and the programming. You may decide to move to another provider at some point, or you may decide to serve the pages yourself. Your contract with any service provider should detail the ownership of every piece of your project. That may very well include your domain name, if your provider registers it for you. Make sure that you still own it if you decide to move! You don't really want to go through this whole process again, do you?

What about forms? Do you plan to have an order form or a request form of some type? Or more than one? What about forums? Image maps? Right. Those affect your eventual price of service.

Updates and Changes

How often do you expect your pages to change? Include in your specification the schedule for those changes—weekly, monthly, quarterly, or whatever you think will be best for you.

As you write your request for quotes, be as specific as you possibly can. Having the provider remind you in two months that the database search you're requesting was never mentioned in your original specification will not be a pleasant surprise, for either of you.

MAINTENANCE AND SERVICE

If you've decided to have the equipment and lines installed at your business site rather than the provider's site, be sure to request quotes for maintenance and repair costs and for the level of service you expect—whether that's for service at any time, day or night, or just during normal working hours. And specify your expectations with regard to response time from the provider, in the event that you need service. Will you be satisfied to wait for 24 hours for response, or 8 hours, or 4 hours, perhaps? Just as with the type of line you need, the faster you expect response, the more expensive the service will be.

Yes, all of this planning and considering is a lot of work, but it will pay off for you in the long run, whether you contract the entire job to the service provider or not. It's the foundation for your Web site.

PRICE COMPARISONS: APPLES VERSUS ORANGES

As the providers' quotes begin to filter back into your hands, you're going to wish you had a seat belt to buckle on your office chair. Quite a few people know how to do the work associated with building and managing a Web site, but there aren't so many of them that supply exceeds demand. You know what that means: You can get it wholesale, but you probably crossed most of those people off your list for one reason or another, and your reasons were probably good ones.

Even if you were prepared to see some reasonably large numbers on the quotes, they may seem to be arriving at those numbers in odd ways. All of the quotes may be reasonably equivalent with regard to access charges, but the costs per page and how they quote the ongoing charges is a mix of magical potions:

- ◆ Based on the amount of storage space you may (or may not) use on their computers
- ◆ Based on the number of hits per day, week, month, phase of the moon, or something

- Based on the number of bytes transferred
- Unlimited access (no charges based on hits or transfers) but eye-popping charges

Internet and Web service providers are in business to make money, just like you are. The business is still young, and there are as many ways to charge for the services as there are services. Most reputable providers try to structure their prices in a way that's fair and will give them a reasonable income and you good service. Some providers are in it strictly to get rich, and some may do exactly that—but more will fail. They know what we all know in this industry: The skills that they offer, in many cases, are going to be replaced in two to five years by software that will do the same things. But right now, the software either doesn't exist or is too primitive for most people to take the time to learn to use. Your mission is to try to sort out the decent offers from the totally outrageous ones.

Your pages don't just drift around in the air waiting for someone to request them; they take up space on the provider's computer. Let's see if we can put it into some kind of reasonable perspective.

COST PER PAGE

The first chapter of this book is (in its electronic form) in the neighborhood of 100KB of data. That's about 40 pages of textual information. Text doesn't take up much space, really. Graphics, however, can take up a *lot* of space. And you're certainly planning to use at least a few graphics to brighten up your pages. Sound files tend to be even larger than graphics files, normally.

If each of your Web pages is in the size range that's presently considered optimal for serving across the network (20-25KB), 4 or 5 of your pages is the equivalent of the first 40 pages in this book. What looks to you to be a very small graphic may easily be 25KB all on its own. It doesn't take long at all to consume a great deal of hard drive space on a computer when you start adding graphics and sounds and the other gadgets for Web pages.

The service provider will have to add disk space to the computer as those files start filling up the available space. That costs money; the provider in turn charges you for that space. Nothing to it. Those are legitimate charges. If you bought or leased the same computer and filled up the space on it, you'd have to either delete some files at some point or buy more memory space.

The cost per page is a seemingly arbitrary figure arrived at by a combination of what the market will bear and the self-confidence factor of the designers, word-crafters, and/or marketers involved in the process. (There's a rumor that slaughtering chickens and studying Tarot cards are involved in the process too, but that hasn't been verified by any knowledgeable source.) What the market will bear is easier to understand than the self-confidence factor of some of these people. The quote that, in all seriousness, lists $5,000 per page for your home page plus one other page that's especially important to you in-dicates the self-confidence level of the provider. You can decide whether you have that much confidence in their work. It may very well be that the page or pages in question are important enough to warrant the costs, but you must be the judge.

Cost Per Hit or Per Bytes Transferred

Charges by the number of hits per whatever cycle the company uses or the number of bytes transferred fall somewhat in the same category—but only somewhat. A *hit* is the transfer of one file across the network. Not too com-plicated—except that one page is likely to be more than one hit. Yes, you read that right. If your page has graphics, each graphic is a separate file, which also counts as a hit on your site. So if your home page has one text file and three graphics (a graphical bullet, an image map, and a picture of your product), that's four hits, not one.

The number of bytes transferred (which will be more like megabytes, actually) has to do with loading your pages across that line you're leasing so that it will eventually be seen by your prospective client. If your page is 25KB, including the graphics, you can deliver that page about 40 times to equal 1 megabyte transferred. That doesn't sound too bad, until you remember that you have not just one page but 3 or 5 or 20—do the math.

The eye-popping access charges are a valid cost of doing business. Someone has to pay for the lines, for the equipment to make them work, and for the maintenance to keep them running.

The average manager tends to descend into either fits of rage or a catatonic state on receiving quotes from Internet and Web service providers. Supply and demand, remember? Even the most abysmal of those service providers has skills that you don't have and that you don't think your staff has. For the short term, it may very well be a perfectly sound business investment to get your Web site up and running. But does it make sense for you to pay for those skills, any one or all of them, on a long-term basis?

If the Web, or whatever it evolves into next, is the future of communications, you are at some point going to need people on staff who know how to work in the medium. If you've been in business more than 10 years, you can remember when not every desktop had a computer. The immediate future is the Web. In two years, if you don't have people on staff who understand how it works and know how to manipulate the information that you want on the Web, you'll still be paying service providers and consultants to do the work.

Take another look at the bottom line on those quotes. If they look reasonable for a one-time investment, approach it that way and put your business on the Web. In the meantime, determine what staff you have who can do the work (or who can learn). If the quotes don't look reasonable even for a one-time investment, take a hard look at what you can do yourself, and what parts you absolutely need to contract to someone else.

How Much of the Work Can You or Your Staff Do?

If you don't already have Internet access and the associated equipment and staff, you're going to be forced to pay someone for that part of the work. Determine which of the providers is the most reliable and the most reasonable and contract with them for that part of the service.

You need someone who can write your Web pages or adapt the information you already have for the Web. You also need someone to do the necessary HTML coding. You need (or will need) at least one person on your staff who understands the technology of the Web, or, as one provider puts it, "You are in for a huge bill somewhere down the line." Ignorance may sometimes be bliss, but it can often be very expensive. Someone needs to design or locate the graphics you want to use on your Web pages, and someone else needs to do the programming necessary to make your forms or other specialized pages work.

It isn't as much of a production as it sounds, actually:

◆ Someone is undoubtedly already writing the information you're using in your present marketing efforts.

◆ Someone on your staff is probably a budding graphical artist, if not a professional one.

◆ New programs are appearing daily on the market that take the mystery out of the programming you'll want done, so you don't really need a programmer dedicated to the task. HTML coding is really quite simple, though time-consuming. And it's getting easier as new products are introduced that easily convert documents prepared in most word processing programs to HTML.

THE COMPLETE TRUTH
ABOUT HTML CODING

At a bare minimum, you want someone on your staff who can do HTML coding, so that your documents can be easily and quickly put on your Web site, no matter where that is. You don't want to depend on someone else and their schedule to do this piece of the work. So let's talk about HTML coding. Not the specifics. You don't have to know how to do it yourself yet. If the coding is the part you've been most concerned about, you're about to justify your purchase of this book.

HTML coding is easy. HTML coding is *very* easy. HTML coding is so easy that it's deadly dull after the first 50 pages or so. Up to that point, the gratification of having pages that actually work on the Web will be enough to keep the budding HTML expert going. After that, eyes begin to glaze and the fun goes out of it. After the 100th page, it's just plain boring. Unless of course the HTML standard changes, as it does on a fairly regular basis, and the soon-to-be expert can figure out a way to include the latest feature in your pages—and he will, whether or not you want that feature included.

▶ **NOTE**   The `<blink>` tag that the folks at Netscape so maliciously added as an "enhancement" is just such a feature. The rumor is that it was added as a joke. Ha. Blinking pages starting showing up everywhere. It's the single most annoying "enhancement" ever to be added to HTML, but bored HTML coders everywhere embraced it just because it was new. Thankfully, the `<blink>` tag has not been adopted as part of the HTML standard specification (though that doesn't stop people from using it). ◀

It is indeed possible to learn the basics of HTML coding in a week. The finer points take longer. Because the standard does change regularly, you can't learn it once and then never change your approach; that's the only thing that keeps it interesting.

72

HTML coding is absolutely, positively not a design language. This drives graphical artists totally nuts. You can attempt to trick HTML into presenting information the way you want it seen, but you can't guarantee that every browser will interpret the code the way you want. Sometimes you just have to live with a reasonable alternative to a designer's fabulous idea.

GRAPHICS—THE GLITTER FOR YOUR WEB SITE

Yes, you want graphics. Absolutely. Well-designed graphics can add a great deal of appeal to your site. However, graphics that are very large or that don't have some useful function are a waste of time and do nothing but slow down the speed at which your pages can be served.

You can use your existing graphics if they're in electronic format. A number of excellent software products can convert most graphic formats to the types of formats that are most easily viewed by the majority of graphical browsers on the Web—either GIF format or JPEG. If you have the graphics but not in electronic format, they can easily be scanned into files that can be used. The trick then becomes one of reducing the size and complexity of the image so that it doesn't take forever to load over the network. If you have graphic artists on staff, they should be able to do that for you. If not, contract with someone who can.

If you don't have graphics or graphical artists, you're not completely out of luck. There's a wealth of freely available graphics on the Web. Put someone to work scouting them out. Protect yourself from copyright infringement, though, by requesting permission from the owner to use the graphics. Some will be happy to have you use their work in exchange for a link from your site to theirs. Others may request payment for use of their work. (You've just found yourself a graphic artist who already knows how to design for the Web. Aren't you the cagey one?)

Programs to Make Your Customized Pages Work

No programmers on staff? No problem. Your local university, technical college, or perhaps even high school has a bright young programmer who will be more than happy to work on your project for a reasonable fee. Of course, the programs must work on your provider's system, so your programmer should work closely with the provider to ensure compatibility. On the other hand, it may actually cost you less in the long run to have the provider's staff prepare these programs, because of their familiarity with their operating system. In addition, because those programs can pose a security risk, you may be required to pay someone on their staff to review the programs. If the programs are being written to be used on your own server, you obviously want to take care that the person with whom you contract is mature and responsible.

Though most Internet businesses hate to admit it, the truth is that software products are now coming onto the market that are *designed* to work with Web server products—giving you easy-to-learn and easy-to-use integration with the forms and databases that you want to make available to your audience. (We don't like to admit it because we thought at least this one area of Web site design would remain a bastion of technical people and a complete mystery to the rest of the world. So much for job security.)

3-D Worlds, Java, and Such—The Glitz

Ah, the *real* excitement of the Web. These technologies allow your Web site to move, to be three-dimensional. They're exciting, and they're the parts of the Web that Web developers dearly love. They can turn a boring page into a real world; they can animate the dullest of pages.

If your plan involves the most creative areas of Web site development and you don't have graphic artists and programmers on staff, you'll need to subcontract for that work. These areas are really technical, and they require considerable investments of time and effort. Undoubtedly, someone is writing software applications to simplify these processes even as this sentence is being written, but for now what's available is still rather tricky to learn and use.

For the most part, these are specialized, developing areas of Web sites. They require specialized skills. That's not to say that someone on your staff can't learn how to handle them, but the investment of time for that learning process won't be negligible.

When Is Enough Too Much?

The work associated with Web site development is not, for the most part, terribly difficult. The difficulty is more in juggling all the pieces and parts and in paying very close attention to all the details of coding and design that make the site work as it should. The details and the juggling can become overwhelming as a site grows. Don't wait for your Webmaster to come to work carrying an Uzi before you either add staff to the project or subcontract some of the work.

Superhighway Tolls and Traffic Jams

Your Web site, no matter how simple or how complex, is an investment. Treat that investment as you would any part of your company's investment plans. Determine a budget, and inform the people involved with the project what that budget is. They can't make good, realistic plans for your Web site unless they know the limits of your financial commitment to the project.

The Obvious Costs

You may decide to make a minimal investment initially. It's entirely possible, if you or your staff can write and code your pages and locate or design your graphics, to place a few pages on your service provider's site for less than $100 initial investment and a monthly fee as low as $25. At the other end of the spectrum, if your plan includes a large number of documents housed on your provider's site, served by a full T1, and you subcontract design services, your initial investment may very easily exceed $100,000 and may go as high as $1 million. (Well, that certainly is the other end of the spectrum, wouldn't you say?) Your monthly charges for T1 access alone will be $1,000-$3,000. If you have Internet access at your site and need only designate a computer to serve your pages and people to prepare them, you still may want a consultant to help guide you and your staff in the initial stages. You can expect to pay Web consultants $60-$100 per hour or more, depending on your location and their level of expertise.

Your Internet access charges are an ongoing expense, whether or not you already have service. You may find it necessary to upgrade the type of service that you do have, if your Web site is a busy one.

If you are operating your own Web server, expect to add software to handle special processing needs over time. You can also plan to upgrade the computer within two years at a maximum—sooner if you aren't starting this project with a reasonably up-to-date, fast machine.

Staff salaries will be involved for coding, designing, and maintaining your site. Whether you budget that time directly or indirectly, it's still a very real cost of doing business on the Web. As your site grows, so will the time necessary to maintain it.

COSTS THAT AREN'T SO OBVIOUS, BUT ARE JUST AS REAL

Don't you just love meetings? That's good, because the number of hours expended by you and/or the people involved with your site (and those who want to be involved with it in any way, however remotely) will increase far faster than you anticipate. As with meetings on any other project in your business, some will actually be worthwhile. Just as many will be nothing more than dog-and-pony shows, and an equal number will be of little or no value.

Your staff has to learn the skills necessary to make your site work. That isn't a one-time investment in training. It's an ongoing process in an industry that's changing daily—sometimes twice a day. For the most part, staff training won't be structured, but rather self-motivated. However, you should budget for some amount of structured training for your key people, just as you would for other projects. Those key people also should be teaching others in your company how to do what they do. The reason Web service providers are in such demand is that there aren't many who know how to do the work. Spread the knowledge, and your investment in staff training will eventually pay for itself. Allow it to be guarded, and you'll pay.

Your priorities for your Web site will change over time, and those changing priorities will require changes in your site. Your original plan for significant changes every six months and minor changes monthly will evolve into seasonal redesigns and major overhauls. That fact translates to more staff time.

THE BALANCE SHEET

Once you have determined the facts and figures—you know what you need and what it's likely to cost—you'll probably have to convince someone a bit higher up the food chain that the idea is a good one, worthy of the investment required. If you're in the enviable position of being the final arbiter, and your investment really isn't much more than $25 to $100 a month, your risk is minimal. You can hardly place a newspaper ad for less. But if your investment is going to be substantial or you have to convince someone else that a Web site is worthwhile, combine your plan for your site with your facts and figures and start deciding how best to present the information to those who can commit the resources for the project.

Can You Sell It?

Quick—without pondering or rereading the first chapter of this book—what exactly is your purpose for your Web site? Managers in most companies aren't typically impressed by a purpose statement that says something similar to, "We think this will just be great fun and it's really cool." If you want to have fun and do cool things, management would generally prefer that you do that on your own time. Your plan needs goals that reflect the real concerns of the company as a whole. Make a list of precisely what you hope to accomplish with your Web site: Do you want to provide customer support, sell your products, educate, or simply maintain a competitive edge because your competition is already on the Web?

Whatever the reasons, list them one by one. If you were required to judge those reasons with a critical eye and back them up with your own money, would you buy this project? If you wouldn't, you're not likely to convince someone else to spend their money. Refine your plan until you would buy it.

Take into consideration your corporate culture. Is your company typically on the leading edge of new technologies, or is it more conservative and cautious? Your approach will have to be modified to reflect that overall culture. Even a very cautious company may have extremely good reasons for investing in a Web site; it's your job to find those reasons.

Did Someone Say ROI?

You're armed with cost projections for your project, but when was the last time you talked management into investing in something that would only cost them money and not demonstrate some measurable return? Is any one of your list of reasons for building this Web site going to add to your company's revenue figures? Are you sure? You can't translate traditional methods of sales-to-customers-contacted on the Web. Sure, your site may draw thousands of people a day, but we've already determined that even the experts don't know the demographics of those people. If you go into a meeting with management and declare that this project will add 10 percent to the company's bottom line, you may not be well-received in a year. Some people do indeed make purchases on the Web, but not as many as most companies would like.

You simply can't guarantee that any specific number of people will visit your Web site or that some specific percentage of those people will make a purchase. There are no verifiable indicators available to you—no hard and fast facts that will back up your claim. The likelihood is that some tried-and-proven method for secure payments will eventually be put into place, and that the Web will continue to grow and become a mature medium for sales. In the meantime, you'll make some sales; as the medium matures, and you learn more about who your site attracts and how to appeal to the audience you want, you'll make more.

You can take reasonable steps to encourage people to visit your site—and you may even make it worthwhile for them to purchase your product on the Web by offering special discounts—but you can't at this point offer any more than anecdotal claims for actual sales. You can estimate what you hope to sell, but both you and management should understand that your estimates are only that. In truth, they should probably be labeled *guesstimates*—and on the Web, your guess is as good as the next person's.

That doesn't mean that a Web site can't make a return on investment. Rather, it means that you need to measure it differently. How much does one call to your technical support group cost the company? How many calls do they take in a day? Is your goal to reduce the number of calls, thereby saving telephone charges and staff time? Suppose, for instance, that the average support call costs your company $25 and your support staff fields 200 calls a day. If your goal is to reduce the number of calls by 10 percent, you are offering a significant savings.

The same measures can be applied if you routinely mail out product specifications or other literature that you can make available on the Web. Even low percentage points of line items that routinely make their way into a company's budget can translate to considerable savings over time.

Can you measure goodwill? The IRS made some friends with their Web site. Will you with your Web site? How much is that worth to you and your company? If customer relations is an area that needs addressing, your Web site may be invaluable from the day it appears online.

Consider your reasons for your site and your company's needs and resources. A Web site really is a business investment and you want to be considered seriously when you offer your plan. Unless your entire staff of upper management and/or your Board of Directors has been sailing on the open sea for the past year or two without benefit of radio, TV, or newspapers, they've read at least the headlines in the various business and trade magazines. They see the trend (or what's being sold as a trend, depending on their outlook). They may need only a reasonable proposal that addresses one or two of your key points to propel them to fund your site. Or they may need more. You need to be prepared to give them the best and most honest appraisal that you can.

Your approach to management doesn't necessarily have to be one of "all or nothing." Consider the possibilities of scaling the Web site to address one portion of your overall plan, and testing the Web waters. If you accomplish nothing more than discovering that you need more staff time than you originally planned, or that you haven't yet refined your plan adequately to address the Web market, you'll at least have gained experience that will be useful to you and your company.

As you plan for and make your presentation, don't pull punches with yourself or your management. The Web isn't yet a proven medium for sales, and it's difficult to measure success on other strategies. You may not be able to offer any reliable return on investment for two years or more. It's possible that you can do it sooner, if you have the right strategy, but you'll be better served if you don't make grandiose claims for results in less than six months. It's better to be more successful than your original plan than to look foolish when your predictions simply don't meet the mark.

Now What?

The future of business communications is being written in the applications programming departments of the various software companies. From the largest to the smallest, they're hedging their bets that the Web is the future. They aren't asking you if you want a Web browser to be integrated with your other office products—they're telling you it *will be*. What's more, they're working with one another to make those products more platform-independent, and thus more Web-friendly. The Web is forcing them into alliances that would have been unthinkable as little as two years ago. The handwriting is on the wall, and it doesn't take a prophet to read it.

Joining the growing numbers of businesses on the Web is risky to an extent, but being viewed as a dinosaur is a risk, too. Develop your plan wisely, and you and your company will be better prepared for whatever future the Web brings.

◄ 3 ►

YOUR STAFF, YOUR WEB SITE, AND YOU

WHO'S GOING TO GUIDE THE
OVERALL EFFORT?

◆

WHAT TOOLS DO THEY NEED?

◆

WHEN WILL YOU SEE RESULTS?

◆

WILL THE DOCUMENTS YOU HAVE
WORK FOR A WEB MARKET?

◆

WHEN CAN YOU STOP MAKING
DECISIONS ABOUT THIS PROJECT??

Y̶ou've developed the plan, gotten management support and approval, and you're anxious to get your site built and working. Good for you!

You didn't assign a *committee* to work on the project, did you? We're talking about the Web here; things have to be done quickly, and many times on-the-fly. Do you have a committee that moves quickly? Even one? No, not quickly as in "decisions are made over a three-month period"—which actually wouldn't be too bad for most committees—but quickly as in "sometimes decisions have to be made and implemented in 24 hours or less." That kind of quickly. Cancel the committee. You'll probably end up with one of sorts, but it's likely to be self-selecting.

The amount of work involved with Web site development can be overwhelming; only those who are truly committed to the project are likely to be left standing in three to six months. You're not quite through with making decisions on this project just yet.

YOUR CAPABILITIES

You need staff to get the job done, and you certainly want to know a general time line for creating your Web site. The people you choose or assign or hire to work on this project are critical to your Web site. If you make good staffing decisions, the work will go more smoothly and require less time. If you blunder in this department, the eventual costs could be much more than you are willing—or able—to pay.

Your Web site will represent your company, and your development team will represent the Web site. If anyone of them responds to an e-mail request from the Web in a brusque or impolite way, you may very well lose business. If your Webmaster allows pages that are in violation of copyright laws to be served, you could have a lawsuit on your hands. You need a Web development staff that won't make those kinds of mistakes.

Who Will Do It?

This part of your search should actually be fun. You're going on a scavenger hunt for a Webmaster. One person. Not three. You're likely to eventually have three or more people who are "masters" at some piece of the project, but you need one person who can bring the elements together. Find that person first and the rest will follow.

What Skills Does a Webmaster Need?

Look for an unusual person, a generalist. Your Webmaster should know a little bit about every aspect of your business and Web site design. You need the type of person who loves learning and learns quickly. Because the Web is changing and growing quickly, look for a person who can easily adapt to learning new things. As boring as HTML can be, in two years there were three versions of the HTML standard. And that's just one small piece of the whole. Every new gadget and gimmick will have to be evaluated with an eye to what it can (or can't) do for your site. Almost all of the learning will be self-education, so self-motivation is an important characteristic for your Webmaster to possess.

You may find your Webmaster anyplace in your organization. It's virtually impossible to predict what he or she may be doing at the moment—for the simple reason that generalists tend to change jobs regularly. They're interested in so many things that seldom will one area hold their interest for long. Ask your Human Resources staff to search their files for people in your company who have a background in advertising, marketing, or sales, and in computer hardware and software. Their résumés may simply include long lists of software applications with which they're familiar, or they may have consistently gravitated to positions that allowed them to work with computers while doing their jobs.

Think about the people you know who have a real talent for working with computers—the ones everyone turns to when something doesn't work—

who also dress with uncanny style. The administrative assistant who wears the purple dress with turquoise accessories—and it works for her—who can turn out that 30-page report in two hours, complete with perfect grammar, and installs all her own software? She might be just the person you're looking for.

ORGANIZATION AND PLANNING

Details! A Web site is detail work. Not only does each page have to work, but each must work with the others. Quality control of all that interactivity must be high on a Webmaster's priority list. One broken link on a page can be disaster for a project, especially if the broken link is the one to the order form. A Webmaster who isn't concerned with details isn't a "master."

At the same time, you need someone who has the ability to see how the details affect the bigger picture. Scheduling and implementing a project that's likely to involve a number of people and departments requires very good organizational skills. Just as the individual departments in your company concentrate on their own areas of expertise yet contribute to the company as a whole, your Web site will highlight those departments yet demonstrate how they fit into the whole. Each piece will contribute to the whole. And that necessarily means that each piece must not only *work with* the rest but *complement* them. They're very much interdependent. A good Webmaster always has a mental image of the entire site in the back of her mind as she works with the individual pieces.

In addition to the interdependency of the pages themselves, the various pieces of your Web site have the potential to have an impact on the real workings of the departments that produce them, and on other departments as well. Your Legal department is likely to want to review the pages to ensure that they don't put you in the way of a lawsuit. Marketing may object to the way the Engineering department describes their services. The Sales department may decide that they are entitled to commissions based on sales generated on your Web site. If the Communications department insists that production

86

schedules be published, the Production department may want Communications to provide the manpower to do that. Your Webmaster is going to act as the pivot person for all of that activity. She's going to have to remind each department how their actions affect the rest and at times make sure that they communicate their needs and wishes to one another.

AESTHETIC CONCERNS

Add an eye for design to the mix. In your own surfing around the Web, remember sites that had glaring color combinations that were almost painful? Those are all the examples you need, to know that not all Webmasters have an eye for design. Your Webmaster doesn't need to be a graphic artist, but a sense of what works and what doesn't is a real plus.

She also needs to be able to determine when the use of graphics is desirable and when it's not. The aesthetics of a site shouldn't exceed its content. Finding a balance that's pleasing yet still workable isn't simple. Rainbow-colored pages can be ghastly to look at. If you're considering a marketing person for Webmaster, make sure that he's not the one who says about your print ads, "If we're paying for four-color, why not use color throughout?"

TECHNICAL SKILLS

Obviously, computer skills are essential. Programming experience is a real plus but not a make-or-break factor. You can subcontract essential programming if you must. The ability to quickly evaluate and learn new software applications is more important than programming, but obviously requires more than a minimal skill level.

You need someone who isn't afraid to install new software, who in fact thinks that the challenge of installing it and making it work with everything else is fun. He's the one that you heard telling his friends at the coffeepot that he'd somehow managed to make his entire system inoperable and had to reinstall everything—and laughs about it. Or she may be the one that everyone teases because she has installed every font known to man on her PC just because she likes to see how they look in her documents—and some of them look pretty darned good.

Understanding the hardware involved is also a plus, but again, not a make-or-break factor. Beyond knowing how to turn on a computer and how to do basic troubleshooting if something doesn't work, the hardware is going to be set up on your network, and there's little in the way of hookup and hardware additions that should be necessary.

In fact, that decidedly techy type, who can tell you about RAM and DRAM and how to add SIMMS and exactly what wiring is required in a parallel cable, may not be as well-qualified for this job as one who says frankly, "I don't know the hardware. I get the computer; I add the software; it works. Life is good. If it doesn't work, I call a technician."

GENERAL KNOWLEDGE OF THE INTERNET

Ideally, you want someone who knows the ins and outs of the Internet. The culture of the Internet is very different from that of traditional media. It's more freewheeling and chaotic. But basic rules have developed over time that govern patterns of behavior on the Internet and, by extension, the Web. You would have had to have been totally out-of-touch for the past year not to have heard the word *netiquette*. Netiquette is the etiquette of the Internet; if you're going to have a successful Web site, you're have to know those rules of behavior (or have a Webmaster who knows them). The denizens of the Web *really can* close your site down if they happen to take umbrage at something you do.

If you take that list of people who have registered at your site and send all of them mail that they haven't asked for, you might find that you are the recipient of enough return mail from angry people to overwhelm your Web server. If your Web site is hosted by an Internet service provider, the provider could cancel your account if their site is overwhelmed by angry e-mail. Don't take chances. Learn what you need to learn or hire someone who knows.

Your Staff, Your Web Site, and You

It's important for your Webmaster to understand the various protocols in use on the Internet and to know at least something about the various uses your employees and your clients will make of it. There will be questions to answer that are totally unrelated to the Web; the people asking the questions probably won't be aware of that, but your Webmaster should be. Your prospective Webmaster may be a bit surprised that you know about Web protocols (never hurts to surprise people). The ones that will be used most often are shown in the following table.

Protocol	Description
FTP	File Transfer Protocol. Pretty simple stuff, actually, and it does exactly what it sounds like. FTP will transfer a file from one computer to another, quickly and efficiently. The most common use is *anonymous FTP*. You retrieve a file from another computer electronically, without identifying yourself as a local user of their system. Login: **anonymous**; password: your e-mail address. It's fast, it's easy, it's free, and it gets you the information you want.
Telnet	Remote login to another computer. It's becoming less common but is used by some interactive systems. Telnet allows you to work (or play) by logging onto that remote computer. You may be able to log in anonymously or not. If you were to Telnet to RTI (our site), you would need to have a user name and password to access our systems. If you Telnet to **mediamoo.media.mit.edu**, you can connect as a guest and interact with the people there. Mediamoo is a *MOO*—no cows—it's an interactive site for media researchers.

continues

89

continued

Protocol	Description
	MOO is the acronym for *Multiuser Object Oriented*. It's not a game, it's a place on the Internet where a collection of very interesting people are doing research in this field.
Gopher	Not the kind that drill holes in your yard. Like Telnet sites, gopher sites are disappearing. They were set up originally to provide a place to house information services and software that could be shared. Many of them have been abandoned as Web sites have become more common. Most businesses choose to make information available via the Web rather than via the Web and gopher. They're nice, fast, and intuitively set up menu-style to make them easy to use, but the Web is subsuming them quickly. Our gopher site is quickly becoming a dinosaur because it's easier to maintain one Web site than to maintain a Web site and a gopher site.

There are other protocols: Archie, Veronica (I'm not kidding), WAIS—now you get a slightly better understanding of why Tim Berners-Lee thought we might do well to have one piece of software that could access all of these protocols without understanding what they do and how they work.

▶ **TIP**   Charge your employees and clients for this knowledge. (I'm kidding. But if I had a nickel for every time I've explained newsgroups or the use of Telnet for remote login or how to FTP a file from a site that doesn't have a Web server, I'd be retired to some gorgeous tropical island now.) ◀

90

The Importance of Good Communications

Your Webmaster is going to interact with people at all levels of your business—from data processors to the CEO, from programmers and systems administrators to salespeople and graphic artists—and even customers. Those people will have very different communications styles, and each group will make demands or offer suggestions that require the site to be changed in some way, no matter how small. The Webmaster can't disregard these people, but rather will be the catalyst for the changes that merit real consideration—or the one who has to explain why it can't (or won't) be done or considered. Easy to extrapolate from there that your potential Webmaster shouldn't have feelings that are easily hurt, isn't it? It's also pretty easy to extrapolate that your Webmaster should be diplomatic enough to explain to a Senior VP why her pages aren't going to be ready tomorrow. Sometimes she just has to say "no," but she'll have to say it in a very nice way.

Systems administrators have a tendency to overlook the human aspects of a technical project. Salespeople and data processors don't care about the technical side. The needs of both sides have to be addressed in a Web project, and you need someone who can communicate those needs clearly to everyone involved.

You're armed with the basics; ask questions. Can your candidate explain FTP or Telnet so that you understand it? Listen carefully. If she confuses you, she'll confuse anyone who calls her to ask that same question. Can she regroup when it's obvious that someone doesn't understand, and explain the process in very basic terms? Ask basic questions: "But aren't FTP and Telnet the same?" (No, they're not. One transfers files; the other allows you to work interactively.) "What's the difference between Archie and FTP?" (Quite a lot, actually. Archie searches for information; FTP retrieves it.) Listening is essential in the Web business. Your Webmaster must listen carefully and determine the skill levels of the people with whom she interacts. The Senior VP may not understand any better than the clerk in Purchasing. Patience and diplomacy count.

OTHER NECESSARY ADDITIONS TO THE MIX

Your Webmaster must have the self-confidence and skills to guide the project—to coax, cajole, and goad as necessary to meet deadlines—and the foresight to plan to punt when some piece of the project doesn't arrive on time. The plan always has to be flexible enough that a missing piece doesn't stop the project:

◆ The graphic navigational element that you plan to put at the bottom of each page might not be complete when your site is scheduled to premiere. It just isn't quite ready yet. You've sent the notice out in your monthly newsletter to your clients. Your Webmaster should have a plan that will work around a problem like that—a text element that can be put in place in the interim, for instance.

◆ A key page—your price list—is being changed and can't be delivered on time. An alternate page should be ready to put in its place, stating when that list will be ready, with a phone number and e-mail address for contact information until it is.

Other absolutely essential ingredients for the successful Webmaster include good humor, patience, common sense, and flexibility. There will be times when a carefully constructed priority list will need to be thrown out the window because an important project needs help to implement Web pages pronto. Your Webmaster will need to have the good humor and patience to deal with the situation, the common sense to know whether the project is important, and the flexibility to toss the list.

Oh, and it won't hurt if your Webmaster is a workaholic! Suppose that Arthur in Accounting forgot to mention that he's demonstrating the pages tomorrow at a conference and he has the URL engraved on his promotional information. Those changes have to be made tonight—it can't be done tomorrow.

STARTING YOUR SEARCH

The addition of "workaholic" to the mix probably makes your search a little easier. Your future Webmaster is probably already at the office at all hours of the day and night. You may want to follow your cleaning crew around for a couple of evenings, checking trash cans. You're in search of a closet nerd—an obviously social animal with computer nerd tendencies. Look for Jolt Cola cans covered by junk food wrappers. It doesn't count if the trash is from a computer programmer's office. They live on such fare. Okay, it counts if the computer programmer in question is also known to be an engaging and approachable type. (Are you sure this person is a programmer?)

Yes, it's true that all programmers don't fit the stereotype of the computer nerd. Enough do, though, that those of us who are in the business of computers can laugh at ourselves. Programmers have typically been seen as slightly deficient in social skills. That's not necessarily true, however, and less so now than it was 10 or 15 years ago, when those in the profession were less likely to need to interact regularly with the end users of the computers, and those users were numbered by the handful. Today, it's the rare desk that doesn't have a computer and the rare programmer who can avoid working closely with the people who will use his programs.

No luck with your late night sortie? You're in big trouble. You may have to ask for volunteers for this hazardous duty. Better block out plenty of time for the interviews that will follow. People are fascinated by this new technology and eager to learn it—at least, most think that they are. Choose carefully. Your Webmaster needs the combination of social and technical skills to make your site into a seamless whole.

In addition, your candidate needs a commitment to your company's future growth. The word *lucrative* has been used before, and with good reason. Web site management and Internet skills are in great demand. Without a commitment to your company, your Webmaster may learn the necessary skills at your expense, and then take them to your competition. Not good. Notice, though, that the emphasis is on the *company's* growth, not some special interest within the company. If you install a Webmaster who has another priority, whether to build his own little fiefdom around this project or to further the aims of a single department at the expense of others, you're going to have a problem you don't want and don't need. Your Web site will reflect that imbalance.

Ask your candidate whether he has Internet access. That's a very good sign. Find out how long he's been connected. New users often learn the jargon and assume that they're experts in the subjects of the Internet and the Web. The truth is often far from reality. On the Internet, a little learning can sometimes be a very dangerous thing. The fact that he's read the newsgroups for two days (or even a month or two) hardly makes him an expert. A post to one of them that isn't on target for that group can seriously offend, and, if it contains your URL, your company could bear the brunt of the group's reaction.

There are more than a few people around who've been learning and working on the Internet for years—not many of them will profess to be expert at it. It's just too big and there's just too much to know to become an expert in any short period of time.

You may have people on staff who've had some experience coding and designing Web pages. Many providers allow individual accountholders to prepare their own Web pages. Personal pages are, of course, quite different from what you want for your company, but they can give you an idea of the talent and skill level of your candidate.

Have your candidate provide you with the URL for his pages; take a look at them later. Does the design please you? Are the pages well written? Personal pages can be amazingly blunt sometimes. You may be quite surprised at the tone (and subject matter) of some of them. They're likely to give you quite a different view of your candidate than you might have expected, based on your personal interview.

You're Going to Pay People to Have Fun??

What most of your candidates will think is that you'll pay their salary while they surf the Web. To an extent, that's true. They will get paid to surf the Web—in order to learn what they must know to function as a Webmaster. What they don't know yet is that being a Webmaster is demanding and frustrating as well as being challenging and exciting. When you're operating on the bleeding edge, well, you know why it's called "bleeding." The technology is evolving so quickly that staying on top or ahead of those changes can cause even the most pragmatic person to feel as if she's teetering on a tightrope only a millisecond away from freefall.

Looking at Web sites and studying details of design and implementation can be great fun, and it can be boring in the extreme. Some days, all the challenge and excitement pales, and a rubber room is more inviting. Those deadlines for redesign that seemed so easily attainable during the planning processes will suddenly be just around the corner, and the pieces will seem to be scattered to the four winds. A critical graphic will still be missing two hours after it was due, and it won't work the way it was supposed to when it does arrive. It's just Murphy's Law applied to cyberspace. You need to understand those things in advance, even if your candidates don't (or choose not to) believe it. People with low frustration thresholds aren't good candidates for this particular job.

Should You Hire a Webmaster from Outside?

Finding someone with the necessary skills may not be easy. We've already determined that people who have them are in demand. And it may be difficult to justify hiring someone for a project that isn't yet producing income—and may not do so for some time.

To hire someone who has the experience and skill you want, be prepared to pay him well. Various trade magazines are estimating salaries for Webmasters these days. Salaries can range from $25,000 for inexperienced people who can do the basics of HTML coding to $70,000 for those with technical and managerial skills.

If you hire someone who doesn't already have the skills and experience, you run the serious risk that it will take you longer to implement your plan because the new person must learn not only the work associated with managing a Web site but your corporate culture as well.

It may be easier and less expensive to hire a part-time administrative assistant to shift duties from one of your regular employees than to hire a Webmaster from outside the company. An insider will better understand how to get things accomplished. A Web site that needs input and work from any number of departments requires knowing who to call when that deadline is close, and that can mean the difference between success and failure. The person who knows which arm to twist to speed up the production of page content or who to schmooze to get the graphic production moved up in the priority list is going to get your site up and running faster and with fewer ruffled feathers than one who doesn't know your company culture.

What Will the Webmaster Actually Do?

The scope of the project will have a decided impact on the role of your Webmaster. A corporate site will of course require broader knowledge than a departmental or division site, but the same basic skills are necessary at all levels.

Ideally, your Webmaster will handle all the details of server administration:

- Attending to quality control and scheduling updates
- Adding new applications and functions as they're needed
- Doing routine maintenance
- Attending to the details of security and statistics
- Responding to and/or forwarding e-mail from the site as necessary

This list quite obviously doesn't include writing and designing. The ideal isn't always the same thing as reality.

The reality is that most companies don't have, or choose not to commit, the resources (people) that will allow a Webmaster the luxury of concentrating fully on administrative duties. Your Webmaster may do everything from writing to designing to coding or any combination of all the tasks involved in the process.

At a minimum, though, your Webmaster will keep an eye on the content, design, and coding on your site. That will become a matter of self-preservation. Any error in any of those parts will be laid at the Webmaster's doorstep initially. And, unfortunately, people who produce pages for the Web tend to take a somewhat cavalier approach, apparently deciding that because it's fast and easy to add, delete, and change pages, that they don't need to apply the same standards of editorial and design review to Web pages that they would to print. Unfortunately, that simply isn't true. A good Webmaster will roll that editorial and design review process into the quality-control function, checking for and correcting obvious errors, and requesting corrections or clarification from the originator when in doubt.

At first, your Web development staff are likely to examine every page microscopically, but as the work increases and the number of pages that are added expands, it will become increasingly difficult for them to maintain that level of scrutiny. Pages will arrive for inclusion that haven't been proofed by anyone at all, and your developers are likely to be too busy to do much more than make sure that the HTML coding works. The people who provide the content have to be responsible for it. Suppose that the pages sent over by the folks in Software Development are riddled with "minor errors"—little things like a wrong price, or a sentence that makes absolutely no sense whatsoever, or three locations for training being omitted. A quick look before publication on the Web would have (and should have) caught those errors. Now your Webmaster is likely to become a rather highly-paid word processor. Make plans now to vest the basic responsibility for content on those who provide it.

ADDING A GRAPHIC ARTIST TO THE TEAM

Depending on your resources, your Webmaster may be the only person involved to any great degree in the project. If you're lucky enough to have graphic artists on staff, however, you surely will want at least one of them to contribute to your pages. Once again, though, you're looking for a combination of skills—design and the desire and willingness to approach design from a new angle. It's not as easy as it sounds. Graphics that work wonderfully in print can take days to load to a Web browser.

The graphic artist that you need for your Web site must possess some of the same skills your Webmaster needs. Good communications skills are important because your graphic artist and your Webmaster will have an ongoing dialogue throughout the project. There will need to be interactions with other people in your company who have special graphics requirements for their pieces of your Web site. Here, as in the case of the Webmaster, the overall design should always be considered when adding new pieces.

Your engineers may want artwork that reflects their technical accomplishments with chips and circuit boards, while Human Resources wants artwork that puts a human face on their work. Your graphic artist can give each of those departments what they want, while giving the entire site a cohesive visual component. A company that sells boats might have a "fluid" look overall, or a company that rebuilds machine tools a crisp, technical look. The circuit boards and the human faces will be added to the design, but the overall look will remain the same.

Software companies understand this concept very well. Microsoft Word's toolbar is very much like the toolbar in Excel, Microsoft's spreadsheet product. That makes it easier for you to use both of those products, because you're already familiar with one. You don't feel lost with the graphics. The same should be true on a Web site. You want your visitors to always know where they are and how to navigate within the site, and the visual components simplify that process.

BASIC SKILLS REQUIRED

Self-motivation is essential for the graphic artist. He needs to have a sincere desire to learn designing for the Web. It's a completely new medium and as such requires constant re-education as new tools and products are introduced. Neither your Webmaster nor your graphic artist will have the luxury of waiting for someone else to take the initiative. The Web is evolving too quickly for those on the front lines to wait for someone farther back to instruct them on the details of actions.

Your graphic artist is probably going to spend many hours studying the designs of Web sites, determining what works and what doesn't. He'll test his own designs, adjust the colors endlessly, and then start over because it just doesn't feel right or the color doesn't work.

▶ **NOTE**   One of our projects gave our graphic artist fits. She spent hours attempting to duplicate the shade of green used in their print ads. She processed and reprocessed the image and was never completely satisfied, but finally hit on the shade she felt was as close as she could get. We were closing in on a deadline and rushed to put the pages into test production. One of their first complaints, naturally, was that the color was wrong. *Really* wrong. They'd forgotten to provide her with the most recent print ads—blue, not green at all. ◀

Designing for the Web requires a combination of talent and skill that isn't easy to find. Your graphic artist will quickly learn that his 256-color file that's a masterpiece of shading simply doesn't translate across various computers and browsers. While it looks gorgeous on his Mac, it simply looks fuzzy on the PC down the hall. You need someone who doesn't faint at the very idea of designing graphics in 16 colors instead. Images require more crispness to stand up to the rigors of computers that simply can't handle the intricacies of shading.

TECHNICAL SKILLS FOR A NEW MEDIUM

The graphic artist has to be able to balance design and content. There is a very strong interrelationship between the medium and the message. That interaction takes on more importance in an emerging medium because there are no truisms to rely on. The rules are being written as they are learned.

A print ad will look the same in every issue of the magazine in which it appears. The artwork will be placed precisely to achieve the designer's intent. On the Web, that same design will display differently when viewed with one browser or another. Internet Explorer will interpret it one way, and Netscape another. Mosaic might display it entirely differently from the other two—and there are dozens of different browsers and dozens of versions of those browsers that all work differently. Your graphic designer will be forced to think of his artwork in relation to the content of the page, rather than focusing on its placement. Will it sell the product or idea, achieve the proper look, even though it doesn't necessarily appear precisely where he'd like?

You absolutely need a graphic artist who has experience producing graphics on a computer. He can learn the characteristics of the Web as he studies, but you can't realistically expect someone to learn to produce computer graphics at the same time. It doesn't matter what platform he uses (Mac, Windows, UNIX), because graphics developed in any of those environments work quite well for the Web.

Obviously you want to choose a graphic artist whose work you like. That doesn't mean that the artist who does fabulous watercolors you absolutely love is going to be able to translate that talent to the Web, however. Designing for the Web involves much more than simply adding a few nice pictures to your Web site. The elements of navigation on a Web site are enhanced by the graphical design (or they can as easily be destroyed). Whether your site has 10 pages or 200 or more, the one talent your designer should bring to this project above all others is the ability to apply a design that's consistent and increases the overall functionality of the site. Those watercolors may be outstanding, but you're looking for someone to provide visual organization as

100

well as aesthetically pleasing graphics. Experience in something like book design might be a traditional skill that would translate easily to the Web.

▶ **NOTE** Our graphic artist says, "Raw multidimensional navigation and expansion offer more potential for chaos than for information." What that translates to is that it's unbelievably easy to get completely lost in a Web site, and without good design for both graphics and content, your visitors will get frustrated and leave. ◀

As previously mentioned, designers tend to get more than a little frustrated with Web pages because the results of coding can be unpredictable. That graphic that was supposed to go right **there** on the page just won't, for some unfathomable reason. The reason is a combination of coding and how individual browsers interpret that code, so it will be of enormous benefit to find a graphic artist who knows (or is willing to learn) at least the rudiments of HTML. If you're really lucky, you'll find a graphic artist with a technical bent. There are some out there, but they're rare. If you have one, treat her well. She's priceless in today's market. If you don't have one, you need someone who can devote sufficient time and energy to learning the ways of Web graphics.

So what you're really looking for is a pioneering designer with computer nerd tendencies. Well, get as close as you can to the whole package, at any rate.

You certainly don't want to produce completely new graphics if what you have works for you or is easily recognizable and associated in the public mind with your name. McDonald's has its arches; you have your logo or trademark graphics that are uniquely your own. You want those existing graphics translated for inclusion in your Web pages, so your graphic artist has to learn some new tricks.

Your Webmaster and your graphic artists will work closely to design and refine your Web site. Their goal should be to produce a Web-workable design on some specific time line, whether that is two months or six months or a year.

ANYONE ELSE?

Staffing requirements depend entirely on the scope of your site and your resources. If you can reasonably commit a team of people to the project, you should definitely include people from Marketing, Sales, and Communications. You may have writers devoted to creating content and programmers working on applications that will entirely customize your site for your visitors.

You may assemble teams to study and analyze your design to make it as appealing and navigable as possible. Sun Microsystems hired focus groups to test their pages and spent a great deal of time making sure that their site was easy to navigate. If you have the resources, you can easily invest them in a Web site. Only you can determine the scope of that involvement. Your staffing can be as simple or as complex as your Web site.

The same rules apply for every member of your development team, however. To borrow a phrase from a famous auto maker: "This is not your father's marketing medium." Everyone involved must be willing to take completely new approaches and they absolutely must be willing to study and learn on their own to a great extent.

You can assign people to begin learning what they need to know while you develop your plan. There is no lack of books available to guide them in every area of the technical aspects of Web site development. There is a wealth of information on coding and design on the Web itself. Web site management isn't rocket science but it is management—that act of balancing people and priorities with the added dimension of technical implementation. The technical implementation is changing fast and your staff is going to have to be prepared to follow and adapt to those changes.

▶ **NOTE**   Interested in examples of good sites to see? Check out the appendix. ◀

How Will They Do It?

You can't build a Web site without tools, of course. The sophistication of a Web builder's tool set can be scaled to fit your budget.

Document Converters

If you're planning to use legacy documents that are already in electronic format, you'll want to have one of the many document converters that are available. These tools take standard word processing formats and convert them to HTML-coded pages. As with most things Web'ish, converters are available at no cost on the Web for some formats, and commercial products are also available. Your Webmaster should evaluate those products based on their compliance to the HTML standard. You want to make your documents available to as broad an audience as possible, so it's important that they comply with the standards. What looks just perfect with one browser may not even be viewable by another if the standards are ignored.

The various browsers can keep life very interesting around your Web site. There are so many of them: Netscape, Internet Explorer, Mosaic, Arena, and NetCruiser to name only a few. If you want a real feel for how many, go to Yahoo's listing of browsers at this address:

http://www.yahoo.com/Computers and Internet/Internet/World_Wide_Web/Browsers/

It may be true that the largest percentage of people who surf the Web use Netscape, but quite a few of them are using versions of Netscape that have long been rendered obsolete. What those people see on your site won't be what people who have the most recent version will see. Their browsers were written when HTML 1.0 or 2.0 was the standard. Many people simply don't upgrade their software because what they have *works*, or because they don't have the technical knowledge to be comfortable with making changes. A headline that appears on one browser in **BIG BOLD LETTERS** will appear on another in SMALL CAPS—maybe bold, maybe not. So your best policy is to make sure that the pages you serve are coded to the most recent standard. That will generally be *backwardly compatible* (work with older versions) but allow most of the functionality that's written into the most recent browsers.

WEB PAGE EDITORS

Software packages are available that can assist a novice coder in setting up new pages, in addition to converting documents from other formats. These products can be especially helpful in the beginning stages, if they force at least minimal compliance with the HTML standard. Those that do automatically apply the correct coding for the basic pieces. In time, those basics become second nature in the coding process.

▶ **NOTE**   The specific products that are on the market now may or may not be on the market when your developers begin working on your site. If they are, the likelihood is that they'll have changed. If they haven't, they're probably not good candidates for use. ◀

None of the converters or document preparation packages are perfect, however. More often than not, coding is accomplished simply with a text editor or a word processing package. In many cases, it's simply easier and faster to code and make changes manually than to use one of the tools. That will change, of course, as the standards develop and the software developers standardize their products for the Web market.

GRAPHICS DEVELOPMENT

Graphics can be developed in any of the standard graphics software packages. They then have to be customized for use on the Web. The choice of programs depends on the experience of your staff and the task at hand. The specific tools for Web graphics are, like everything else related to the Web, in constant flux. Programs are available on the Web at no charge, and commercial products are also available. (Specific recommendations for any software for Web development would be out of date before this book is published. The industry is changing very fast.)

There are also reasonably-priced software packages that can take a computer screen "snapshot" of an image and interlace it and apply transparency to it, too. These can be a real help in situations where you have a graphic that's in computer format but not set up for the Web. They don't always produce exactly the image you might want, but they go a long way toward helping you and others get a feel for the eventual design of the page.

▶ **NOTE**   *Interlacing* is the method used to make graphics appear to load faster by presenting them a little at a time rather than all at once after the entire image is loaded. *Transparency* removes a certain color from the graphic—usually a background color—so that the graphic appears to float on the page rather than having its own background.

Obviously, you don't *need* to know this technical information, but you might just find it useful to know some of the more esoteric terms that your Web staff will be throwing around. ◀

Your graphics designers should evaluate various packages based on their own needs, and consult with the Webmaster on issues of size and complexity of the images. They will want to make sure that those images load as quickly as possible, of course, and retain their clarity.

▶ **NOTE**   One iteration of our site included a design that we considered "interim" (it lasted six months), which included an image map that had a background that was a marbled black on white. When it was first uploaded, I called our graphic artist because I couldn't read portions of it on my computer, which doesn't have the best of video cards so isn't always as clear as I might like, but is probably not too different from many of the computers that

continues

continued

are used to view our site. She took out a bit of black here and a bit of black there while I constantly reloaded the image to see what she was doing and how it worked. I was never completely happy with it, but we agreed it was acceptable.

As just a matter of aesthetics from my point of view, I said, "It needs to be wider. It doesn't come close to filling my screen." I thought she would cry. Her reply: "You can have almost anything else you want on this page, Linda, but it would take me way too long to change the size. The file is over 1.5 megabytes in its original form and 18 layers of graphics and text."

I allowed as how I could live with the size. She reduced that 1.5 megabyte file to one that was under 20KB and loaded pretty quickly. You don't argue with graphic designers who can do that kind of work, if you want to keep them around. ◄

ADVANCED TOOLS FOR SOPHISTICATED PROJECTS

You may need to add other tools based on your plans for your site. There are software packages that can be used for form preparation and processing, database integration, conferencing, and many other applications. They're getting better and simpler to use by the day. You may want to invest in several, a suite, or none. It's entirely dependent on what you want your site to do and who controls it. If you're running your own Web server, you can add as many gadgets and toys as your budget will allow. If your pages are being hosted by a service provider, you're limited to the tools they have or will allow you to have.

How Long Will It Take?

How long it will take from the time that you make your staff decisions until you have a functioning site is dependent on any number of factors. How's that for a nice definitive answer? If you have people on staff or hire people who have the requisite skills, and you have a focused plan that doesn't include hundreds of pages, you may easily go from plan to implementation in a month or two. If your people have to learn the necessary skills, it may take six months or a year. Competition may drive you to move very quickly, or there may be budget issues that frame your decision. You do need to set a definitive time schedule based on your staffing and the market issues surrounding your site. And you should focus your efforts so that you accomplish a credible site when your pages are debuted. One of the better-known manufacturers of office wiring equipment recently announced their Web site in the regular newsletter to their customers. They probably shouldn't have been quite so eager. They are a high-tech company with high-tech customers. They put in place a few nicely-designed pages that would be entirely acceptable for a company of one-tenth their size and reputation. There was not one product specification, price, e-mail link for technical support, or even an e-mail link for their Webmaster. Oh, but you can order their catalog online.

They should have hired a consultant, but they obviously didn't do their homework. Those of us who use their far-from-inexpensive products can only hope they get a clue, sooner rather than later.

You don't want to make that kind of mistake, so set a realistic schedule and make your pages work for you in some way from the very beginning.

Still insistent on a committee approach? If you didn't disband that committee you assigned to this project originally, you may be retired before this project is completed, unless each and every one of them is already Web-literate (literacy in this arena can't be achieved in two months of Web surfing; it takes study and it requires reading, not just looking at graphics on the Web) and they all agree completely with the actual plan for the site and how that plan should be implemented (*exactly* how it should be implemented). Once a brand new Web site project is launched, "experts" appear magically from every corner of the known universe; you'll be amazed at how many you have in your own company.

Consider other committees in your company. Politics come into play. The priorities and schedules in one group conflict with priorities and schedules in another. Endless meetings result in no workable decisions being made. The Web will not wait on your committee, unless you don't plan to have anything ready to serve to the world for three to five years. If that's the case, you can keep your committee. Of course, unless they're constantly studying the Web and its markets over that period of time, your Web site—when it does appear—will be out of date. Committees! Do your part for Web ecology and don't create another one because of it.

Instead, gather your key people, study what you want done and how it should be done, and set a schedule for the implementation. You can be flexible enough to build in some delays. They happen in every project, and this one is no different. But set the schedule and hold your staff accountable. (It's the constant refrain you will see in this tome. This is a business project. Treat it as such.)

Your Resources

Before you spend too much time concentrating on what content and design you think you need for your sight, there are some things you must consider about your audience. Your present marketing pieces are undoubtedly targeted for a specific culture, whether that is based on certain demographics that define your product, the media in which it is used, or the geographical area(s) in which you market.

THE CULTURE OF THE WEB

Your Web pages should reflect the culture of the Web. Whatever the demographics, there are basic cultural attitudes that make it unique. Let's start with the most obvious—it's a somewhat exclusive audience.

That's right. The media may be doing an excellent job of leading you to believe that everybody and his brother and their cousins have access to the Web, but it simply is not true. Those who do have access are, as a general rule, literate and well-educated. The odds are that their incomes are slightly above average, or they wouldn't be able to afford Internet access. It's a luxury, not a necessity. And businesses on the Web? Believe it or not, not every business has Internet access. It's difficult sometimes to separate the truth from perceptions. The intense media scrutiny and constant barrage of information surrounding the Web combines to give the perception of ubiquity. That simply is not the case. It is, in an emerging global marketplace, becoming much more likely for companies to have Internet access, at least to the extent of having e-mail for their basic inter- and intra-company communications, but full access simply isn't yet a reality for many companies (that's right, yours isn't the only one that is home-page-less).

ENGAGE THEIR EYES AND THEIR INTELLECTS QUICKLY

Given that exclusivity, the people and businesses who do have access consider themselves just a step or two ahead of the rest. That somewhat exclusive group you are talking with (not to) expects you to treat them just a little differently. They think they're special—and in some ways they are. You must tailor your pages for them.

Consider these other basics of the Web. There are over 155,000 Web servers (at least) operating now. Many of those servers host multiple domains. If you don't have Web pages that are visually pleasing and supply quality information, your prospective client is only a point-and-click from some other destination. You must engage those people quickly. You can't do that with a *home page* (the primary gateway to your site) that's a huge graphic that takes too long to load, or with a page of text that's confusing and cumbersome.

Your present clients are presumably visiting your site to get information about your products (old and new). Truth to tell, they don't concern themselves overly much with how your site looks, as long as it isn't glaringly obnoxious and difficult to read.

▶ **TIP**   Remember that you're talking with a huge audience. Every page on your site says something about you. You obviously want those pages to say something good. ◀

Users come to your site for a specific purpose; they simply want to accomplish that purpose as easily as possible. They want to find out how much that piece of statuary costs, or what the product specs are for that lawnmower you advertised. You may entice them to consider other products or services, but probably not before they've found what they want.

You must find ways to provide pages that are attractive enough to draw that prospect and functional enough to allow both the prospect and your present client to access the information on your site with ease. If your clients are typical, you may have about 30 seconds to convince them to invest more of their time in your site. They don't tend to be a patient lot.

IT'S A SELF-SERVING GROUP

The Web is personal. Never forget that. Your site visitors are not sitting across a room using a remote control, nor are they curled up on a sofa pointing and clicking. (Well, some of the old hands may have figured out new and novel ways to achieve that, but most of your visitors won't have.) They have some purpose for visiting your site and it is a personal one. Whether they're simply curious to see what your company does or to retrieve information, they're there for *themselves*, not for you, and you must think about how to make your pages relevant for each of them. This simply can't be stressed too often; you must involve the user in your site. Give him something to do, to learn, to experience—whether tangible (a product) or intangible (information) is entirely up to you, but he expects something from you, and you should be ready to deliver.

You want to talk to each visitor to your Web site personally. That doesn't mean that every document you have designed for a mass market has to be completely rewritten, but it does mean that you should tailor key pieces at least to the point of acknowledging that you're talking with one person.

The folks at Ragu (**http://www.ragu.com**) accomplished personalization with rare style. Mama's Dining Room is a pleasure and Mama talks to her visitors through the pages. Who could resist registering at Mama's site when she says, "Mama knows you're busy. If you want me to send you e-mail whenever I do something new to my site, or whenever Ragu sends out coupons or makes a new sauce, just put your e-mail address in the box below and choose 'Send.' And don't worry—Mama knows how to keep her mouth shut: I won't give or sell your address to anybody without asking you first, OK?" Somehow you just know you can trust Mama.

The Web isn't your traditional marketing medium and it shouldn't be approached with traditional thinking. The one-to-many approach is all wrong for an interactive medium. You can literally tailor the information you provide for the individual who's visiting your site. It's true that that may be a bit difficult, but programs are making it easier every day—by the time you're prepared to build your site, it may be very easy indeed.

BORING JUST WON'T CUT IT

Remember those Super Bowl commercials, though. People really do like them because they're fun and creative. Your annual report may be one very slick production, but if you translate it wholesale to your Web site, it's still going to look like your annual report. How many customers did it attract for you last year? Aren't there more creative and interesting ways to tell people about your products and your company?

It doesn't matter what business you're in, or how conservative your corporate culture—a little humor goes a long way. Don't you prefer to work with people and companies who can see the humor in themselves? When you entertain a client, you want to see her smile or laugh. Certainly some aspects of your business simply aren't funny or suitable for humor, but you should look for ways to show people that your company has an approachable, friendly staff—in spite of all your fancy titles and all-business attitude about your core products.

Consider letting your corporate hair down in your introductions to your company or your products. This is a tough audience you're addressing. If you can make them smile, you may keep them at your site a little longer and encourage them to look at your business a little more closely.

Some companies have wonderfully creative pages introducing their staff members. Most corporate sites seem to take the approach of having an introductory message from the CEO, at least. Consider introducing your staff on your Web site. You've hired them for their skills, and this is certainly a way to demonstrate to them that you're proud of them. It also puts a human face on your company for your visitors. Yes, you run the risk that your competitors will be as likely to contact them as your clients, but your competitors already know they're working for you in most cases. It's the rare business or industry that isn't somewhat incestuous in its hiring practices.

▶ **NOTE** One of my favorite Webmasters recently remarked, "…Most commercial sights don't bother with people, except for some fluff from the High Muckety-Muck. If someone is doing a site, they should include people sketches, if only lists by divisions with titles and e-mail addresses. It's obvious that the product is paramount. Fine, but who makes it?" ◀

112

The Internet takes some of the mystery out of your corporate hierarchy—or it can if you allow it. While a customer might visit your physical location, he probably will never ask to speak with your CEO. But that same customer might have no hesitation to send e-mail. Want to know if your staff is offering the kind of quality technical support your customers want? Ask the customers—and give them an e-mail address directly to you on one of your pages.

Your Web site may be designed for a business-to-business approach, but remember that the companies you are targeting aren't logging in and surfing the Web—their employees are. That's especially important if you're interested in attracting good employees as some part of your overall plan for your site.

WILL THE DOCUMENTS YOU HAVE WORK ON THE WEB?

Now look at those documents you were considering using on your Web site. Will they work? Will they appeal to this particular market? Content: Does it deliver? Is it sufficiently engaging to attract that well-educated group? Does it assume a certain level of sophistication and knowledge? If it's at all condescending, trash it. If it doesn't add depth to your product, service, or company, it's not going to work the way you'd like. If it makes you more approachable, rather than less, you're probably on the right track. You're a company on the front of a leading-edge technology. That makes a statement to your visitors. Don't dilute that statement by pontificating. These people will not be impressed.

You can take that boring but useful complete product specification and put it on the Web just like it is. If your customers, or your potential customers, want it, you should make it available to them someplace on your Web site. Your marketing pieces, though, should involve and engage your audience.

▶ **TIP**   Whatever approach you take for your Web pages—fun, creative, or conservative—give your visitors an opportunity to contact at least one person on every page on your site. Otherwise you aren't gaining much ground for your investment. ◀

IF THE DOCUMENTS WON'T WORK, WHO'S GOING TO FIX THEM?

You've looked at your existing marketing and you've decided that some of it really is okay for translation to the Web without more than fixing the occasional typo or restructuring and rewording a few sentences (and this is probably true of all those product specs and the questions-and-answers that have been assembled over time for your tech support staff). You do want something a little more creative for your company home page and your main products or services. If you have a Marketing or Advertising department, obviously someone there can take a shot at creating the Web pages.

Let your staff know that you're looking for new ideas for your Web pages, and ask them to let their creative juices flow. They'll have fun, and you may discover the one talent that the Web is still waiting for—the person who can make a Web site pay for itself in sales. Anyone who enjoys writing is a candidate for the job.

If you don't have staff who can write marketing pieces, consider subcontracting those pages to an outside advertising agency, or even one of the traditional advertising people who call on you regularly from your local newspaper, radio, or TV station. They already know you and your product, and they might love a chance to design a Web page for you; they may already be doing just that for other people.

If you decide that you do need outside help for key pages, don't assume that any good advertising or marketing firm can do the job. The Web is a new marketplace; some of those firms don't have a bit more experience with it

114

than you do. You wouldn't hire an advertising agency to produce your print media without seeing samples of their work. You don't want to spend a king's ransom on Web pages that aren't right for the Web.

Your best choice if you go outside your company for help with the project is to find an agency that has done work on the Web. Even at that, though, make sure that what they've done works for *you*. View samples of their work on the Web (as stated previously, though, don't count on a canned presentation from a laptop—view it on the Web).

Make sure, too, that they fully understand what you want and when you want it. Involve your Webmaster and graphic artist in the selection. What the agency designs and writes has to fit into the entire site. Your Webmaster and graphic artist are likely to have a feel for the Web-savvy level of the representatives, too.

Finally, if a service provider is hosting your site, ask what their experiences have been with the agencies. They may be able to suggest two or three that have just the level of experience and skill that you need.

How Much Managing Is Necessary?

Got your project staffed, decided what existing literature you can use and what to have customized, and assigned the work. We're moving right along here. Good thing, too, isn't it, because you actually do have one or two other projects you could be spending a bit more time working on. You're definitely in luck, because the last thing in the world a Web site needs is micromanagement. It does need to be managed, however. That's especially important for a corporate Web site. How you go about managing can make a real difference to your Web site and the staff working on it.

It's Just Another Project

In most regards, managing a Web site is little different from managing any other project. The goals need to be clear and clearly communicated to the appropriate staff. The time line needs to be set. The work needs to be assigned. The lines of authority need to be clearly defined.

In other respects, though, a Web site project is different. Because you're dealing with an emerging technology, time and resources must be considered differently. Unlike a project in which your staff can hit the ground running, with experience and tested skills, a Web site requires more time for learning and more time for evaluating tools. It also calls for your staff to approach even work with which they're very familiar in new ways. There are a number of things that you can do to make it all easier for them.

Time to Surf

Support your staff in discovering, evaluating, acquiring, and learning new tools and techniques. There's no better way for them to learn about those tools and techniques than on the Web itself. If they wait to learn from the trade magazines, they're likely to be two months behind the curve.

Surfing the Web for information about tools and techniques, for design guides and tips, is time well spent. In fact, it will save you money. Your staff can learn the vast majority of what they need to know to make your site work for you simply by sitting at their desks and reading the information available online. Rather than spending thousands of dollars for staff training, you simply need to give them the time to study what's already there. Any staff member who tells you he's learned all he can possibly learn on the Web is either a true genius (in which case you really should be paying him more) or not interested in learning (in which you should replace him on this particular project).

116

TESTING THE TOOLS

Time spent downloading and trying new tools is also time that can save you money over the long haul. This is a time of rapid development of Web tools, and the emphasis now is on automating tasks that hitherto have been extremely time-consuming (like coding the pages and writing the programs to integrate a database into the pages you serve on your site). That means that the wise choice of emerging tools has a probability of both improving your site and saving you money in production time.

LIST MAIL—A NUISANCE, BUT IT CAN BE USEFUL

Your Webmaster should subscribe to any e-mail list that discusses Web servers, or at least the ones that discuss your server of choice. Yes, that may easily mean that she's sorting through 50-100 e-mail messages daily. In the beginning, she'll read them all and few will make sense. As time goes on, she'll learn to skim subject lines for topics of interest and, even more importantly, determine which of the people who send mail to the list are the most knowledgeable. Those people can become invaluable resources. Likewise, your graphic artist and any other staff you involve in the project should be monitoring discussions in their areas of interest.

All of these things are easy to accomplish as long as you're willing to allow your staff to accomplish them. Manage their time, as best you can, so that they have time to learn. Unless you made a miscalculation about the motivations of the individuals, they're likely to be spending an equal amount of their own personal time extending that knowledge.

BOOKS AND MAGAZINES MAKE IT ALL EASIER

You can also provide your staff with subscriptions to trade magazines that will help them. Even the most diehard Web surfer gets tired of sitting at a computer reading. Besides, they can take a magazine home to read in spare moments.

Provide the necessary resources to buy new books as they're published. Encourage them to read, read, read. The information is available and new ideas and better techniques are being developed and published regularly. Give them access to the information, and give them the time to find those books on company time. Indeed, insist that they take time to shop the shelves during the day. In the first place, there'll be less traffic, and in the second, they can spend their own time reading (which they want to do anyway).

The time and money your staff needs to learn their jobs from the Web and from published magazines and books can pay off for you in unexpected ways. Your Webmaster may learn that the server software he had been planning to buy for thousands of dollars is only marginally more functional than one that costs only a few hundred. That's the kind of surprise every manager appreciates.

UNDERSTAND STAFF LIMITATIONS

Specifically with regard to your graphics staff—but it may very well apply to others involved with your site—remember that in spite of the fact that they may be producing work daily on a computer, your staff members aren't necessarily computer-savvy. Work on a Web site involves a network, not just a standalone computer. If something breaks, whether hardware or software (and they're not likely to know which), don't let them waste two days trying to figure out what's wrong. They're not likely to figure it out, in any case.

Provide the support they need to get the problem fixed. "That guy over in Sales who's good with computers" doesn't qualify as support. He may actually have other work to do, and though he'd love to help, isn't going to be available for a week. Be prepared to provide someone within 24 hours—a company tech or someone from outside—and follow up to make sure that the work is accomplished. In the meantime, encourage and reward workarounds that continue productive work that can be accomplished without the "broken tool."

REWARD THEIR EFFORTS

Reward the people on your staff for learning. Rewards, as you know, don't necessarily have to be money. A well-placed compliment is often all the encouragement an employee needs to increase his efforts—if it's honest and sincere. A simple "thank you for your hard work" costs you nothing and can bring you large rewards.

WHO'S REALLY IN CHARGE?

Because you had the foresight (okay, let's not be overly modest—brilliance) to assign smart, dedicated, and eager people to the project, your plan now is to simply get out of the way and let them do what needs to be done. That's a fine plan as far as it goes. But a certain amount of guidance is going to be necessary. If you don't provide it, you'll find yourself in any number of unfortunate circumstances.

Have you ever managed a project that didn't require someone to make a "go–no go" decision at some point? The only difference here is that you're adding some technical issues that make the project slightly more difficult to understand.

WHO SETS THE PRIORITIES?

Depending on the scope of your Web site, the pieces that make up the whole are likely to be coming from different departments or divisions. Who has the authority to set the priorities for each of the people producing the parts? If you have a budget for the site that includes the key players and those people either report to you or to your Webmaster, it will be much easier to get the job done on a timely basis.

What tends to happen in the case of a Web site, which can generate overwhelming attacks of eagerness among managers and staff during the planning process, is that the reality of the amount of work and time it takes to produce the first (not final) product can be a real surprise. Other projects suddenly take priority. That's a real problem for a Web site, because you have a schedule for the work and you don't want it to slip. It becomes even more important after the site is functional. It will be constantly changing and evolving.

If your management counterpart isn't sincerely interested in the project, it will be easy for her to find other, more critical work that must be done in lieu of the Web project. Other factors may come into the equation. The manager may be wary of the technology or worried that her staff won't be able to keep up with the work. You have to judge the situation carefully. If you have the time and the inclination, you can attempt to educate your counterpart. If you don't, consider other avenues for getting the work done, including outsourcing. Whatever approach you take, however, should be taken quickly and handled decisively; otherwise, your Web site could be held hostage for much too long.

If staff can't be committed on a regular, ongoing basis, they shouldn't be committed at all. You must know that, and you must be sure that you know the level of commitment of other managers. Otherwise, the project will flounder or you will have one terrifically overworked and frustrated Webmaster (in which case, listen very carefully if she develops a sudden interest in firearms).

If you can't set the priorities for all the people involved in the project (and that's the case, more often than not), work closely with your Webmaster to at least help her set her priorities and suggest alternate approaches if other people simply don't deliver their pieces of the project. That's right. You not only have to plan for late delivery, but the occasional no-show.

Problems most often arise when a manager assigns people to work on some piece of the project without taking into account the level of self-motivation and desire to learn new things. If the person is afraid of change, he can be easily overwhelmed by the Web and those who embrace it. You're probably in a better position than your Webmaster is to work with other managers to encourage them to assign appropriate staff.

WHO'S CONTROLLING THE PROJECT?

The priorities could be the least of your worries, however, if you happened to have the bad luck to hire a Webmaster who is very technically inclined and controlling. Determining who's really in charge may be very difficult in that case. This Webmaster will assure you that everything is going perfectly and the plan is moving right along. It will be, in the Webmaster's view. What may actually be happening, though, is that she's busy coding a Web site to show off her talents, effectively shutting out input from anyone else and giving you the occasional "all's well" status report. Because it's likely that others who are involved in the project assume their ideas are being implemented, they may not even realize that anything is amiss.

How bad could that be? Depending on your perspective, it may not be bad at all. She may be designing pages that can be viewed well with only one browser. That may mean that 10 or 15 percent of the people who visit your site either don't see it the way you do (because it's only been demonstrated to you with that one browser). You may not be concerned about a 10 percent attrition. Then again, 10 percent of 30 million people is… well, let's be a bit more realistic, and assume that your site is visited by 1 million people over the course of a year. Can you really afford to miss a chance to talk with 100,000 people? Your call—but it *is* your call.

In the case of one university department's Web site, the situation became a bit more involved. The Webmaster had not only taken complete charge of the design of the site, but owned parts of the equipment involved. Sorting out who owned what before resuming control of the design of the site was maddening and upsetting to everyone involved.

YOUR INVOLVEMENT AND THEIRS

In between frustration and control is the world of minutiae. Even the smoothest functioning, most congenial staff will disagree on approaches to take and technologies to adopt. Most of those disagreements will work themselves out, but some won't, of course, and someone (you??) will have to make that "go–no go" decision.

The people who are involved in the development of the site will become personally involved. Most of the time that fact will work in your favor; they'll give you their very best effort because the work will reflect you (and them) to the world. Sometimes, though, they need to be reminded that their view is too personal. An overworked staff that drops every other priority to fix pages that someone else should have done sooner and correctly will soon have their real priorities completely out of order. That's the time for you to remind them that sometimes it's necessary to let other people fail. They probably won't take your advice, because they take the success of the project personally, but they'll appreciate your support at any rate.

You should, if you have hired talented people, be completely uninvolved in the day-to-day management. They should handle all requests for specific tasks. Your Webmaster will not be able to schedule anything with accuracy if tasks and projects are scheduled by more than one person. Multiple priorities aren't impossible to balance. Multiple priorities that land on your Web site staff unannounced or priorities that are garbled in the translation from one department to another can cause major problems and confusion. Simply being aware of a deadline so that other priorities can be adjusted accordingly can make a real difference to your staff.

▶ **NOTE**   In the course of one particularly hectic three-week period, we had the misfortune to have two previously unannounced projects and one announced-but-miscommunicated one dropped into our work schedule. That wouldn't have been too frustrating had we not already been scheduling a complete redesign of the site and an upgrade in hardware and software at the time. The hardware upgrade and part of the software upgrade made it into the final schedule, but additional software and a redesign were forced into a holding pattern for what eventually became almost three months, as additional projects migrated into the schedule. Frustration levels reached record highs. ◀

If you manage technical projects now, you know all the pitfalls. If this is your first attempt at management in the technical arena, remember these two rules:

- ◆ Refer technical questions to your technical staff. If you answer a technical question incorrectly, one of two things will happen. You will look unnecessarily foolish when the correction is made; or your staff will cover for you, but you will have gained no respect from them.

- ◆ Don't commit your staff to a particular course of action without consulting them. For instance, if you assure another department that your staff can administer their Web site, and that requires additional hardware and software for the actual implementation, your budget is going to take a nasty hit.

You don't have to learn everything there is to know about Web sites. You do have to understand enough and be willing to learn enough to know which decisions to make and which to defer.

WHO IS ULTIMATELY ACCOUNTABLE?

Accountability may seem unimportant in the early stages of your Web site, but the management process requires that someone be responsible for the site. Your Webmaster will not only be the target for the day-to-day planning; she'll also be the regular target for suggestions, criticisms, critiques, and questions from people both inside and outside your company. The perception for most people is that the Webmaster is responsible for the site. How your site is staffed simply isn't likely to be apparent to people who visit it. That's the way it should be. You may have one or two staff members or you may have 100 working on the project, but its cohesiveness should indicate to your visitors a single entity. They will associate that entity with your Webmaster. Actual control over the process may reside anywhere.

In truth, if the budget overruns or the site simply doesn't accomplish what it was designed to accomplish, who will management invite to explain it? You sold them the concept and you hired the staff. It's somewhat unlikely that they'll ask the Webmaster for explanations. *You* may, but *they* probably won't.

WHY WOULD YOU WANT TO DO THIS?

Because it's fun! Because it's exciting to be out there involved in a completely new medium that offers tremendous potential for you and your company. It won't be the easiest project you've ever undertaken, but it's likely to be one of the most challenging. It may be one of the most gratifying, too.

It's sheer pleasure to watch a person who has been struggling with the basics of HTML coding look at his first completed page with a Web browser, or watch that "light bulb" moment when a graphic artist determines just the right palette for an image map. Beyond that, it's a real pleasure to be involved with people who love their work (and most Web workers do).

This project will test your management skills. If you're up to the task, you won't have to advertise for new employees. They'll come looking for you. Good managers are as rare as graphic artists who can program; everybody wants to work for one.

Oh, and one other thing—if you do this right, the visibility associated with a Web site can't exactly hurt your career options, either.

4

Got People;
Got Documents;
Got Cold Feet

This project was moving right
along. Now it seems to be
stalled. What's the problem?

◆

What can you do that will
get things back on track—
and on time?

◆

Will you need outside help to
get things rolling again?

The first flush of Web fever is evidenced by serious attacks of Web surfing and study. The most ecologically inclined staff person will have no hesitation to kill whole forests of trees as she prints every page she finds that appears to offer good information about building a Web site. So much for the paperless office! As the fever takes hold, enthusiasm is high. Great plans are hatched; wonderful ideas are bandied about and considered, then rejected or embraced.

The fever doesn't go away, but the reality that a project deadline is getting closer and there's still a huge amount of work to be done overcomes some of the enthusiasm. A Web site can die before it's born if this stage isn't handled properly.

The signs that your staff has reached this critical juncture are obvious:

- They express ever more serious concerns about whether anyone will even notice the site.
- They assure you that the original plan just isn't quite good enough or that it's just not working.
- There's a decided slowdown in the pace of development.
- You see less evidence of self-confidence in their ability to complete the project.

You can help make the transition from a plan to a working Web site easier if you know what to look for and how to address their concerns.

IF YOU'RE NOT WORRIED, YOU'RE NOT PAYING ATTENTION

Your concerns and those of your staff aren't likely to be the same, though they may intersect. You're concerned about completing the project on time and within budget. If the staff is stalled, for whatever reason, both of those items are in danger.

You're also concerned about the usefulness of the Web site to your company. This isn't exactly charted water, and you may be experiencing your own case of jitters—especially if you haven't seen some tangible proof that all the time your staff has spent learning about the Web is going to result in a workable Web site.

This isn't the time for a staff inquisition, though you may feel sorely tempted to set up the rack and summon them one at a time. Curb the urge. Odds are good that they need nothing more than a bit of hand-holding.

When Bad Sounds Good… And Great Sounds Awful

There's simply so much to learn and so many new developments being touted on the Web that sheer nervousness will make even the most self-confident employees quake. When a Web site debuts, the world is watching. It can be a terrifying thought. At this point, making Mirsky's Worst of the Web seems preferable to finding your site on one of the "mediocre" site lists. At least, if you make a "worst" list, you can only improve.

Oddly enough, the fear of success is just as great. What goes through the minds of your staff is, "If they really like our site, what will we do next? We've given this our best shot; if it works, we're in deep trouble." It's nothing more than growing pains. In truth, every Webmaster and Web site development team feels the same thing, to at least some degree, each time they try a new design or approach.

The odds are that their best effort is good—not great and not terrible. If they manage to arrive at "great" on the first shot, and your site is a fabulous hit and makes money for your company immediately, you've got one very valuable staff. Give them all raises and encourage them to greater heights. Your site will be the exception to what very few rules exist on the Web right now.

Quite honestly, so much can go wrong on a site that your staff is justifiably concerned, to an extent. For the most part, though, they've got nothing more serious than a case of opening night stage fright. Part of the problem is that they're probably just beginning to realize how much they don't know. At the beginning of the project, the challenge seems easily surmountable. If excitement alone would get the job done, your Web site would have been built in less than a week. But now you're looking for tangible results and they're worried. We're talking about feet that are icy cold here.

They don't know whether to show you what they've done (if they've actually done something). Will you laugh? Scream? Curse? Applaud? Take voluminous notes, applaud what's good, and throw out questions to the staff about possible improvements of those sections you doubt.

Maybe they haven't quite gotten around to details like coding a page or installing the Web server or producing the graphics. It's not that they don't want to. It's just that they've studied enough to know that what looked terribly easy in theory isn't quite so simple in reality. (Well, that's what they think, anyway.) There's absolutely nothing wrong with that thinking. They're obviously conscientious or they wouldn't have the good sense to worry.

YOU KNOW THIS AILMENT

Arriving on the Web with a slightly cocky attitude is fine; arriving with delusions of grandeur is not. The former will get you a grin and a tip of the hat from the best and brightest; the latter isn't going to be well-received. Your staff knows that fact, if they've been studying and they've reached the point of second-guessing their every move.

As a manager, you know that second-guessing can be deadly. The fact is that many times it makes much more sense to take a chance and apologize later than to procrastinate until you've missed an opportunity. Your staff is probably not engaging in the garden-variety type of procrastination. It's the second-guessing kind.

So what are you going to do about it? Until you determine the reasons, not much.

There's one thing you should know as you look for reasons, and one thing you can assure your staff as you ferret out the causes: There are no experts in this field.

There are people who've been working at it longer. There are experts at individual pieces like programming browsers and writing new applications. There are plenty of people who've been studying and working at Web site development longer than your staff, and some of them have a great deal of knowledge in the field. That only makes them (I suppose I should say *us*, but I'm no expert either) more experienced. At best, they've been where your staff is now and learned a few lessons along the way.

Do that thing you do best—listen. Talk to them and listen carefully to their answers. The most common fears can be easily addressed.

WHAT IF NO ONE VISITS OUR SITE?

This one is almost laughable—almost. It's not likely to be a real problem, but your staff may think it will be.

Those many, many indexes ensure that this isn't exactly "Field of Dreams" stuff but it comes really close. As soon as your site is listed on any of the major search engines, they'll come. Okay, "they" might not be who you hope to attract, and they may not arrive as quickly or in quite the numbers you would like, but they'll arrive anyway. It's all but impossible not to be listed by at least one of the major search engines. Alta Vista (**http://www.altavista.digital .com**) is so quick to find new Web sites that it's almost frightening.

Your staff is probably already planning to submit your URL to a number of search engines for inclusion in the databases. One simple submission at Submit It (**http://submit-it.permalink.com/submit-it**) will enter your URL to 18 (at last count) of the indexes on the Web. You do, however, want to counsel caution on two fronts:

◆ **Better to be fashionably late.** In spite of the fact that it may take a month for your URL to be entered into the various databases, you don't want it published *before* your site is operational and you're prepared for visitors. That doesn't mean that your staff should wait until a month before your site debuts to make submissions—they shouldn't even be *that* eager. Not every index will take a month for registration. If your listing begins to attract people even two weeks before your site is actually online, there's simply no way to know how many of the people who try it and fail to find you won't try again. Better to attract a crowd a little later than you might like than to attract them too soon and run the risk that they won't visit when you're ready.

◆ **But we *make* screws.** Before your staff makes any submission to those databases, have them run searches based on any keywords they intend to use in your listing. The results can sometimes be a bit surprising. If you're in the business of manufacturing screws, you may be a lot happier with the company you'll find in search results based on the term *threaded fasteners*.

Trying out searches on the various sites based on the keywords in your listing may, at the least, provide your staff with hours of good laughs and any number of red faces. This isn't an exercise for the timid, but it's almost always educational.

Conducting a Search

Take a quick trip to Alta Vista at the URL mentioned earlier in this chapter. Enter the keyword you're looking for in the form provided at the beginning of their pages, and play this game yourself. The keyword *screws* turns up 20,000 responses and *screw* 40,000. And yes, a lot of manufacturers or distributors of screws are there. So are (in the first 4-5 pages) a page that offers you ways to screw the IRS, and Screws Home Page (a college student's efforts, apparently), among others. Actually, some references that turn up are very interesting, and quite a few aren't interesting at all—to me, at least. We're talking about the Web—there's the good and the dreck.

THOSE TRICKY NEWSGROUPS AND MAILING LISTS

Newgroups and mailing lists are part and parcel of the Internet. Usenet News has been around for years and hosts thousands of newsgroups, each with its own focus for discussion. Some are serious, some are silly, and some are sound and fury signifying nothing. People who have Usenet newsfeeds, either through a provider or at their places of business, can take part in the discussions by posting directly to the groups. Some Web sites carry all or a portion of the many newsgroups (**http://www.zippo.com** is one that does at this time). Quite a lot of long, involved, and very interesting discussions can be found among the newsgroups. And quite a few of the people who are involved in those discussions are very knowledgeable about the various subjects—from computer operating systems to networking hardware to pet care and yachting.

Mailing lists, on the other hand, are subscribed to by the members of the mailing list, and the posts to the groups are delivered by e-mail. As with newsgroups, if there's a subject in which you have an interest, there's at least one mailing list for you. Some of the lists are very, very active, producing hundreds of incoming mail messages daily—others aren't.

Both newsgroups and mailing lists generally have a set of questions that have been asked and answered so many times that they demand their own documentation. They're called *FAQs*—short for *Frequently Asked Questions*. If you or your staff are going to post to a newsgroup or a mailing list, read the FAQ that's available about the group—or enter at your own risk. Things have gotten a lot less friendly among veteran Internet members in the past year or so. A question that would have drawn nothing more than a polite, "It's in the FAQ," two years ago is likely to draw a completely different response now that will sizzle your hair (which is one reason they're called *flames*).

Any number of newsgroups and mailing lists may be appropriate for announcing your site's opening. The newsgroup **comp.infosystems.www .announce** is set up specifically for general announcements of new Web sites.

If your staff plans to use any of the newsgroups or mailing lists, however, they absolutely should be reading those lists and groups regularly. It's imperative that they understand the nature of the group to whom the announcement will be made and the acceptable standards within the group. It may be much more acceptable for them to post messages to some groups with no mention at all of your site other than a reference to your URL in their (short—no more than four lines) signature. If they don't thoroughly understand the purpose and culture of the newsgroups and mailing lists, they simply shouldn't attempt to publicize your site in any of them. They can easily do more harm than good with a misplaced announcement.

Your *signature* line for your e-mail might contain your name, e-mail address, and the name and URL for your company. That's plenty. Keep it as short as possible.

▶ **CAUTION** This can be a very serious business. Two lawyers, whom I won't name because they've already gotten more publicity from their stunt than they deserve, posted blatant advertising for their firm in several thousand newsgroups. The Internet community wasn't pleased—to say the very least.

It's true that they received a tremendous amount of publicity, but certainly not the kind that most businesses would hope for. The people who read newsgroups and mailing lists spread the word about offenders very quickly. You don't want to make that kind of splash with your Web site. Your business might never recover. ◀

Brief announcements to the newsgroups and mailing lists are completely acceptable, if the message is targeted to carefully chosen groups and is in keeping with the standards set by those groups. That makes it doubly important for your staff to do their homework and study the groups to which they intend to post (and no, reading a group for a day or two isn't enough). *Lurk*—read the group but don't post any messages—for a month or two to get a feel for the relationships and the ongoing dialogue of the group.

Assuming, however, that your staff is regularly reading the lists that are targeted to their areas of interest in your Web site, those lists may be helpful for determining where and how to publish information about your site. They can contact others on the list who have already publicized their own sites and ask them for information and advice on how to publish yours.

▶ **NOTE**   In the past six months, I've received around 30 announcements of new sites via one mailing list to which I subscribe. Of those 30, I've taken the time to look at fewer than 10. The authors of those announcements generally posted a message to the group to the effect of, "We've worked hard at making our site ready—please take a look at it and tell us what you think." The ones that announced their fabulous new sites in screen after screen of nothing more than self-serving advertisement went straight into the *bit bucket* (a techy-term meaning that I deleted the messages without so much as a glance at the URL). If their sites are that great, I'll hear about them from other sources, no doubt. ◀

Targeting Your Audience to Increase Your Visitors

You have in mind a specific audience and you need to plan to attract that audience. This part of your staff's dilemma can be reasonably easy to address. The timing may be a bit tricky, or at least a little slower than they'd like, but it's hardly insurmountable.

You're already targeting specific audiences with your traditional marketing tools. Plan to add your URL into those marketing devices within a week of your Web site's debut. As soon as your site is ready for prime time, add your URL to your signature line in your e-mail messages. As new business cards and stationery are printed, make sure that the URL is included. These are simple, but very effective and inexpensive ways to promote your site.

The Numbers Don't Lie, But They Don't Tell All, Either

Most new Web site developers take an inordinate interest in publicizing their sites immediately and are more concerned with the number of hits on the site than with the quality of those hits. High hit counts are fine, but they don't really tell you much about who's visiting your site and why. That's the information you need.

Rather than concerning themselves with numbers, encourage your staff to think of ways to determine the "who" and the "why." Obviously, requesting that visitors register at your site is one way to do that. But what are you offering them that will encourage registration? Unless you give them some good reason to fill out a form and give you information about themselves, they're not likely to take the time. There are plenty of other sites to see.

Can you offer them special pricing arrangements for their effort? Will you let them know of special discounts on your products and services before you run your print ads or send out your regular customer mailings? Will you give them a deeper discount for placing their order electronically, since it will be less labor-intensive for you?

▶ **NOTE**   Whether you choose to accept payment online is entirely up to you. You can take faxed or phoned purchase orders or credit cards, or you can provide a mailing address for mailing payments. The details depend entirely on your normal business requirements for payment. ◀

Consider adding value to your site by offering a special service—an addition to your regular newsletter that's available only on the Web for registered visitors, for instance. Some of your customers might prefer to receive the information electronically that you normally send via snail mail (the U.S. Postal Service). Offer to remove those customers from your regular mailing lists and send them e-mail instead. Now you not only get a better idea of who your visitors are, but you have an opportunity to quantify real savings to your company.

▶ **TIP**   As you go about your daily duties, keep an eye out for obvious ways to replace some function in your business by displacing it to the Web. It's the displacement of effort and time that will make your site work for you in the real world. ◀

Junk Mail Is Still Junk Mail—Even in Electronic Form

Just as people toss bulk mailings and flyers that arrive via the U.S. Postal Service, they delete junk e-mail without reading it. Many of us receive hundreds of e-mail messages a day, and many of those messages go completely unread. In many instances, even those messages we'd like to read must go unread because there are a limited number of hours in any day. If you send e-mail at your customer's request, make the subject line brief and descriptive of the content of your note so that your customer can quickly determine its priority. Yes, you might get away with one message with a subject line of "This is VERY Important," but it had better *be* important, or others you send won't be read.

Can you give the visitor something for his registration? You might offer a sample of your product, for example. Wouldn't you rather send a sample to someone who actually requests it than wonder how many of the ones you included in a bulk mailing actually were opened and used? Consider asking your Web visitors not only to register for the sample but to come back later and tell you what they thought of it. Ask whether they'd like to receive e-mail from you when you offer other product samples.

If product samples aren't an option, what about other promotional items— hats, pens, T-shirts—one to every x number of visitors registered (your choice: 10, 25, 100). This type of promotion takes a bit more processing for your Web site developers, however, so consider the experience level of your staff as well as your business needs. Right now, your immediate goal is to get your staff back on track so that your Web site debuts on time.

A TRIP TO EUROPE WOULD BE NICE

How about a contest? Certainly, it's an idea. The question is whether it's a good one. Some businesses offer contests based on answering questions about the contents of their site. It's one way to entice people to explore your site a little further, and it does result in registration. There are sites that track and list ongoing contests, so you could get additional exposure there.

There's little doubt that a contest will increase the numbers of visitors to your site. Whether they're the audience you want probably depends on the prize. A hardware manufacturer who awards a set of tools as a prize is more likely than one who's giving away a trip to have registered visitors who are interested in hardware.

The point of registration is to determine more about your audience. Increasing the numbers of hits may look good on the quantity side of the ledger but won't necessarily do much for the quality side.

▶ **CAUTION**   Be very careful how you use personal information that visitors to your site choose to give you. If you specify that you will send them e-mail, be sure to create a list with one alias for all the people registered. One business simply set up a list of names and sent e-mail to all of them. The result was four screens of e-mail addresses to page through before the text of the message could be read. Worse, people responded to the message and each response went to the entire list. Can you say "dissatisfied customers?" Not a good entry into the electronic world at all. ◀

E-mail Isn't Necessarily Confidential, But It Is Private

Don't share e-mail addresses with anyone unless the person with whom you are corresponding gives you express permission. Many people don't share their e-mail addresses with others, or have certain accounts that are private and others that they consider public. If you send e-mail to a long list of people, each of those people can see the others' addresses. That may not sit very well with some of them. For all you know, the list you send could contain the address of a spouse, a child—or a boss who is (or was) previously unaware that the other address existed. That's not likely to make quite the impression that you would like.

▶ **CAUTION**   Unless your visitors explicitly give you permission to use their personal information in any way other than for your internal use, don't use it. Good business ethics go a long way with your Web audience. So do poor business ethics—a long way in the other direction. ◀

You can take any number of approaches to encourage people to register at your site. Without a doubt, one of the best is taken by Amazon.com Inc. (**http://www.amazon.com**)—a bookstore that offers to shop the shelves (and stock them) for their registered visitors. In return for information about their visitors' reading tastes and buying habits, they send them e-mail when favorite authors publish new works or when new books are published on specific subjects. Theirs is an approach that works not only for the customers but for Amazon.com. Readers love the service, and surely it's easier for Amazon.com to place their orders for specific titles, authors, and subjects based on the information they have about what their customers want. That's win-win registration—precisely the kind you want your staff to be considering for your site.

MAY WE OFFER YOU A COOKIE?

One recent approach to Web statistics involves the use of *cookies*. Briefly, this technology attaches an identifier to a particular visitor to your site and can allow you to track them as they browse. It's used on sites that sell a range of products so that customers can go from page to page, acquiring items and purchasing them after they've looked at as many pages as they'd like.

If you have the technical capability to implement this approach, it can help you determine the navigational approaches to your Web site, at least. It can also give you some clue as to why people visit your site and how they use it. It's not likely to be as useful as registration information yet, though it certainly has potential.

Some of the more enthusiastic supporters of the technology tout it as useful for determining how long your visitors linger at your site. Certainly, that could be useful information. There's some question about its reliability, however. Does the fact that the visitor spent three minutes studying your home page and then ten minutes studying the next page before moving on mean that she was truly interested in the second page? Or does it mean that she took a phone call or went to get another cup of coffee and got stopped in the hall?

Before you decide to use the cookie approach, you should know that there has been quite a bit of discussion among Webmasters and the Web community about the ethics of gathering information about visitors this way. The cookie can remain with you and track your viewing habits until the next time you visit the site where it originated. At that point, a program can gather that information. As a marketing/statistical analysis tool, the information could be invaluable. The question of surreptitiously gathering and using that information is likely to be hotly debated before any conclusions are drawn.

Web servers have logs that gather at least some of the information your staff will want. They can tell you the IP address of your visitor, and that can be translated to a specific domain (**net**, **com**, **edu**, **gov**, etc.—pop back to Chapter 2 if you're not familiar with domains). Software is currently available to translate the information quickly and easily. Other information that is (or can be) tracked from your server logs includes the date and time of the visit, the browser that was used, and what pages attract the most visitors.

Until all the issues surrounding the ethics of other types of information-gathering are resolved, your server logs are tried and true, if not always as specific as you might like.

A LITTLE LINK EXCHANGE

Your staff could be considering ways to encourage *reciprocity* in links. If one of your pages links to another site, they can send e-mail to the Webmaster there and request a link back to your site. Your staff should be careful to use this type of linking discriminately. Again, you're looking for quality rather than quantity of hits.

Put the Web staff to work considering realistic and useful ways to determine who will be visiting your site and why, rather than spinning their wheels worrying about numbers. That's useless worry. Worrying about the *quality* of those numbers is not.

Everyone Will Hate Our Site!

Well, some people will indeed hate it. That's quite simply one price you pay for being willing to take risks. A Web site is ripe for criticism. Your staff is likely to be more critical of it than anyone else. They've been studying what works and what doesn't. In truth, very few people will waste time hating any site. The opposite of love isn't always hate—in the case of a business, at least, it's apathy. They'll simply move on to another site. You need to determine whether you're dealing with real concerns or phantoms, and reassure the staff where necessary.

What, Exactly, Will They Hate?

And who, by the way, is "they"? Expect rather nonspecific answers to these questions. More than likely your staff has spent time reading reviews of Web sites on the major indexes, and they've probably read some reviews by individuals (there are a wealth of pundits on the Web). "They" are likely to be precisely those people. And those people may or may not be impressed by your site. Who's to say, at this point?

More importantly, does it *matter* what those people think? Of course you want your site to be admired—that's perfectly understandable. But you want your clients and your potential clients to like it and use it. They are the people you and your staff need to be concerned about pleasing and serving.

If your staff is seriously concerned that the audience you are trying to attract will hate it (and more than likely "hate" is just a wee bit extreme), that's another story entirely. Can they give you concrete reasons for their concerns? Do they think the content or the design lacks clarity or sophistication? Perhaps it doesn't offer enough in the way of a personal approach? If they can offer specific examples of inadequacies, together you may be able to address the problem.

It's entirely possible that the people who are creating content haven't done their homework as well as your staff has done theirs. A rewrite might very well be in order.

But it's just as likely that your staff is simply thinking in terms of attracting the broadest possible audience—without regard to who that audience is.

Your Virtual Geography

There's absolutely nothing wrong with having a very focused Web site. A legal firm that specializes in corporate law should concentrate on attracting business concerns to its Web site—not people who are interested in writing their wills or looking for information about domestic law. Making that type of information available is sure to attract a reasonably large audience, but not necessarily the audience the firm needs.

A Web site isn't very different from your physical location. Most businesses choose their location based on the clientele they want to attract. Your Web site should be populated with documents and information based on those same criteria.

Unless your staff can show you why your desired audience will not be attracted to your Web site, you're probably just dealing with a serious case of anxiety.

Sigh—The Politics of a Web Site

On the other hand, some measure of in-house politics or rivalries may be causing problems. Developing a Web site may look like a rather glamorous job to some people. There's no doubt that it's a project with high visibility. There may very well be some people who would be just as happy to see your staff fail as succeed. And they may be taking shots at the plan and/or the implementation at every opportunity.

It's not easy to ignore criticism offered by people who should have the company's interests uppermost. It's even harder to determine which of those criticisms (offered as "suggestions") are entirely well-meant—and many of them are. Unless your staff is familiar with the politics and rivalries, they're likely to be trying to incorporate every suggestion into the eventual Web site. Now *there's* a sure-fire way to keep this project from reaching completion.

You can determine how much of that kind of delaying tactic is coming into play. There may be none, but it's worth taking a quick look to be sure. Even if every suggestion is completely sincere, you need to make sure that your staff isn't straying too far from the original plan, and that anything they decide to incorporate (some of those suggestions may be very good ones) isn't going to affect the schedule adversely. A Web site can expand exponentially from plan to execution—especially if the schedule is allowed to slip.

It's Just Not Good Enough

It's true. Well, it's true in the sense that a Web site is simply never good enough in the eyes of the people who are working on it. This is another one of those (very few) rules of the Web.

Technology—The Hero and the Villain

During the time that your staff has been studying the Web, they've been bombarded by new ideas and killer applications. *Killer applications* (*apps* for short) are the latest, greatest gadgets and technologies. Your staff may now be convinced that introducing a Web site without including one or several of these killer apps is corporate suicide. It's not. At least, it's not if your product isn't one of those gadgets or technologies.

The *early adopters* (those who are always on the forefront, trying and using new technologies—the ones who download the newest browsers within 20 minutes of their announcement on the Web) embrace each new technology and immediately begin to tell others that this is simply the one thing the Web has been waiting for. Some of those technologies will stand the test of time and be incorporated into what will eventually become the mainstream of the Web. Others will go the way of the dinosaur, but much faster. Is your staff experienced enough at this point to make a prediction?

FUNCTIONAL IS COOL—HONEST!

Your staff needs to be concentrating on building a functional Web site that works for your business rather than being intimidated by the technology. It's much more sensible for a new Web site to take a slightly more conservative approach and add the technologies later. Of course, if your product is one of the new technologies, it wouldn't exactly be a brilliant tactic not to demonstrate it on your Web site. Then again, it seems more than a little unlikely that you'd just now be setting up a Web site if that were the case, doesn't it?

Attempt to apply a dose of reality if your staff members are letting themselves get sidetracked by gadgets. Functional is cool. Functional, combined with good (even if specialized) content and navigational qualities can get you kudos and a good review from "them" (you know, the pundits).

And what will happen if your site does get a good review at some point? Your staff will be delighted—and then assure you that your Web site just isn't good enough. Count on it. Then, of course, they'll go back to work making the site better. Praise can be quite an effective motivator.

OVERCOMING FEAR

You need to see tangible results. More importantly, that's what your staff needs to produce in order to get past their own hesitations. You already knew that, right? They'll be less concerned once they move from the world of theory to reality, so it's time for you to assess the actual progress of the project, by answering the following questions:

- Is the Web server software installed and has it been tested?

- Have all of the documents been developed?

- Part of the documents?

- How many of the documents have been coded?

- Have the graphics been developed?

If your server is hosted by a service provider, or if the software has already been installed and tested by your technical staff, that item at least is a non-issue.

INSTALL THAT WEB SERVER!

Depending on how far along your staff is, and on their technical skills, installing the Web server software and coding the documents may be easier if you consider having a consultant come on site for a day or two to simply guide your staff. You don't want the consultant to do the work—only to give assistance and guidance as necessary to get things back on track.

If you plan to run your own server, you certainly don't want a consultant to do the installation for you. Your Webmaster will be better served by doing the installation himself. He's going to have to do the upgrades (which will come around sooner rather than later) and deal with any problems that arise. Some experienced guidance can be useful, though—if only to advise on tricks and "gotchas."

READ THE F——— MANUAL

Yes, your staff can, indeed, "Read the *fabulous* manual." (Or *frivolous* or *fantastic* or any other word beginning with the letter *f* that you prefer.) Unfortunately, not all server documentation is perfectly clear. (If there were awards for understatement, that sentence would definitely be a candidate.) Having someone available either on-site or by phone to answer questions and offer explanations can be of tremendous benefit. Most experts won't start an installation of important software without at least having a number for technical support. (They don't like to place the call, though—admitting defeat is hard for these types.)

The installation process can be anything from simple to maddening. Even simple installations can have their frustrating moments. The maddening ones can drive even reasonably sane technicians to distraction.

▶ **NOTE**   Back in the dark ages of Web servers, after we had already moved our Web site from UNIX to VMS (an interesting exercise) and had pretty much decided that Windows NT would be our platform of choice, I installed three evaluation packages. I was ready to pull out my hair before I managed to get the first one working. The second was an absolute breeze, but the software carried a price tag that was rather overblown considering the features. The third was up and running in less than 30 minutes and was half the price of the second with equivalent features. That software now operates on both our intranet and our external Web server. ◀

Get the software installed by whatever means it takes to get it installed. It's possible to code pages on any computer and view them from a browser locally, but it just doesn't feel the same as having them on a Web server. In fact, depending on the platform and tools your staff is using for development, there actually may be differences in the way files are structured and links coded, which can be very confusing for new Web developers. People who are experienced with coding find it very easy to ignore what appears to be "broken" if they know that once the page is installed on the server it will work perfectly; those new to the process have, understandably, less confidence that something that appears to be broken actually isn't.

Now, About Those Documents...

If the content isn't available, little else can be done. It makes very little sense to spend hours coding pages that will never be used. HTML coding is entirely too boring for such an exercise. In the very best of circumstances, it's not likely that all the documents you want for your Web site will be ready before your server is installed and simple pages have been coded.

Naturally, you'll want to read and approve (or not) those pages that are being newly written or rewritten specifically for the Web site. Always read the pages with an eye to your Web audience. The people preparing content must understand that audience, or your pages won't work for you. If you aren't satisfied with them, send the writers back to their writing desks with instructions to chant a mantra of "literate, well-educated" several times daily, until they produce well-written copy that stands on its own without obvious references to links. "Click here" simply isn't acceptable. Why? What's the first thing your customer will do when he finds one of your Web pages that's particularly useful? He'll print it out, of course, for reference. (You just have to laugh, given all the talk about this "electronic medium.")

"Click here" makes no sense at all on a printed page. The page may include links to other documents, and will, in all probability, but those links should be apparent only on the Web, in the context of the page.

Preparing good documents for the Web is usually an ongoing item that will require any number of revisions and rewrites. But some documents probably are ready for inclusion without more than a minimal amount of massaging.

CODE IT NOW!

In all probability, if the documents weren't being delivered your Webmaster would have made you aware of that fact. It's much more likely that some documents have been attempted. One of the funniest characteristics of Web site development is that people will code documents, view them, decide they look okay, and then immediately assume that they did something wrong because it was just too easy. They may have done something that isn't strictly "by the book" but, let's face it, the purpose of this exercise is to produce

146

pages that can be viewed on the Web. If they doubt their code, the pages can easily be submitted to one of the HTML validators, which will return a full report of any coding errors. The HTML validation services are very helpful for finding errors in code. They check only the code and can be reassuring for people who doubt their own efforts. Your developers can find a list of the available validation services that Neil Bowers at Khoral Research, Inc., maintains at this address:

http://www.khoral.com/staff/neilb/weblint/validation.html

If the documents really haven't been coded (certainly a possibility), you may simply be dealing with people who don't learn as easily by reading as they do by hearing the process explained and seeing examples. Hiring someone to do training for a day is probably all it will take to get things back on track.

Getting documents coded and working on your Web server may be the boost your staff needs to get everything rolling along smoothly again. The project begins to take on a reality at that point. No matter how simple those first documents, they're proof—not just to you—that your Web site can happen. Once you or they break that particular logjam, things should move more quickly.

Purple Text on a Paisley Background—Ouch!

What you can expect to see happen almost immediately is that those first simple documents will take on more complexity than you ever expected (or wanted or needed). That dark green fractal background with pink type is probably not precisely what you had in mind for your Web site. Don't worry—standard operating procedure is for pages to be completely overdone before they're judged bloated (not to mention ugly) and pieces begin to disappear.

Believe it or not, excess is a good sign. In fact, it's a far better sign than pages that take on no life at all. It indicates a certain creativity and willingness to take risks. More importantly, it indicates that the people who are doing your coding are learning. Coding a basic HTML pages doesn't take a great deal of talent; understanding when you've done too much is more difficult.

WHAT'S HAPPENING OVER IN GRAPHICS?

The tone set by the writers will affect the graphics design, so it's unreasonable to expect graphics production before content development. These two pieces must work together. However, it isn't unreasonable to expect your graphic artists to be producing at least some graphic devices to *try* on the first pages that are coded. They should definitely be attempting the techniques necessary for Web graphics. It makes no sense at all for them to wait until they have final copy for the site before learning how to apply their artistic talents on the Web.

Designing for the Web is unlike designing for other media. Make sure that your graphic artists are at least learning the basics of the process. The last thing you want to hear a week before the site is scheduled to debut is that they "have this really perfect design but just can't seem to make it work on the Web."

REALITY CAN BE SUCH A NUISANCE

Now, in theory, your Webmaster should be monitoring all this activity and you shouldn't really have to concern yourself overly much with any of it. In fact, if your Web site is being developed by an experienced Webmaster, who either supervises staff assigned to the project or at least reports to you on a regular basis regarding what is or isn't getting done, you should be involved only to the extent of prodding or providing motivational support as necessary.

Most people don't live in a theoretical world, unfortunately. Experienced Webmasters don't grow on trees, and experienced Webmasters who have managerial skills are decidedly hard to find. Let's assume that your chosen

148

Webmaster, and the associated staff, are of the more common inexperienced variety, and that you'll simply need to stay reasonably well-informed about the status of all the pieces of the project.

After you determine the stage of development of server software, documents, coding, and graphics, you can apply whatever encouragement or outside help you deem necessary to ensure that the project moves ahead.

Don't rule out replacing project staff who are too timid or too firmly entrenched in old technologies to work well in this new one. All the talent in the world won't give them the necessary motivation to overcome fear or a hesitation to try new things. It's better to replace them with less-timid souls now than to allow them to hold up the project (now or later).

First Look

Now that you're ready for anything, it's time to take a guided tour through the pages that have been coded, however hesitantly or daringly. Your staff should develop good habits for Web page development from the very beginning; these are the warning signs you need to watch for:

- ◆ "Under construction" signs or apologies in any guise
- ◆ Links to pages or graphics that don't exist
- ◆ Sending your visitors off to other sites too quickly

Drop That "Under Construction" Notice in the Bit Bucket

You don't want to see one—not even *one*—page that announces that it's "under construction." *Every* page on the Web is under construction—or has been abandoned entirely. Your staff shouldn't be making apologies for their Web pages, even in the earliest stages of their design. It can become a habit.

Think of the absolute worst TV show you can name. Does it carry a prominent disclaimer that the writers are still working on the scripts and the set designers aren't really pleased yet, so you should tune in next week to see how they're doing? Of course not (though some probably should, come to think of it). Why waste time watching a show the producers aren't proud of ?

Your staff shouldn't be wasting your time now or your visitors' time later. Those Web pages, whatever the level of experience and time allotted, are the best they can do right now. They may not think the pages are very good, but they shouldn't announce that fact on the page. Would you send out a print announcement that says, "Here's our new product! It's not very good, but we'll improve it later"?

A 30-Second Commercial with 15 Seconds of Dead Air?

The question of the quality of the pages becomes more critical the closer your site comes to production on the Web, of course. A business simply shouldn't have a Web site with pages sporting "under construction" signs or links to pages that don't yet exist. Even the least experienced Web surfer will grow weary of following links that result in the dreaded "404" error message (which announces that the page doesn't exist) or links that go to pages that have no content beyond a header announcing that this part of the Web site is "coming soon." It's entirely preferable to have a few good pages with valuable content than to have 50 partially completed ones.

You would never consider sending a mailing to your clients (or placing an ad) that was only half-written, would you? It's fine to tell your Web site visitors about future plans for your site, but not with pages that are incomplete. The Web is a different type of medium, but it's not that different!

The same principle applies to the graphics on your pages. If the graphic doesn't yet exist on the Web server, it shouldn't be linked into your Web page. Your visitor is likely to assume that her browser isn't working correctly

150

at first and attempt to reload the page (only to have it not work again). While that isn't quite as annoying as incomplete or nonexistent pages, it's still annoying.

But the sign will be removed and the links will exist later, right? So why not include them in these early stages of development? Because they're entirely too easy to forget in the press of a deadline and a myriad of other details, especially if you have a Web site that's extensive. Yes, if your site is composed entirely of less than 10 pages, those apologies or "dead" links are probably going to be caught and expunged before your Web site debuts—*probably*. Most Web server packages now have some type of link-checking feature that makes finding those "dead" links easier, but not all of them do. None of them are yet advertising "apology detectors."

Oops! One Click and They're Gone!

The third item on the list qualifies as a "caution," for the most part—don't encourage your visitors to leave too soon. That sounds pretty easy, doesn't it? Just don't offer links outside of your Web site, right? WRONG! (Sorry, didn't mean to shout.) Wrong. You absolutely should link to other sites that add value to the information you provide, whether that's more in-depth information about a subject, or information that's peripheral to the subject. Consider, for instance, a medical practice that specializes in geriatrics— linking to information other sites offer on the topic makes sense; there's no reason to reinvent the wheel (in this case rewrite what's already been published on the Web). Peripheral information may be very helpful, too—links to information about elder care or support groups for families of seniors are good and useful resources people will greatly appreciate.

That doesn't mean that you want your visitor to your site to rush right off to other places. Your staff should be concentrating on providing outside information quickly and easily for those who need and want it, but not at the expense of your core information. It's a balancing act, but not one that's terribly difficult. For the simple reason that HTML, when used correctly, is context driven, text with links to external resources don't necessarily have to be located in the first paragraph on your site. If your goal is to make those resources readily available, you can place a link on a separate page of links for such things. It's all a matter of what you want your site to do and be.

You may find that those external resources are as valuable to you and your staff as they are to your visitors.

▶ **NOTE**   In the course of preparing some pages for inclusion on our Web site some time ago, I came across a reference to traumatic brain injury (TBI). A friend had recently set up a Web site about TBI, so I called the researcher responsible for the study we were referencing and asked that he take a look at the TBI site to determine whether it was the type of quality information to which we would want to provide links. He called me back within 24 hours (after he figured out how to use the Web) and said "I'd have saved hours of time on my own research if I had known about this site." ◀

Don't encourage your visitors to leave but, at the same time, do put links in your text that enhance your site and provide your visitors with quality information—no matter the source. *That includes linking to your competition.* Yes, you read that correctly. The Web is an entirely new medium—entirely new. You've probably sent customers to your competition before, in one way or another, but it somehow feels wrong to do that on your Web site, doesn't it?

We're not talking about not competing here. We're talking about incorporating the spirit of the Internet—the culture of the Web—into your Web site. It's impressive for a business to point people to their competition. It indicates complete self-confidence. Remember your audience—you are talking with a pretty savvy bunch. There's nothing at all wrong with linking to your competition if they have, however inadvertently, posted something on their site that adds value to yours. (And isn't that just wonderfully Machiavellian?)

ASK AROUND

When you determine that everything is moving along as it should, and as your Web site begins to take on some substance, it's important to get some input from people who aren't closely involved in the project. Since we've already determined that your Web site developers will never really think the site is quite good enough, they're obviously not the best judges of the site. It's time to expose this work to a wider audience.

FROM GREAT TO HO-HUM

Obviously, other people in your company should be asked to take a look at the site and comment on it. Some will; some won't. It's not real to them yet. This phenomenon has never been sufficiently explained, but perhaps it's a combination of the unreality of a Web site that isn't yet "officially" on the Web and a lack of understanding that these pages actually will, at some point, represent your business to a very large audience. Whatever the reason, however, you and your staff can expect reactions varying from "Fabulous!" to yawns.

One other phenomenon that's almost beyond explanation is that even pages that have a direct impact on specific areas of your business may be ignored by the people who really should be looking at them. There's simply no reasonable explanation for this behavior; just accept the inevitable. As long as you can be sure that those people have been informed of your desire for them to view and comment on the pages that affect their part of the operation, there's little else you can do. You can point them to your Web site but you can't make them click, so to speak.

You'll get a certain amount of reasonable input from inside your own company. Some of it will be very helpful, especially if you have Web-literate employees. Oddly, those who do offer input are likely to comment more often on technical implementation than on content. At least they're likely to find that one link that doesn't work (that everyone else missed) and in itself that's helpful. If your staff isn't generally Web-literate, their comments and suggestions may not be relevant to your Web audience, however.

LIFT THE CURTAIN JUST A LITTLE

When you're reasonably sure that you have gotten as much help as you can from people within your company, it's time to broaden your exposure. This next step is somewhat akin to opening a play off-Broadway. Send the URL of your site to friends (yours and your Web site staff's) and ask them to take a look. If you're all feeling especially brave, ask your families to take a look.

▶ **NOTE**   The second part of that process netted me a two-page critique on everything from my grammar to the tone of our site (and a few choice comments about the design) from my sister—tough audience! ◀

This is actually a much better test of your site for several reasons. The people who will visit your site won't know as much about your business as those who work in it. People inside the company overlook jargon that's familiar to them and that may not make sense at all to your wider audience. Your friends and families will judge your pages without an "insider's eye"—and that's exactly what you need them to do. If something isn't clear, you want them to tell you about it.

An additional benefit is that this audience is more likely to be looking at your site the same way many of your later visitors will be—from their homes or offices, over various types of lines and connections. You probably won't find it necessary to ask about the speed of the transmissions—that's one thing practically everyone will comment on, if they deem it to be too slow.

THE DETAILS ARE IN THE DIFFERENCES

They'll also be viewing your pages on a wide variety of monitors, and that can be extremely helpful. A graphic that looks just wonderful on one monitor may be all but incomprehensible on another.

154

Got People; Got Documents; Got Cold Feet

Different browsers display the same page in different ways, too. That can be more important than you know. Did you know, for instance, that not every person who surfs the Web has the latest version of Netscape or Internet Explorer? Gasp! It's true, and what's more, there are actually people who will visit your site who won't be using graphical browsers at all. No kidding. Making your pages friendly for visually- or hearing-impaired visitors is also a very good thing.

And just because your Web developers have the most recent browsers installed doesn't mean your visitors will. Many of them will, in fact, be viewing your site with older versions of the vast array of browsers that are on the market. That means that your Web site may look very different to them than it does to you. It's very important that your developers check your Web pages with several browsers, and one of those should be text-only. Try it yourself at least once with a text-only browser—you'll get a completely new view of your Web site. It may not please you, but it's how some people will experience your site.

You Don't Have a 17-Inch Monitor?!

It's hard for us techy types to imagine that! We tend to assume that everyone has a CD, a sound card, SuperVGA with 1024×768 resolution. Lots of people don't. Those of us who design and code pages can be brought up short by those limitations. In one instance, because I *don't* have those things on my own office setup, and because our designer purposely designs for the less-than-optimal viewing experience, one of our cohorts in another department sent along a caution about our page. The graphics that fit very nicely on a 14-inch monitor, one above the other, displayed beside one another on his 17-inch one. It took some real playing with the coding to make it work for both environments. More often the complaints will be from people who *do* have the 14-inch

continues

155

> *continued*
>
> monitors and don't have the sound cards and spectacular resolution.
> They are quite likely to be the majority of visitors to your site.

▶ **NOTE**   In the course of one of our major redesigns, I allowed the time
pressures involved to let me break my own first rule for checking Web pages.
I didn't check our site with a non–graphical browser. I mistakenly thought
everything was just fine until about a month later, when I received e-mail
advising me that none of the links on our home page worked beyond the second link. The note went on to state that the visitor really did like our new design, however. Sure enough, a quick check with my Lynx (text-only) browser
confirmed the sad truth. Incorrect coding ignored by my latest, greatest
graphical browsers *wasn't* ignored by older versions of those same browsers or
by text browsers. I don't even like to *think* about how many people that might
have affected in the course of a month! ◀

REVISE AND REGROUP

Your off-Broadway production will give you a real sense of what works on
your site—and what doesn't. It may be difficult for your Web site staff to
summon the courage to invite outside criticism, but it will be worth making
the leap into that unknown. Take the information you gather from all of your
sources and look for common points.

If only one person commented that the site was slow in transmission, it may
be that he simply had a bad connection; if several did, your staff needs to be
looking for ways to trim the file size. Split one page into two, or make the
graphics smaller—not necessarily in their size, but perhaps in the number of
colors displayed.

You really should never disregard comments about slow transmissions. You're
going to have a very limited amount of time to attract the attention of a Web

audience, after all. The best test of your pages isn't from your site but over a modem. That will give you and your staff a much better indication of what most of your visitors will experience when they visit your site.

Test the site yourself—from home with a PC and modem. Even a 28.8 connection (which sounds like it should be pretty quick) can be agonizingly slow if your site isn't well designed. And not everyone has a 28.8 modem. Honest. They're becoming more common, but plenty of people will access your site over 14.4 or 9600 through their Internet providers. As with their browsers, many people just don't see the need to upgrade their modems. What they have works. Why spend money on something faster?

▶ **NOTE** On the Web, speed doesn't kill—*lack* of speed does. Several months ago, one of my coworkers was telling me that a graphic artist friend of his had just become enamored of the Web. In the course of the conversation his friend said that he just hated that everything was "so slow!"—and this person had a state-of-the-art setup. My coworker showed him how to disable loading graphics through his browser and thrilled his friend entirely—just what he wanted—a fast connection, or at least as fast as the Web gets over 28.8. ◀

▶ **NOTE** Our graphic artist telecommutes from a very rural area in Mississippi to our office in North Carolina. Her phone line is literally run across a cow pasture, and until very recently it wasn't even buried. She is always the first to know if we've overdone any portion of our site since transmission speeds are decidedly a factor for her. Though her remoteness has its disadvantages in some ways, it is a real advantage to have someone testing the site who is remote and not necessarily accessing the site over the most advanced lines and equipment. ◀

Confusion about textual elements should be addressed. You're probably dealing with a very small group of viewers at this point—one person who doesn't understand the content could translate to many on the Web.

Did they like the overall design? Find the site easy to navigate? (Okay, it's not too easy to get lost in five pages, but it can be done.)

Now Do It All Again

Take all the comments from in-house and your first "focus group" and have your Web developers address as many of those issues as they can. Some may be more crucial to address immediately than others. Certainly it's more important to address issues surrounding textual items and overall design than to spend time learning how to do animations just because someone thought they'd be a good idea.

When the important issues have been addressed, and as more pages are added, encourage the same people to take a look at the site again. Invite others to have a look as well—the broader the audience during preview, the better.

And Now, a Kind Word About Those Newsgroups

Your Web site staff should definitely invite at least a few individuals from those mailing lists they're monitoring—if not the entire list—to preview the site and comment. It's especially useful to have people who are experienced in Web site development offer suggestions. They may notice things that most people wouldn't, and offer creative solutions to problems that your less-experienced staff wouldn't have considered.

The people in the Web community really can be extremely helpful; most are more than happy to offer advice and assistance if your Web developers are willing to listen and learn. All they need to do is ask questions and request help from more experienced people on those mailing lists or newsgroups. While it can be very intimidating to post messages in the beginning, the rewards can be terrific, and having those people visit and comment on your site can be wonderfully helpful. You would be hard-pressed to find consultants who are any better informed than some of the people who frequent those groups. The people who code the browsers and the servers, and the folks who are designing some of the most eye-catching sites on the Web, show up with surprising frequency to answer questions and offer new ideas. Few companies can afford that kind of expertise in their consultants—and they're there to share their knowledge freely with your staff, for no more than the time and effort it takes to read the groups.

YOUR MISSION—
QUELL ANXIETY ATTACKS

Preparing your site for the Web will have its moments of everything from nervousness to sheer panic for your development team, but none of those feelings should be allowed to interfere with your ultimate goal—putting your business on the Web.

You may be called on to guide the process more than you'd like in the initial stages of development—or you may have little involvement. You are the best judge of the experience and maturity of your staff. Unless you have the quintessential Web site staff, you may be assured that a certain level of trepidation about the site is a normal and even smart reaction to the various pressures that they will be experiencing.

As long as you keep at least a finger on the pulse of the project—being aware of any apparent stalls in the process—you can avoid letting nerves and second-guessing drag the work to a halt.

◄ 5 ►

WHICH TECHNOLOGIES TO PURSUE AND WHICH TO LEAVE BEHIND

WHAT DO OTHERS IN YOUR
BUSINESS EXPECT FROM YOUR
WEB SITE?

◆

SHOULD YOUR WIDGETS REALLY
DANCE AND DIP?

◆

IS THAT MINI-BLAST
OF SWAN LAKE
QUITE THE RIGHT APPROACH?

◆

IS CAUTION A DEADLY APPROACH
TO A WEB SITE?

While you're busy making sure that everything is moving along according to plan—overseeing the details and soothing frazzled nerves—other people in your company are waiting to see which gee-whiz technologies you'll incorporate into the final design. Still others are trying to determine whether your Web site will address their needs. Some of them aren't waiting nearly as patiently as you may like. You might as well go ahead and add a few other duties to your schedule (well, maybe add them to your Web developers' schedules), as discussed in this chapter.

Talk to People Who Know What They Need

Your Web site will make its debut as a site devoted to those specific purposes in your original plan. It will evolve, however, in ways you never even considered. If you prepare for that evolution, the result will be a site that works in many ways. If you don't, you may find yourself with a site that's completely out of control, with various design elements and nothing to tie the pieces together. So, as if you weren't busy enough already, it's time for some in-house public relations. Delegate, of course, unless you really understand the technical aspects of Web servers and what can and can't be done with them.

Your purpose is to meet with people in various departments to determine what your Web site can do for them:

- Do they have an audience on the Web?
- How can that audience best be served?
- Are there specific things you can do to help them with your Web site?
- Do they have special needs that you haven't considered?

In many instances, people won't understand enough about the technology to know how they might use a Web site. Others will immediately see uses that are not only good ones, but the kind that will help you measure the success of your site—for example, a report that's requested often and has to be copied and mailed can be put on the Web instead. While you may expect the folks over in Engineering to have ideas for using your site, the people in Manufacturing and Accounting are just as likely to have good uses for it.

Meeting with them now—before the site is fully functional—serves several purposes:

- Giving you an idea of areas that your Web development staff should be considering for the future

- Encouraging other groups to begin thinking of ways to displace functions, if they haven't done so already

- Perhaps most importantly, serving notice that the plan is to present your business as a cohesive unit, which may serve to avoid some kicking and screaming in the future; at the very least, no one will be able to say they weren't consulted in the equation

WHO IS THEIR AUDIENCE ON THE WEB?

Even in a business that has a narrowly focused purpose, the audiences for different departments or divisions may be very diverse. Sales and Marketing may target the end users of your product, while the target audience for Human Resources is qualified candidates for available positions, and Communications may target groups that could reduce their budget for mailing newsletters and magazines by putting those items on your Web site. In a business that has many different groups that might be considered "end users," the audiences, and the needs of those audiences, can be diverse indeed.

Manufacturing may not even think that they *have* a Web audience, but do they have schedules for producing specific orders? If they do, the people who placed those orders may be extremely pleased to know when they're scheduled for production. Shipping might make some of your customers very happy by posting regular updates about orders shipped and by what method.

By the same token, a Web site is a great place to advertise/explain the occasional business difficulty. You do most of your shipping by rail and there's a rail workers' strike? Post a page with details about the situation, when and how you expect to make alternate shipping arrangements, and news updates on what's happening with the strike.

CAN YOU CUSTOMIZE YOUR SITE FOR THAT AUDIENCE?

As more and more business functions have been automated, clients and customers feel more like numbers than names. Some of that reaction is inescapable, but the Web can be one way to make those people feel more "special." Most businesses have voice mail, much of it automated—so customers seldom have a chance to talk with a real live human being. Encourage your staff and other departments to consider ways to tell your customers the things they normally might place a phone call to determine.

At this point in Web development, when your customer can find something specific to her needs, she feels special. That will change as more and more businesses go online, but you can take advantage of the uniqueness now. Five years (maybe less) from now, it'll be old hat. People will be as bored with it as they are now with your voice mail. Right now, however, you have an opportunity to build some customer loyalty. Being one of the first to make such a service available will be remembered—your customers will enjoy telling their friends that you were offering the service before your competitor (whom, of course, *their* friends are now praising for their foresight in using this technology).

BE PREPARED TO MAKE SPECIFIC SUGGESTIONS

The people who will meet with representatives from the various functions in your business should know enough about the department to know what the department does, and they should be able to make specific recommendations for using your Web site if the department representative isn't familiar with the technology. While this may seem like so much "cheerleading," the actual purpose is to encourage them to think of ways to make your Web site pay for itself. If enough mailings or phone calls can be eliminated (actually, replaced), you'll see a return on your investment. If you (or they) view your Web site as simply an additional element of your business, that's likely to be what it will become—an addition—and it could prove to be an expensive one.

You and your Web developers should encourage people at every level of your business to suggest ways to use the site that can reduce your costs. Your Web site is never going to completely replace general mailings or the need for support staff. Universal access is a nice-sounding phrase that politicians and the media have latched onto, but it's not going to happen for a very long time— maybe never. But you don't need to *completely* replace certain functions in order to save money.

KILLING SEVERAL BIRDS WITH ONE WEB PAGE

Encourage people to honestly consider their audience and how that audience should be approached. What can their department do that would attract the right people to your Web site? The people in Research and Development may have papers they've authored that can be shared with other researchers. They may find that offering those papers on your Web site will open channels of communications with other researchers that could be very useful—and potentially lucrative—for your business.

▶ **CAUTION**   Copyright laws extend to the Web. If you own the copyright, you can reproduce the work on the Web. If you don't, the copyright holder must give you permission for that reproduction. In some cases, copyright holders are willing to sell the rights for electronic publication. Just be careful not to infringe a copyright—you certainly don't need that kind of hassle. ◀

Offering research papers can be useful to your Human Resources department in attracting qualified employees. If Shipping provides information about when it ships a particular order and how, Sales takes fewer calls requesting that information. When Human Resources takes résumés electronically, they save the costs of copying and sending those résumés through interoffice mail. The people who are interviewing and hiring get the résumés faster, and may fill positions more quickly. Each department should consider its own audience, but your Web site developers should be considering the larger picture and offering suggestions for ways to make the individual pieces work for more than one department.

You may be very surprised at the diversity of the audiences your staff will identify. Manufacturers of high-end computing equipment may decide that their audience is primarily people who already have reasonably high-end computing power and connections. If that type of audience is indeed your primary target, it's reasonably safe to assume that a site designed with extensive graphics and rich technologies (movies, animations, large sound files, etc.) won't overwhelm your visitors. Their own computing speeds and connections will be quick enough to accommodate those special features. It's the unusual business, though, that can target one audience only.

It's much more likely that your audiences will access your site from a vast array of computing equipment and over any number of different types of connections. Your visitors may run the gamut from people using text browsers on *dumb terminals* (terminals that don't have any real computing power) over 2400 baud modems—yes, there still are connections made in the real world over very slow modems—to those fast workstations with T3 access. Customers who are interested in your manufacturing schedule may be accessing it from their offices with powerful computers or from their homes over less impressive equipment. Researchers looking for published papers may be working in impressive labs with high-tech equipment, or they may be working in university labs that are far from high-tech.

How Will That
Audience Perceive Your Site?

How you view yourself isn't nearly so important as how your audience views your site. Their perceptions of *your* attitude toward *their* needs can make a very big difference in how your Web site is received. If you disregard their needs or limitations, they may choose to disregard your Web site.

If yours happens to be a business that your clients perceive as wealthy (no matter the reality), they may expect you to have a Web site that looks like you spent a great deal of time and money to develop it. But if yours is a not-for-profit concern, you hardly want your Web site to appear to your clients or contributors as though you've spent unnecessary sums in the development.

As departments or divisions within your company consider their own ways to utilize your Web site, they should be encouraged to consider the importance of their audience's perceptions.

Put the Nerds to Work for You

Adding all these other functions to the site sounds like a very large job. It can be an overwhelming job, actually, but each department needs at least someone who can do the basic HTML coding. Because it's easy and because any number of tools are available to produce new pages or convert existing ones from standard word processing software, there's no reason for your Web development staff to be required to do all the work.

Save a Little Time and Money

There are extremely good reasons for the various departments to have at least one "Web expert" of their own. From a strictly financial aspect, it simply doesn't make sense to pay upper-level staff to do what is essentially a clerical job. Basic Web page coding is little more than word processing. Most of the revisions, other than those required for overall site redesign, are simply revisions of the textual content of a page:

```
<HTML>
<HEAD>
<TITLE>Castle Books and Music</TITLE>
<META NAME="description" CONTENT="Home page for Castle
Books and Music, a retail bookstore offering books of all
kinds and ages, movies, computer software, an extensive
children's section, and a fun café">
</HEAD>
<body>
<h1>Castle Books and Music</h1>
<p>Welcome to our electronic bookstore. We hope you'll find
just what you're looking for here. Check out our newest
titles:</p>
<ul>
<li><a href="gaugin7.html">Gaugin's Years in Ireland by M. C.
Scott</a>
<li><a href="wheel.html">The Wheel Turns Slowly by P. C.
Tiredbody</a>
<li><a href="muggy.html">Fresh Air: Not Really a Necessity by
E. S. Stale</a>
</ul>
</body>
</html>
```

Those book titles at the bottom of the page are going to need to be changed regularly. It's a simple matter to replace them and doesn't require vast amounts of time, even operating with the slowest and least-easy-to-use text editor:

```
<HTML>
<HEAD>
```

```
<TITLE>Castle Books and Music</TITLE>
<META NAME="description" CONTENT="Home page for Castle
Books and Music, a retail bookstore offering books of all
kinds and ages, movies, computer software, an extensive
children's section, and a fun café">
</HEAD>
<body>
<h1>Castle Books and Music</h1>
<p>Welcome to our electronic bookstore. We hope you'll find
just what you're looking for here. Check out our newest
titles:</p>
<ul>
<li><a href="pet145.html">Your Pet and You by G. U.
Pushover</a>
<li><a href="messy.html">Housecleaning Eliminated by C. U.
Cann</a>
</ul>
</body>
</html>
```

In addition, if the departments need revisions and have no one who can do them, they are simply forced to wait for more experienced (and expensive) help, who may not be able to do the work as quickly as desired. That causes a bottleneck that will frustrate everyone involved.

HARNESS THAT ENTHUSIASM!

Your Web developers should be evaluating new tools as they have time, and should be prepared to suggest the ones they find to be good and intuitive. As they talk with people in the various departments, they should recommend those products and they should encourage people who are obviously interested in the technology to learn the basics. There's at least one such person in practically every group. You may be quite surprised at the energy and enthusiasm some people will bring to this new challenge.

Granted, some will see the opportunity to learn Web skills as a way to position themselves for better jobs. Some may actually find better jobs. The other side of that coin is that you'll be encouraging your staff to learn skills that they're quite likely to need for your company's future.

▶ **NOTE**   In many ways, Web publishing now is in much the same situation that desktop publishing experienced ten years ago. If you wanted a special look for your printed documents, you needed a specialist to produce them. Luckily, the speed of development of the tools required for producing good Web pages is moving at a much faster pace than the tools for desktop publishing. ◀

Other people will embrace the technology and go far beyond the basics of Web page coding. That can actually be to your advantage, because it may relieve your Web development staff of a significant amount of work. At the same time, someone should be monitoring the overall site for consistency of quality and design—one department's poor Web pages may reflect badly on the site as a whole.

Additionally, the question of the experience level of staff working on Web pages isn't insignificant. There may be very good reasons for high-level engineers to be producing Web pages—if a project requires it or if the audiences being addressed expect advanced technologies that your Web development staff is unable to handle due to lack of time or programming skills. It doesn't make quite as much economic sense for those engineers to be coding Web pages for the fun of it, though. Those are management decisions you may need to address—if not now, at some time in the future.

WHAT CAN YOU DO TO HELP THE EXTREMES?

Jean in Research and Development insists that R&D's audience is extremely high-tech, and it's simply impossible to address their needs without Web pages with dancing widgets. Wilbur in International Relations assures you that many of *their* clients not only don't want dancing widgets, they don't need graphics at all, thank you very much.

Whether you can convince either side that they may, perhaps, be exaggerating just a little may test your patience severely. It's probably not worth the effort. The Web isn't going to unravel because both of them are probably wrong, at least to some extent. Your Web site, however, may become a bit more complex than you originally planned—or you may need to consider some shuttle diplomacy.

It's sometimes easy for people who have Web sites and for individuals who have access to the Web to make the assumption that access to computing power is the equivalent of access to the Web. That's simply not an equation that works. Researchers may have very powerful computers located in older buildings that just aren't adequately wired to support more than the most fundamental of networks. Businesses in rural areas may have exemplar networks installed, but not have local access to the Internet. That doesn't mean that individuals don't have access to the Web and use their personal accounts or text-based browsers (in the case of inadequate networking capabilities) to look for information about products for their businesses. Nor does it mean that all of the people who browse the Web from remote areas are using primitive equipment. Some may very well have industrial-strength computers with excellent Web access.

Realistically, even if your business develops and markets products to people with visual impairment, the fact that your end user is unable to view graphics doesn't mean that other people can't and won't appreciate them on your Web site. You may want investors or distributors to be able to view specific products. Good Web pages can balance content and design to accommodate both ends of the technological spectrum.

Virtual Reality and Text-Based Pages *Can* Coexist

It isn't difficult to code one set of pages that's technologically advanced and another set that's quite simple. That's not an ideal solution, of course, because it requires two sets of pages. Each time the content is changed on one set, it must be changed on the other.

Doing Multiple Tracks Well...

A manufacturer of high-tech media equipment at one time had what may very well have been the most polite and agreeable set of duplicate pages ever assembled. The first page had nothing more, graphically, than their logo. That was followed by "How May We Serve You?" and a brief explanation of the technological levels of their pages:

- High bandwidth for those with the equipment (or time) to view them
- Medium bandwidth for more technologically-challenged visitors
- Low bandwidth for the completely impatient or those who were seriously challenged technologically

The site worked on several levels. It wasn't in the least disdainful of those without the time, patience, or equipment to deal with graphical (or other) capabilities, and no one felt like a second-class citizen on their Web site. To top it all off, their grammar was impeccable—something that simply can't be said for (far too) many Web sites.

172

...OR NOT QUITE SO WELL

Contrast that level of discernment about the needs of their visitors with a site that offers beginning graphics of a tortoise and a hare to lead into the high- and low-bandwidth tracks on their pages. The second carries the implication of second-class citizenship for those who may not be connecting over the best of lines or those with lesser computing power. People who use the Web for business applications—and some who are simply surfing but understand that graphics take time to load and often add little or no value to a site—simply disable graphics on their browsers. They may be quite the opposite of "tortoises."

▶ **NOTE**   I often am forced to remind my own coworkers to turn on graphics if we add some graphical element to our pages. They simply don't have the patience to wait for graphics to load on a regular basis; if I want them to test an image map or look at a design, I have to try their patience for at least a day or two. Few of them are technically challenged. Computing speed and connection times aren't issues with which they're concerned. They're simply doing real work in a real world and graphics (or other technologies that re-quire unnecessary time) are a nuisance, not a pleasure. ◀

It's not completely necessary to maintain duplicate pages to accommodate opposing (or at least what would seem contradictory) needs. Graphical ele-ments of a page can be coded so that text-based browsers present alternate text for those elements. Other, more involved features like tables and frames (a feature that can be viewed only with Netscape, at press time) can be coded so that they can be viewed without more sophisticated browsers. Even those Java applets—the ones that your engineers may want to include to make a cal-culator dance across their pages—can be coded so that people who are unable to view the calculator dancing will know what they would have seen if they had a browser that was capable of such a display.

COMPROMISE CAN WORK

Consider a compromise approach to the extremes—a basic design that balances text and technology, but can be added to or subtracted from without detracting from the basic information that needs to be conveyed. You may decide that specific items about site design are non-negotiable. Your logo, for instance, may very well be an item that you want displayed on all pages, along with basic navigational tools—a link back to your home page and an e-mail link to your Webmaster. You might provide departments with a template of the core design that they can use to develop more technology-rich pages or simply add the necessary text to the template. In that way, your basic design and navigational tools can be implemented easily throughout your site.

If your business is particularly diverse, it may be entirely acceptable to have specific portions of your Web site that aren't obviously identified with the overall site design. It depends entirely on the nature of your business and the corporate attitudes toward the Web site. Some businesses require strict adherence to specific design details; others take a more freewheeling approach, allowing individual groups or departments to produce and design Web pages based on their own perceptions of the market they want to address.

YOU CAN'T PLEASE ALL THE PEOPLE ALL THE TIME

The choices you and your development staff make for your site aren't likely to please everyone. So what else is new? Your efforts at designing a site that offers good content and appealing design will be appreciated by some and deplored by others as simply unacceptable, given the state of the technology. That's assuming, of course, that you have Web surfers of one sort or another on staff. Those new to the technology and those who are technologically inclined are likely to insist that at least one of the latest, greatest fads is essential on your Web site.

174

They may very well be convinced that the entire site needs the addition of scrolling headlines or that at least the portion of the site that addresses their department will miss the mark entirely if it doesn't include an animation of their (complete) manufacturing process. Better yet, they may insist on a full-color photo of their plant, coded as an image map so your visitor can click an office and see who currently inhabits that space.

The fact that those scrolling headlines can't be viewed by people with many browsers—and would be a complete distraction from more important information on some of your pages—will be conveniently ignored. That the animation and the full color photo might take an hour (or more) to load—not to mention that it's difficult enough for your staff just to keep the internal phone book up-to-date with office locations—are likely to be glossed over by those who are quite simply enthralled with the Web. Your best approach to begin with is to nod sagely and assure them that those are excellent ideas to consider for future development on the site. (They may be—but not for right now.)

Evasive tactics are a completely acceptable form of self-defense for those who are new to developing Web sites. Those people who don't understand the technology—and those who do understand but simply want the latest gadget incorporated—will have found some other technology to tout before your original Web site is ready for visitors.

Life Without Java/VRML/Shockwave/ Technology du Jour: Is It Worth Living?

News Flash! A Web site is not yet like having your own little television station. If it took you ten minutes to see the first two minutes of the evening news, it would hardly be worth your effort. It can take considerably more than ten minutes to download the equivalent of the first two minutes of the evening news on the Web. Most of the fabulous new technologies are designed to do things that TV already does—and does better. Certainly animation on a Web site is interesting, and the addition of sound is an enhancement, but your Web site can't deliver enough frames per second of video to equal even the poorest quality television transmission. The quality of sound on Web sites is improving, but there are so many competing technologies to deliver that sound that it's the rare visitor who'll have the specific helper application installed so that he can hear it on your site.

WELCOME TO THE WAR—INTRODUCING THE ARMIES

The Web is one huge battleground for competing technologies at this stage of development. Building your site design around one or more of them increases your risks. Granted, it might also increase your audience in the immediate future—but will it cost you in redesign time later, if some other application wins the battle for that market?

A CONTENDER WITH RESOURCES TO SPARE— GOLIATH (AKA JAVA)

Java applets, little pieces of programming code, can do some very nice things on Web pages. You can use them to rotate pictures automatically on your Web pages or to animate graphics. Java has a great deal of potential for producing interesting and quite functional pages; it's a very serious programming language that may be incorporated into any number of your software applications—and possibly your toaster. The good folks at Sun Microsystems developed Java with an eye to incorporating it into various electronic systems. It's based primarily on C and C++ programming and can be used in some heavy-duty applications.

▶ **NOTE**   A truly whimsical discussion at a Web development seminar in February of 1996 took hysterical turns as developers considered the uses of being able to interact with their toasters. The yet-to-be-answered question: Given the technology, will those lovely devices still burn our toast? ◀

Java code may very well be worthwhile for you to use if you have staff that can write it—or it may not. Not so very long ago, C++ was touted by many applications developers as the future of object-oriented programming.

Plus, serious Java programs won't be written by less-than-serious Java programmers—not for some time, at least. It's more likely that applications will be developed that use Java's underlying strengths, like security and the ability to customize interactions, to make it easier to integrate for mere mortals (as opposed to "real programmers"). Java isn't likely to disappear, however, because too many of the major players in the Internet/Web development companies are basing at least some portion of their applications on Java code. Learning to write Java *applets*, however, is easier than writing the full-blown code if someone on your staff is interested in making use of the technology and you have a need for it.

THE UNDERDOG—DAVID (AKA VRML)

VRML (pronounced verm-ul) is the acronym for *Virtual Reality Modeling Language*. It can do some of the same things that Java does but, unlike Java, which was financed by Sun and originally developed as proprietary code, VRML developed more slowly—without the financial support. Originally conceived and championed by Mark Pesce, Tony Parisi, David Ragget, and Tim Berners-Lee, VRML is based primarily on code that was developed by Silicon Graphics and Template Graphics Software. SGI and Template Graphics gave the code to the Web community (for all practical purposes) with hopes of, perhaps, peripheral sales of other products. The intention for all involved was to add a third dimension to Web sites.

VRML was not designed to be the type of programming language that Java is. It was instead designed to give depth to the Web spaces that incorporated it. You might use VRML to design a 3D Web space that would allow your visitors to "walk through" your manufacturing process, for instance. At this point, most of the applications that are developed with it aren't particularly exciting, and require very-high-speed connections to deliver. But there's great potential, and the Web community is a strange one—they may very well choose David over Goliath. But whether it's worth the effort for your development staff to learn to use is questionable at this point. The Web has simply begun to develop so quickly, and so many proprietary applications have entered the competition, that, unfortunately, without some infusions of monetary resources VRML is likely to be eclipsed by other applications.

At the same time, VRML 2.0 (the second iteration of VRML—not yet an accepted standard on the Web) appears to offer some very exciting functionality that its predecessor (VRML 1.0, what else?) did not. And, in keeping with the Internet and Web culture, it will allow the inclusion of programming code from any number of standard programming languages, including C, PERL, and Visual Basic, in addition to Java. Look for a wave of new applications to become available to make VRML a serious contender for 3D-rich sites.

THE NEW KID ON THE TECHNOLOGY BLOCK—SHOCKWAVE

Developed by Macromedia, *Shockwave* is yet another proprietary product that can make those graphics you're going to use twist and turn, and make your pages sing as well—if your visitors have the Shockwave client installed and if you have the Shockwave server. It's a much-touted addition to the Web. If you need to deliver multimedia applications over the Web, Shockwave may be the best candidate for the job. Your demonstration of how to assemble the bicycle your customer bought could be delivered this way. At this point, the majority of the applications that are "shocked" are logos that turn, spin, and twist, and menus that change. The technology has a great deal of appeal but also requires a fast connection (for both you and your customer). By the time you read this, it may have been eclipsed by some other, newer technology that will make your pages delightfully different and amazingly appealing. Microsoft is even now touting their ActiveX controls, which are likely to deliver the same multimedia applications. Yes, there's a place for this type of technology. In all probability, the delivery of real-time multimedia over the Web isn't likely to happen for several years, though.

Client? Server? Huh?

No, not your customer in this instance, and not, precisely, your Web server. In this instance the software that delivers your multimedia applications is the *server*. The helper application that your potential customer uses to view/hear that application is the *client*.

RealAudio, StreamWorks, Those Other Audios

Right—sounds! They're cool, no doubt. You can produce pretty nice sounds on your Web site—if you're willing to pay for the servers. RealAudio was one of the original players in the game.

You may very well have a good reason to include sound files on your Web site, especially if you're publicizing a recording artist that you represent, or planning an arts festival that will feature music. You might consider producing a sound file from your CEO, welcoming visitors to your site. Radio and TV stations make use of the technology to deliver weather and news briefs.

Sound on the Web has come a very long way. It seems almost impossible that a year ago we were delighted with sound files that might take 45 minutes to load and that translated to a 2-minute recording whose quality approximated our grandmothers' era (okay—*my* grandmother's; your grandmother may not be much older than I am). The technology has improved greatly since then. Streamed audio takes those same audio files and delivers them as they're received, rather than after the entire file has downloaded. The quality still isn't perfect, but it's improving, and will only get better. The question is whether people will be willing to wait for the delivery of the sound. Like graphics, the larger question is the value of the content of the information you are delivering.

The Web is an audio battleground in full conflict. Will there be a clear winner? Or several? Place your bets and take your chances.

DECISIONS, DECISIONS!

As you consider any of the advanced technologies, or even some of those that aren't so very advanced but may be based on extensions to HTML that are specific to one or two browsers, remember your audience and think of the future of your Web site. If your development staff is careful to take into consideration the people whose browsers won't be able to interpret those extensions to HTML, you'll have a Web site that works even if those extensions are never incorporated into other browsers—or even into the next versions of the browser for which they were originally developed.

The more advanced technologies, however, require a much greater commitment of your staff's time, and possibly some very real financial investment in server software. Committing your site to those technologies may be perfectly sensible for you if you have the resources—and/or a crystal ball that guarantees that your choice of technologies is good. (If you have a crystal ball like that, my e-mail address is **lgb@rti.org** and I'd certainly appreciate the occasional tip or two.)

You must weight the cost in time and money against the purpose of your Web site. Consider the strengths and weaknesses of the Web in the equation. For all its graphical (and other) capabilities, the Web is about communication and providing information. It's not sound bites and animated snippets that will bring people to your site on a regular basis. Those may serve to attract some people for the novelty on more than one occasion, but hearing a sound bite or seeing an animation over and over is no less boring than those same things would be on television. Remote controls allow us to channel surf past them on TV, and a click of the mouse does the same for the Web.

Quality content and helpful information, presented in an engaging and useful manner with well-designed graphics, will win repeat visitors. If that

180

information can be customized specifically for those visitors, you may very well have a Web site that will be surprisingly successful with your visitors—and for you.

If You're Really Staying Current, You'll Survive the Killer Technologies

It can be positively depressing. Each new magazine or newsletter that crosses your desk targeted to the Internet/Web markets will extol the virtues of at least one of the latest technologies. There are days when the sheer number of new things to learn and try is daunting. Worse, if you believe each of those magazines and newsletters, no Web site can survive without the very latest and greatest. From the wonders of Internet phones to the thrill of Java-enhanced pages to the joys of adding 2,127,386 plug-ins (give or take) to browsers so that Web surfers can experience every possible combination of applications installed on Web pages, the magazines that cover the Internet and the Web make it all sound so easy and so necessary.

Oh, How They Gush

Reality check! The trade magazines *survive* by those new technologies. HTML is boring, remember? Without the gizmos and gee-whiz technologies, they'd have very little to tell you about—reviews of Web sites can be helpful, but that's not what sells those magazines.

Unfortunately, your resident Web surfers are probably reading the magazines, too, in their hunts for the latest helper applications or plug-ins to add to their browsers—not to mention the perfect Web site that incorporates every single one of those technologies they've read about. The simple reality is that most of those magazines are directed at the end consumer of Web applications—the surfer—not toward Web developers, though they can be helpful for developers, too. They feature reviews of the plug-ins and browsers and applications that make Web surfing fun (for those who have the time and leisure to install and use the software).

▶ **NOTE**   My editor suggests here that I mention how many programs *I* currently have that I downloaded and haven't yet installed. Great idea, but my hard drive crashed recently and I just decided to start over. I must have had at least 20 pieces of software that were just sitting around doing nothing, and were unlikely ever to do anything because I couldn't remember why I'd picked most of them. They had interesting names like **id5mb2x.exe**—pretty intuitive, eh? Probably a spell checker or something. I'm better off without them, but very soon I'll probably start picking up new ones that I won't use and won't remember what they do. ◀

What's Your Number?

But this is a reality check. Quick, without looking at your Web browser, what version are you using? If you know, you're probably an early adopter, and you likely downloaded it within days, if not hours, of its introduction. You're a nerd at heart, aren't you? Lucky you. You're going to have a wonderful time with this project.

If you didn't know your browser's version number, not to worry. You're not very different from the majority of people who surf the Web, except that you probably understand a great deal more about it than many of them. (Well, you've read this far—you certainly should understand more than most.)

The Web is being surfed quite well daily by people who don't have the latest browser or umpty-dozen plug-ins. Poor benighted souls they are—muddling along without seeing those VRML worlds and unable to hear William Shatner vocalizing over their computers. Such a pity. They can surf but they're not necessarily taking the time to upgrade their software or add bells and whistles. What's the point, if they are using the Web as it was originally intended—as an information resource?

Besides, more than a few are a bit afraid of attempting to plug anything in. What they've got is working and they're completely sure that anything they attempt will upset that status quo. They'll break something and be forced to call the neighbor's child yet again to straighten out the mess. Worse, they'll have to call their company computer gurus and admit that they were wasting time playing when they should have been working.

WATCH THE TRENDS

It's important for you and your Web developers to be aware of the trends and technologies. Some may be useful for you; some may not. Reading the available information will make the decisions to adopt the latest trend—or not to adopt it—a bit easier.

Scanning the magazines for trends is a good idea, as it will give you a taste for where things are going. But keep in mind that the writers who hype these technologies can be just as wrong as anyone else. They simply have the opportunity to be wrong very *visibly*. And by following their advice, so do you (as described in the next section).

TRENDS DON'T ALWAYS WORK AS ADVERTISED

There's almost always a tendency to incorporate the newest technologies into some portion of a Web site. Web site designers and developers are always looking for new ways to make sites more appealing and more intuitive for their visitors. Limited adoption of a new approach can help developers determine whether the technology will work in a larger way. Unfortunately, early adoption can have its pitfalls.

A number of Web sites adopted *frames* in major ways when the extension was added by Netscape. The idea was certainly a good one, in that it gave designers more control of Web page presentation, but the implementation hadn't been fully considered. Those who decided to use the extension were virtually forced to take a multi-track approach, because no browser other than

Netscape supported it. Worse, because visitors to Web sites that used frames could quickly find themselves in Frames Never Never Land—hopelessly lost in a Web site and unable to determine how to escape without simply closing down their browsers—sites using them came in for more than a few complaints. Even Netscape removed frames from their own pages after receiving complaints. Good idea, used too soon.

▶ **NOTE**   Frames were the newest thing on cyberstreets in the fall of 1995. Our graphic artist was seriously fascinated by the idea; I was seriously skeptical. By February of 1996, she was only slightly less enthralled, but admitted that she was abandoning the idea—not without reservations. Lately she was considering them seriously again.

If you happen to have any influence with the HTML standards body, do me a serious favor and urge them to give us something similar that works better. She needs more control on the design side and I absolutely, positively do not want to maintain a multiple-track site. There's a gracious plenty of work to do without that! Thanks! ◀

Trust the Developers

It's important for your Web site developers to be monitoring mailing lists and newsgroups devoted to the Web—and specifically for developers. The people who are participating in those groups are on the real front lines. They're trying the technologies and experiencing their strengths and weaknesses. They know whether that new technology can even be implemented yet on your platform, or if it works with your Web server software. If the software has a bug that will crash your server regularly, they'll know it first, and your developers can forgo that particular joy until the bug is fixed.

Those developers who are working and writing about their experiences can be trusted to tell the whole truth—many times in much more detail than the designers of the application software might like. There's no one quite so critical of a technology as a Webmaster who has been tracking erratic server glitches for weeks—only to discover that one killer technology is intermittently killing another killer technology because of one small problem that puts them in conflict. Webmasters can be killingly articulate under those circumstances.

Waiting Can Be Wise

You need to stay up-to-date on the technologies but not get caught up in them and make—or let your Web development staff make—needless work as a result. If the technology is one that will stand the test of time, waiting a month or two or six isn't going to ring the death knell for your Web site. In fact, if that new gadget or gizmo is going to last, it's going to get better and easier to use—and more widely supported. Make sure that your staff isn't jumping on the bandwagon unless they can give you solid reasons that make sense for your business before they invest a great deal of time learning and implementing that fabulous new feature.

You can easily see that your Web development staff should balance itself on issues of technology. If each of them is easily persuaded to all the new developments, they can turn your Web site into a technical implementation that it will take Rubic to maintain. If they resist all new technologies, your site will become stale. You want them to balance one another—there should always be a devil's advocate for or against new proposals. They'll talk the details to death, but in the process they'll determine very good reasons on both sides of the issue. That will obviously make it easier for you to make an informed decision in the rare instances in which they can't reach consensus.

How Fast Can You Learn— and Do You Want To?

Into every Web site, too much work falls. Whether you have a development staff of 2 or 200, the time will come when you can't buy any more time. Your development staff will simply be too small or too overworked—no matter the staff size—to take on another development project.

As more departments add pages, and those pages become more complex, simply keeping the core pages updated and fresh can become a logistical nightmare. Scheduling and implementing design and content changes isn't too tricky when your entire site consists of ten or even fifty pages. Those same changes on several hundred or several thousand pages—yes, Virginia, there really are Web sites with thousands—is not unlike planning an international conference.

INSANITY CHECK

The details and decisions that must be taken into consideration can drive even a reasonably sane person off the deep end. The most stable of Webmasters considers announcing that the Web server is dead, the technology will never generate enough interest to make the Web work, and he has just decided to take an extended vacation in that hitherto unheard-of tourist Mecca: Podunkville, ND (where there are no computers and no telephones). If he looks perfectly serious when he makes this announcement, or worse, if he cries or laughs hysterically, it's time to make some adjustments.

▶ **NOTE** I have all-too-vivid recollections of returning to my office following a meeting in which absolutely nothing was accomplished beyond a dozen people (who had yet to read more than the headlines about the Web in the popular press) telling me that they knew how to "fix" our site. Since they'd been telling me that for more than eight months without producing so much as the first piece of work that might accomplish that goal, I was just a tad frustrated. Since I was less than a month away from a complete redesign of our site, I was truly angry at the waste of my time. The first phone call I had upon my return was from someone who was proposing yet another project for our Web site that was going to be complex and take still more of my time.

I was nearly ready to throw the phone and the job out of the nearest window. But what really, really iced my cake was that I couldn't figure out who I should give my resignation to! That quandary alone kept me in the job. The moral of the story: Don't tell your Webmaster who he reports to; it'll make it very hard for him to quit. (Just kidding.) ◀

Your Web developers would probably love nothing better than to take on adding a virtual reality world in that corner of your site designed to appeal to teens, but if taking on that project means other, more boring but no less important maintenance is overlooked, it's not in your best interest. Obviously, this isn't going to happen very soon if you have a large development staff, but even businesses with large Web teams have to weigh the tradeoffs of taking on some wonderfully challenging project at the expense of less exciting, routine projects. If the new project requires jumping in and learning some new skills, you have to weigh the advantages of adding those particular skills to your developers' repertoire against the overall impact on your Web site.

YOU CAN'T KNOW IT ALL, BUT YOU CAN KNOW A LITTLE BIT ABOUT ALL OF IT

Unless your company has virtually unlimited resources to throw at a Web site, and few do, it's all but impossible to have a full team of writers, designers, and programmers devoted to Web site development. Not only are they busy working on your Web site, they're quite likely busy writing media pieces for more traditional markets, designing graphics for advertising and packaging, and tracking down the problems in that statistical program that Marketing and Accounting installed last week.

At this early stage of Web development, most of us wear several hats. That makes the job challenging without the addition of virtual reality projects or Java-enhanced lightning bolts on our Web pages. It doesn't make those technologies any less interesting or beckoning, though.

STUDY AND MORE STUDY

Your development staff should be able to give you some indication of the time it will take to add that new technology to your Web site, the specific skills that it will require, and an assessment of staffing needs necessary to accomplish it. That requires that a certain amount of study be given to each new technology. It may appear to be as simple as adding a new piece of software to your Web server, but even the most simple application requires time spent in learning to use it effectively.

Time spent reading and studying the trade magazines, and following that up with more in-depth study of the tools and skills necessary for implementing those most promising technologies or tools on your Web site, is time that's well-invested. It's important for your development staff to be considering not just the challenge of the technology but how it can be used effectively on your site. Technology for technology's sake is fine if you have unlimited resources, but most of us live in a real world that demands we target our efforts toward real-world applications. Those multimedia presentations, for example, while exciting and useful, can cost you thousands of dollars to produce; if your customers then don't have the patience to wait for delivery over the Web, you've got one rather expensive white elephant.

TAKE A ROAD TRIP, SO TO SPEAK

One of the best ways to determine the feasibility of implementing new technologies is to study them as they're being used on the Web. Your developers can look at source code for Web pages to determine the complexity of some applications. Web sites of the applications developers generally offer not only demonstrations of the product but pricing and links to other sites that are using it. Contacting the Webmasters at those sites can offer some helpful information.

If your developers can't locate sites that use the technology to good effect—and that happens as often as not—they may very well decide that it's simply not worth the effort to pursue. That doesn't mean it won't be at some point, however, as the application matures and more functionality is added to it. It's shortsighted to rule out future possibilities on limited applications.

▶ **NOTE**   In the early days of our site, I toyed with the idea of creating a VRML world—before the media discovered this Promised Land of the Web, and I still could find a full day or two to consider projects just for fun. Like our graphic artist and her frames, though, I reluctantly decided that the functionality didn't offer enough to make my efforts worthwhile. I'll be watching VRML 2.0 applications very closely. The desire to tackle a VR world hasn't gone away, and you can place bets that I'm creative enough to find the time and the resources to try it if VRML 2.0 offers functionality for our site. ◀

THERE'S MORE TO LEARN THAN YOU CAN KNOW IN THE WORLD WIDE WEB—LET SOMEONE HELP

Try as they might, your Web development staff may not see uses for technologies that people in the individual departments may see. If someone proposes an application that may very well have been rejected as not workable or simply too time-consuming by your developers, it may be worth a second look. Wherever the idea originates, the usefulness of the application must take precedence over the technology.

THEY WANT *WHAT*??

Interior designers could make a very strong case for creating a virtual reality site that allows customers to manipulate objects with rooms. The question then becomes one of determining who can create that site. Do they have the necessary tools and skill, not to mention the time, to prepare the computer-generated textures and shapes and lighting components? Designing rooms on paper or in the real world is a far cry from designing them in the virtual world at this point. Can your Design department commit someone to the project, or do they expect your Web developers to create the site?

If they're serious about the need for such a site, and it's likely to generate business, it's certainly worth considering. Building a virtual world is a complex project, requiring designers and programmers to make it come alive. Your Web development staff is likely to fall all over themselves volunteering for duty on the project, but if it's not a mission-critical piece of your Web site, their time may be better spent elsewhere.

My editor makes an excellent point on this issue. She says " I hear that it took Disney animators more than a year to create 'Toy Story.' They have more resources than most *any* company, but making it look real and figuring out the technology to maneuver it wasn't cheap—in terms of time or costs."

Depending on the depth of your overall site and the workload of your developers, you might very well need to turn that portion of the project over to the designers or subcontract the work. Consider committing some portion of your staff's time to assist in the graphical design and the programming, if other in-house staff can do the bulk of the work. If the project will be subcontracted, someone in-house should be learning the necessary skills to update and maintain that portion of the site after it's installed, anyway. Even a virtual world must be kept up-to-date. It's not enough for your interior design team to develop a virtual world and then walk away from it. Anyone can produce a one-time project and announce that "it can be done." Certainly, it can be done, but when something breaks, who's going to fix it? When something needs to be changed or added, who's going to do it?

Responsibility needs to be vested in the group that will gain from the project. That applies not only to something as complex as a virtual world, but to something as simple as preparing a few pages to market any other part of your business that's not critical to your core product. If you allow your developers' time to be devoted to planting each flower or shrub, the overall design of the garden may be overlooked.

AVOIDING IDENTITY CRISES

Your Web development staff may very well want to plant not only the flowers and shrubs, but every grass seed, too. They will be identified with every piece of it, from the best to the worst, and they'll want to make sure that the worst is not bad at all. That's an excellent attitude—but one that you can easily see won't work, unless your site remains small or your development staff grows as the size and complexity of the site increases. There's certainly a remote possibility that the tools for building and maintaining your Web site will become so good and easy to use that, two years from now, it may only take four people to do what takes ten now. But you can't bet the business on that—or at least you shouldn't.

Instead, you should concentrate on distributing as much of the basic processing as possible to as many people as possible. The more who understand HTML coding, Web graphics, and Web culture, the better. That means more people who can produce the basic building blocks for your site.

The technology is so very new—in spite of the fact that it sometimes seems we've been hearing about it since just shortly after the earth cooled—that the job of simply keeping up with the new developments and technologies can be intimidating, without adding the work of coding, designing, and all the other bits and pieces that have to be added. But each bit and each piece is necessary for the whole. It really is like every other project—only a relatively small project can be accomplished by only one person, and even then it won't be accomplished in a vacuum.

FIRST CONTACTS—YOUR WEB GURUS

Your development staff should be the first contact for new projects and a resource for those projects. They need to be willing to assist with training and advising on all areas of the site. Unless you're willing to commit the resources necessary to maintain complete control of all of those areas, the basics of the work are quite simply going to need to be distributed as widely as possible.

That won't be easy. The volume of work can more than fill your staff's days, but as time-consuming as answering questions and offering encouragement can be, they are entirely worth the effort. You'll be building a small core of Web experts—well, they may become experts—and that's not a bad thing at all. The Web is in your future, one way or the other, so it certainly makes sense to have as many people working with it and learning about it as you possibly can.

MORE EXPERTS??

You're sighing, right? You just thought that through to its logical conclusion? That's right. The more people who are involved, the more they'll know about the new technologies. Hence, the more important for you to be aware of them. It's true that it's a double-edged sword. Some outside of your staff will push for implementation of each and every new technology—right now. What's more, because they're looking at only their area of concern generally, while your staff is balancing projects that are being tossed their way from every direction, they're as likely as not to have more time to read about the new gadgets and gizmos first.

▶ **NOTE** I honestly don't remember which technology was involved the first time someone called asking my opinion of something I'd never even heard the first word about. It was a completely traumatic experience—which probably explains my memory loss. I was mortified that he—I'm reasonably sure the person was male—knew something I didn't about an area that was supposedly my area of expertise. I'm sure you remember that day; the earth stopped spinning for just a heartbeat. Surely you noticed. I believe I recovered my wits about me enough to sound harried (which I was) and suitably vague (ditto). You can bet your firstborn I wasn't even off the phone before I was searching out information about that technology on the Web. I've become slightly more sophisticated in my approach since I've now had plenty of practice. A simple "I haven't even had time to take a look at it" works quite well;

experience teaches that listening carefully to a description of a hitherto-unknown technology can provide some excellent clues to the importance of immediate research. In other words, I often wait as long as 24 hours before my curiosity overwhelms me and I go in search of the information. ◀

THEY'RE RESOURCES YOU NEED—VERY MUCH

Take an optimistic approach. Those people are doing some of the research for you. The Web is huge; the amount of information available on it is phenomenal. Let someone else sort some of the wheat from the chaff. You can't have time to do it all yourself.

You'll soon come to know those people who are seriously studying what they see, versus those who are simply repeating the latest hype as though it were gospel. Some of their ideas for implementations will be wonderful—and some will be so outrageous that it will take every ounce of diplomacy you have not to tell them they are completely and totally insane and should be locked away for their own safety. You really can't add more bandwidth by adding more members to your orchestra.

Your staff should use the ideas that are good ones and—yes, this is like other projects—they should give credit where it's due. A page doesn't have to announce who conceived the idea, but compliments received for that idea should be delivered to those who originated the idea. Criticisms should be received and acknowledged, but not passed along unless they're very serious. There's no sense in discouraging anyone who's trying to do something that will eventually make less work for your staff. If it's necessary to rework the page so that it works the way it should, so be it. That's what your staff is there for.

THE HARDCORE EXCEPTIONS

Obviously, there can be exceptions to the rules just discussed. Pages that are consistently done badly must be addressed. Your staff won't do anyone any favors by always cleaning up someone else's mess. It's no fun to clean up behind someone on a regular basis, and even less fun to deal with the problem. Your staff may need help with that situation. The regular offenders will be those people who aren't really willing to invest the time and energy to do the job right and follow through with the project—your perennial nine-to-fivers who are more than willing to take credit for the job, but completely unwilling to do the whole job if it means that they might have to work late or study on their own.

Web projects don't always happen according to nine-to-five schedules, unfortunately. They require a commitment that goes beyond regular working hours. This isn't a job for people who are less than professional; as a manager, you need to know whether your staff is being overworked because someone else's staff isn't doing their job. It's penny-wise and pound-foolish for a department to pay people who are unwilling to learn and unwilling to make a commitment to see the job through to completion, when they could spend less money in the long run to pay professionals to do the work, whether that's your staff or outside professionals.

The Best of Help

There will be those who not only understand the technology but can implement it in ways that will be a credit to your Web site. Make sure that your staff doesn't just let them do it, but encourages them in every possible way. Help them when they need help. They're the ones who will save your developers a lot of time in the future. Those Web pages that arrive fully coded and need only testing and checking for compliance to your standards for your site are going to be more welcome than your staff can even imagine at this point.

At first, your Web developers may be intimidated by talents in people they didn't expect to develop those talents. As they learn more and as they develop their own skills, though, they'll be more than a little grateful when they don't have to even think about coding a Web page. They'll enjoy explaining to others how to make their pages work better or suggesting ways that they can be improved. In the process, they'll make some friends they didn't expect to make, and work with some very talented people with whom they wouldn't have had an opportunity to work in any other medium.

It's a Mentoring Medium

The culture of the Internet carries over very much to the Web. Contrary to what you may have read, the Internet is a very friendly place. People help people on the Internet just like they do in the real world. The Web is full of people who are more than willing to help others learn to work on the Web. Every one of us who has been working here for very long has been mentored by someone else who has been here longer. There are those who claim their "expertise" as though they gained it without asking what seemed some very basic questions. They didn't. They may have done their homework and they may have worked hard at learning the things they needed to learn, but they couldn't have done it without the help of one or two (or many more) people who were willing to take the time to answer them and guide them, whether that was by writing about their experiences, or answering questions that eventually became part of an archive of *frequently asked questions* (*FAQs*).

Your staff will very quickly come to appreciate the talents of those people who are honestly interested in working on the Web, since you had the foresight to assign some very bright people to the task. That's one of the real joys of this medium. There's nothing quite so much fun as watching a person who has always had a certain flare for design and a love of words put those skills to use on the Web. You may very well have an artist/wordsmith on your staff who will blossom completely unexpectedly when exposed to this technology. Your staff should not only be on the lookout for that kind of talent but be ready to help as much as possible.

Your developers may not think of themselves as mentors, but rather as overworked drones in an endless battle to keep up with the technology and at least one step ahead of the rest of the world. But they will be mentors if they're doing their jobs right. They can't help but be. The Web is an each-one-teach-one (or more) world. None of us knows it all, and no one can predict who will be the person who will make it all work the way it should for a business on the Web. The competition is fierce, but that doesn't mean that the knowledge won't be shared widely and freely.

EXPECT THE UNEXPECTED

As the circle of people who understand the Web grows in your business, and as they learn more about the medium, your Web developers will become more eager to share the information they've learned, and they'll understand how much work there is to do. There simply are seldom enough hours in the day to accomplish everything that needs to be accomplished.

Your staff will work with (and encourage others to work with) the medium to make your site better and deeper. They'll actually be happy to have the input of those who are taking the time to learn about the technologies and relay the information. One less hour spent looking for that information is one more hour spent putting it to use, if it's something your Web site needs.

You, and they, will be surprised at the people who, given the chance to learn the necessary skills, will spend as much of their own time learning as they can. It's not just the challenge of something new—there's never been any lack of new things to learn, and they've likely managed to resist any number of those opportunities. It's the combination of skills that excite them—the combination of design and content in a medium (the computer) that may have begun to bore them with its ease of use. And this challenge has one advantage—it's very visible. Expect your repressed thespians and artists to be thrilled with a chance to produce work for your Web site. Expect to be surprised by the diversity of those people, too. If you're not, that would be a surprise.

◀ 6 ▶

TWO SIDES—SAME COIN

THEY'RE SPENDING ONE HECK OF
A LOT OF TIME LOOKING AT OUR
SITE. IS THAT WORK?

◆

ENDLESS PHONE CALLS—
THIS IS WORK??

◆

HTML CODING—
BUT YOU SAID IT WAS EASY!

◆

THEY'RE SURFING THE WEB A
LOT, BUT ARE THEY WORKING???

It's not easy to be a nontechnical manager in charge of a project that incorporates some of the newest technology on the block. Truth to tell, it's not always easy for experienced technical managers. The only real advantage for technical managers is that they usually read regularly, at least around the edges of the issues related to the Web, in the course of their regular duties. (It's impossible to miss all the technical articles that are being written in the trade magazines they see daily.) But that only means that they're not easily buffaloed by the jargon, and are a bit less likely to believe that some technical issues simply "can't be overcome."

You need to understand a little about the issues your development staff will face, in order to know when you're getting the straight scoop and when you're getting the runaround.

They Tell Me They're Working on It. Are They?

We're talking about leading-edge technologies. Those who are new to them on your development staff are more likely to be trying to do *too* much, rather than not doing enough. In fact, it probably will be harder for you to keep them from undertaking tasks that are more time-consuming than you would like, than to concentrate on the basics and consider the more complex tasks at a slightly later time.

The early stages of this project, like most other projects, are heady. Everyone's eager and excited. Any delays that occur this early are likely to be the result of your staff attempting to install features on your site that are beyond their level of expertise. They want to learn it all and they want to learn it *right now*.

198

There can be delays and glitches before the site is operational. Any one piece of the site that isn't being delivered on a timely basis can delay all the rest. If your development staff's time isn't completely devoted to your Web site, they may be juggling multiple commitments and priorities. It never fails that major project deadlines originally scheduled to occur months apart eventually reach critical mass within days of one another.

▶ **NOTE**   In January, 1996, a somewhat minor but important redesign of our site was delayed two weeks by our graphic artist due to other priorities that were judged to be more critical to the organization. In the meantime, a large relocation of staff was announced that would require that I don my "network logistics coordinator" hat and determine the easiest way to move network lines for approximately 100 people. Throw into the equation the additional complication that the graphic artist and I were both attending a conference at the beginning of February, and you may come close to picturing the actual fire drill.

I was frantically trying to determine who was going where and when. Eileen (our graphic artist) was frantically finishing one large project and designing and coding Web pages in her spare time. Two days before we were scheduled to leave, she uploaded the revisions to the Web pages. Between phone calls to her about the pages and to others about the moves, I tested and corrected Web pages as necessary, and put them into production at noon before the day we left (not a practice I recommend for anyone, but *certainly* not one for those who are new to the Web). On my way out of the office the evening before I flew to the conference, I picked up the bulk of the move list. Whatever did we do before laptops?? From the conference, I transmitted back information about the moves to the people who were going to have to accomplish them the following weekend—one day after I returned. ◀

Keep check on the priorities your staff is setting, or is having set for them. Other duties may be keeping them from accomplishing things you consider important for your Web site. It's entirely possible that the number of hours required to effectively handle all the work for all the commitments hasn't been set realistically.

Naturally, the other side of that coin could be that your staff believes that you're sufficiently uninformed about what work they're doing—and how long it should take to do it—that you aren't in a position to question any of their excuses for delays. That would obviously mean one of two things: either you're not doing your own homework, or you don't have the right people assigned to the project. You need to know which situation is the case—earlier, rather than later.

WHEN TO TRUST—AND WHEN NOT TO TRUST—YOUR STAFF

Generally, the beginning phases of a Web site project don't cause a manager to wonder whether her staff is doing what needs to be done. The staff is likely to be so excited over every page and graphic that's completed that the poor manager will be sick to death of getting e-mail messages requesting comments and suggestions. The concerns are much more likely to occur after the initial pages are in place and as the day-to-day work of maintaining the site and adding new pieces begins.

Once the pace (apparently) slows down, you may very well wonder what they're really *doing* that seems to take so much time. It's not like they're adding new pages to the site every day. And you don't plan to make additions to the site more than weekly or monthly, so what in the world are they doing with all that time?

200

They Call It "Tweaking"

Technical types aren't the only ones who can't leave well enough alone, but they do seem to be among the worst offenders. Programmers, engineers, mechanics, and, yes, Web developers simply can't leave things as they are. Surely if they just do this one little thing, everything will work more smoothly.

Think of it as a disease. It may be genetic.

It's worse for new Web developers. If you weren't so closely involved with this project, you'd feel sorry for these people. A new Web site, especially the first effort… there's simply no other analogy that fits it quite so well as comparing it to first-time parents marveling over a new baby. Your development staff will spend two weeks just looking at it. Amazed at the fact that it works at all, checking the same links over and over (just in case they mysteriously broke overnight, for no apparent reason), finding the six typographical errors they missed, and being embarrassed to death about them when they do (count on them being corrected within 20 seconds of discovery).

Are We There Yet?

Of course, every 30 minutes they'll drop everything while they make the rounds of the search engines and review sites to see whether your site is listed yet. Your site is, of course, the most important site on the Web, and surely it will be reviewed with inordinate haste—they hope for that and live in mortal terror of it at the same time. They'll check your server logs just as often, to see how many hits the site has received. If they happen to have put one of those silly counters on one of your pages (the kind that counts the number of visitors to the page), they'll swing from wanting to keep it honest and not looking at the page themselves to reloading the page every three seconds just to "make sure it works."

It takes a month or so for all of this to get old. And they're entirely too cool to admit any of it, of course. They're just keeping an eye on things—trying to evaluate how well the site works, don't you know?

Believe it or not, this too is work.

They'll go home at night exhausted from their efforts. When your Web site hasn't been reviewed in a month—and unless you're one of the major players in your league, it probably won't be—they start redesigning the site in their heads. That's when things will get down to real business again. They're convinced now that all the links and graphics work as they should and even the most obscure typo has been eradicated. The site still hasn't been reviewed and it's been all of six weeks, so obviously it's time to start over completely. You can safely ignore this stage. It too will pass, just as soon as one of them reminds another that a redesign means touching and coding every one of those pages again. Whoa! That's a reality check.

THOSE LONG PHONE CALLS

Someone really should do an analysis of how much time is spent by members of Web development staffs on the phone answering questions. The percentage would be pretty interesting. A new Web site generally garners calls from the more technologically inclined members in a business.

Your Webmaster really hasn't gone off the deep end with personal phone calls. Instead, he's enduring the equivalent of an inquisition. These folks want details—exactly what operating system and which version of the operating system and which server software and oh, yes, which version of that are you running? And those are the easy questions. He's now officially a Webmaster and therefore an expert on everything about the Web—or a complete impostor they plan to expose.

Two Sides—Same Coin

You hired the right person for the job if he actually looks like he's having fun with those calls and he doesn't verbally snap anyone's head off at the shoulders. If you ask nicely, he may regale you with a list of all the suggestions, corrections, and comments he's getting.

And remember all those people who didn't have time to review the Web pages while the site was still in the review process? They're reviewing it now, at length and ad nauseum. If you will only take their advice and add that full-color, full-page picture of the "plant"—the one with the unremarkable concrete block building enhanced by the large parking lots full of cars—on your home page, the site will draw visitors by the droves, no doubt. If your Webmaster responds only that you *did* consider that possibility but decided that the graphics were just a little too large, give him the afternoon off. He's a diplomat of the highest order.

Webmasters really should not be inclined to high blood pressure. The job's entirely too stressful as it is, and some of the "help" a Webmaster is offered is not well-meant. Of course, some of it is, and that helps take the edge off the rest.

As time goes on, those phone calls are more likely to be from people who want to know how to accomplish specific things in coding, how to go about getting pages added to your Web server, and how to get hired into your development staff. The first two kinds of calls can be time-consuming.

SHARING THEIR ADVICE

Your staff should be prepared to offer specific publications to new Web page coders to guide them. *Teach Yourself Web Publishing with HTML 3.12 in a Week* by Laura Lemay (published by Sams.net) is an excellent reference. Setting up a page of links to references on the Web may save your staff some time on the phone, but some people simply want verbal instructions or clarifications. Since you want to spread the work around, the time spent in explanations now may be time saved later.

Guidelines for adding pages to your Web server should be established and made widely available. Again, preparing Web pages with instructions is one way to lessen the phone call load. But there still will be questions and further explanations necessary. Nothing about the Web is yet set in stone, and it's highly unlikely that your guidelines can be, either.

▶ **NOTE**   We have only one guideline that's set in stone, or at least firmly packed dirt. Nothing can BLINK!

Mere days after issuing that absolute edict, I saw the only good example of use of the <blink> tag. Our Information Systems staff, who are primarily involved with maintaining our intranet, used it in a game for training new Web users.

Never say never—that applies to almost everything about the Web. ◀

ANY OPENINGS?

The calls involving requests to be added to your Web development staff will certainly serve to remind your staff that other people want their "cushy" jobs doing Web site development. Some days those calls are incentive to work just a little harder; others, it's a serious temptation to suggest that the caller rush right over and take the reins immediately. Secretly, Web developers spend 95 percent of their time amazed that someone is paying them to have a great time learning and working on the Web. That other 5 percent, though, is time they spend deciding that they were completely insane to allow themselves to get trapped in the Web.

HAVE THEY GOT A DEAL FOR YOU!

Then there are the vendors of Web-related products. Webmasters are easy to find, unlike some others in your corporate structure. The vendors aren't satisfied with deluging your development staff with mailings (both through the

U.S. Postal Service and by e-mail)—they call, and they call, and they call again. It's a growing and very competitive market, and those companies are trying hard to claim their share of it.

It's perfectly understandable, if a nuisance. Because the technology is so new, each of those companies hopes to claim the de facto standard, based on its market share. Netscape managed it, for all practical purposes (though that may change) by giving their browsers away. That's not a viable alternative for the majority of the companies marketing document-conversion tools, HTML editors, Web servers, and the scores of other products for Web site developers—so they call.

Your development staff may be up to their eyelashes in electronic technology, but some days it will seem that the only way to remove the phones from their ears will involve surgical procedures. They'll thank you for wire cutters. Unfortunately, voice mail can save them from only an unfairly small percentage of the calls.

WOULD SOMEONE PLEASE TURN OFF THE MAIL SERVER??

Those vendors are sending e-mail. People with questions are sending e-mail. The mailing lists are producing e-mail by the megabyte. Sorting it all out can easily take an hour or more out of the day—easily. Subject lines should make it all easy to categorize, but they don't always do that. Those who love words, and that includes most Web developers, love e-mail and love answering it—at length. Oops! Where did the morning go?

Responses to inquiries from the Web should be handled courteously and promptly. Some of those inquiries require further inquiries to determine their precise nature, while others can be handled quickly. All of them take some amount of time, however small. Even mail that's forwarded along to the proper people for response sometimes requires follow-up and at least a quick, polite response to the originator. If it's not answered after it's forwarded, your Web pages aren't being used to good purpose.

Your Web development staff at some point are likely to be the only people in your company who will be delighted to be Internet-*dis*connected—assuming that the cause is completely beyond their control. Two hours without incoming e-mail will give them time to catch up on the internal backlog. Of course, when the connection is repaired, the megabytes of incoming mail can be a bit overwhelming, but at least a few chores were accomplished in the meantime.

GRUESOME BUT NECESSARY BASICS OF HTML CODING

Depending upon how actively you've promoted your Web site for use by the various functions within your business, your development staff may have additional Web pages or whole projects to begin immediately after the initial pages are in place, or shortly thereafter. Most companies will put specific pages on the Web to begin, and plan for other pages to be added after the initial offering. A regular schedule of new pages will keep your site fresh and your staff busy.

Since your basic design is established—for now—making additions should be only minimally time-consuming. For the most part, adding text between design elements is child's play. It's been said more than once, but the basics of HTML coding are easy and boring. Web developers who are even slightly beyond beginners would rather eat dirt than be bothered with it.

Unfortunately, until others on your staff have developed at least minimal skills in the area, your developers are simply going to be forced to do this boring part of the job. Everybody hates to file, too, but everybody has to do it one way or the other.

Your (Wonderfully Brief) HTML Lesson

You may not really want to know about coding Web pages, but if you don't understand the basics, you're likely to be taken for a ride that will cost you money. Let's get this lesson in coding out of the way as quickly and painlessly as possible.

The ML in HTML, as you may remember, stands for *markup language*. It's not programming, by a long shot. It's simply a matter of adding certain markup codes (*tags*) to text, so that it will display properly in a browser. Most of the codes are paired—a beginning tag, followed by text, followed by an ending tag. Simple concept—simple in its implementation. A completely coded page can be as easy to produce as adding the following tags in the specific order that follows:

Code	Description
`<html>`	Tells the requesting browser that this is an HTML page.
`<head>`	The header information that the browser uses. A number of optional components can be included within the `<head>` element.
`<title>`	This should be a short (less than 40 character) description of the contents of the page. This information will be used by various search engines, and it's the description that will appear in the very top line of the browser—the line above the toolbar. It's also the information that will describe the page to those people who include it in their bookmarks or *hotlists*.
`</title>`	The slash (/) translates to "the end," so this is the end of the title.

continues

207

Code	Description
`</head>`	This is the end of the header (head). Nothing that appears inside the head element will appear in the document, unless it's explicitly repeated in both elements.
`<body>`	Now we begin the actual text (*body*) of the document.
`<h#>`	A head*line* or head*ing* , not a head*er*. The # can be from 1 to 6 (largest to smallest) and indicates the size of the type that the browser will use to display the text in this element. The actual size of the type is browser-dependent (as are most other things about a Web page).
`</h#>`	The end of the headline.
`<p>`	The beginning of a paragraph…
`</p>`	…and the end of the same paragraph.
`</body>`	The end of the body of the document.
`</html>`	The end of the HTML document.

In truth, a couple of those tags could even be left out, and the page would still be completely acceptable—if not perfect, by-the-book code. The `<h#>` `</h#>` pair isn't necessarily required on a page, but headlines break up the text and make the page more readable. You might think of them more as section headings in a document (like the ones in this chapter). The `<p>` `</p>` pair is good form, but simply adding `<p>` at the beginning or ending of each paragraph is certainly acceptable. Obviously, a page that includes only those most basic elements wouldn't be terribly attractive, but it would be viewable by any Web browser. There are lots of other tags that your Web developers will use in their documents, but the purpose here is simply to give you an idea of the very basics of HTML coding.

208

Beyond the Basics—Graphics

Adding a graphic, or a link to another page or site, is only marginally more difficult. The tag that calls a graphic is `<img src = "filename.gif">` and what adds the margin of difficulty is knowing where the file is in relation to the text document. A completely coded page is a combination of various elements: text, graphics, and other files that are included, but each element is a separate file.

Because a URL is a combination address that includes the protocol being requested, the domain name of the company, and the directories on the computer that serves the page, you can generally tell exactly where a file is stored by its address. If you look at the source code for a page on your Web site for which this is the URL:

http://www.yourcompany.com/yourdepartment/ document.html

and you see a tag for a graphic, like this:

```
<img src="filename.gif">
```

that graphic is stored in the directory that houses **document.html**.

If the tag for that same graphic is instead:

```
<img src="images/filename.gif">
```

then the file is stored in a directory named **images**, one level beneath the present one. The full URL for that image file, if you choose to look at it separately from the text document, is as follows:

http://www.yourcompany.com/yourdepartment/images/ filename.gif

If instead the source calls this file:

```
<img src="../filename.gif">
```

the file is one directory level above the present one, in this instance the directory named **yourdepartment**, making the following address the full URL for the graphic itself:

http://www.yourcompany.com/filename.gif

The graphic can be anywhere on the computer, so long as it's in the directory that serves HTML documents. It can also be on some other computer that serves Web pages, but that isn't advisable, because it will take longer to get the image and load it, for one thing (and time is of the essence). It also puts a load on the other computer, and that may not be desirable either.

▶ **CAUTION**   Referencing graphics from another Web server outside your company is very bad form. If the site is busy already, they certainly don't need the additional hits to load graphics for your pages. ◀

Beginning HTML coders sometimes prefer to key in the full URL of a file, rather than use the relational addressing, simply because it's a little easier to address the file directly. Indeed, a site that has many layers of directories can make for some very confusing relational addressing, but it's even more important to use the full URL for a file at large, busy sites that might be mirrored in some other location—as you certainly hope yours will be at some point.

▶ **TIP**   If your documents are being coded with full URLs for every page called from your own server, your developers aren't learning very good work habits. They should be planning for the future, not saving themselves some time now—and very little time, at that, because keying in the full URL in some cases is a lot of keystrokes. Generally, they should use relative addresses for documents that are housed on your Web site and the full URL for documents that link to pages on other sites. There are some few exceptions, of course, but those are a bit outside the scope of this discussion. ◀

Once you make sense of the addressing for that graphic, links to other documents are easy, because they're addressed the same way. A link is properly called an *anchor*. It anchors one page on the Web to another. The tag that accomplishes the anchor looks like this:

```
<a href="filename.html">descriptive text</a>
```

The first a = anchor (surprise); href = *hypertext reference*; and that's obviously followed by the name of the file that's being linked. The descriptive text is the part of a Web page that's highlighted and/or underlined on the page to indicate that it's a link, and the </a> simply tells the browser that it has reached the end of the "anchored" text. If the </a> isn't added, everything in the document up to the next anchored link will be underlined and/or highlighted. That fact makes it very easy to find mistakes of that sort.

Links to documents that aren't on your site simply require the substitution of the complete URL, so a link from your document to Merrill Lynch, for instance, would be coded this way:

```
<a href="http://www.ml.com">Merrill Lynch</a>
```

Yes, HTML coding for complex pages can be a great deal more complicated than just adding the basic tags with a graphic and a link or two. There are many, many parameters that describe where a graphic might be placed or how text should be aligned on a page, and any number of other tags can be used for various purposes. There are extensions to the standard HTML code that can be added to make the page look entirely different to one browser than it will look to another. You don't really want to learn all those, do you?

▶ **NOTE** A programmer friend requested that I help him get started when he decided to learn HTML coding. He assured me that "They don't call it code for nothing," mistakenly assuming that HTML coding was like programming. It simply isn't, except that certain rules must be followed, and when someone is coding pages manually, the design is conceptual rather than readily apparent. Those of us who insist on coding manually see in our minds the design of the page, and code to achieve that design. The converters and

continues

continued

editors for HTML allow people to see the design as the page is coded, theo-
retically. The "gotchas" in that approach are described a bit later. ◄

So How Long Does It Really Take to Code Three Pages?

It's good for you to learn the basics of HTML coding, even if you never code
one single page. Knowing what's involved will give you a better idea of how
long it takes to do at least simple pages. These basics are the abc's of HTML.
They're not difficult in the least. You don't have to be able to write great
marketing pieces to manage a staff that does, but you do need to know, at a
basic level, what it takes to compose a sentence.

Code one short document yourself. It will be a good lesson for you. The
first one may take you 30 minutes because you'll have to refer to the tags as
described. Just take a one-page document and add the tags. Save it on your
computer as a text file with an **.htm** or **.html** extension, and then request it
from your browser by using the Open Document option. If you included
the very basic tags, it should display quite well, though it may look a bit dull
without graphics or links to other documents.

A Few Minutes Should Do It...

Anyone who's familiar with the HTML tags can easily code a basic document
of three or four screens of text, a graphic, and a couple of links in 10 minutes
or less. That doesn't mean the page is going to look gorgeous, but it won't
take long to accomplish the coding.

...or Maybe Not

Using the design that your staff has already developed for your site, adding
pages becomes simply a matter of changing certain text on a page or adding
text to a template. Complete replacement of 15KB of simple text that has the

basic design elements in place can be accomplished in just a few minutes by people who are experienced with HTML.

▶ **NOTE**   That's assuming, of course, that the replacement text arrives in electronic format. You're surely not paying your Web development staff to key printed information!? Leave that to the word processing staff. They're generally much better typists and will take the time to make sure everything is spelled correctly.

The revisions and additions, for the most part, should simply be a matter of cut, paste, and code. Of course, that generalization applies only to short, simple documents. ◀

CAN THE SOFTWARE DO IT?

Even short documents can require special treatment; those with lists within lists within lists, for instance, can take considerably longer to code than simple documents, especially for people who aren't very experienced. Documents that require extensive tables, even those that are accomplished quite simply with word processing packages, can be extremely time-consuming.

If editors and converters are available, why would your staff be coding Web pages manually? Because it's dependable.

The sad truth is that though there are editors and converters that can do some of the work of coding, they don't conform to your special site design. And, in many cases, they just don't work as advertised; even those that do can make some very interesting assumptions about the pages that change the structure of the page. In many cases, the converters assume that any time they encounter a line break, there should be a paragraph tag, and that's simply not the case. You want your address to follow one line after the other like this:

```
Marilyn R. Browning
PO Box 1111111
Your City, NC 45897-0000
```

not like this:

```
Marilyn R. Browning


PO Box 1111111


Your City, NC 45897-0000
```

WHAT YOU CAN EXPECT—BEST CASE

Assume that a document to be added to your Web site is delivered to your staff in WordPerfect or Microsoft Word format. Your staff subjects it to a converter to be reformatted into HTML. The converted text may or may not require additional coding to ensure that it conforms to the style that your developers have established for your Web site.

It does, however, contain beginning and ending code that will probably need to be removed, so that your site's design elements can be inserted. It may require a good deal more revision than that, but for the moment let's assume the best case.

Now your design elements have to be added to the page—probably a matter of cutting-and-pasting, so that's not terribly time-consuming. Now the page is ready to test. That entire process might take 15 minutes.

NOT WORST CASE, BUT MORE IN KEEPING WITH REALITY

The preceding section offered you a look at a best-case scenario. In reality, the converter is more likely to have misinterpreted any number of elements on the page. The document has to be reviewed carefully in the context of the original to assure that basic elements have been maintained. Lists within lists may be been ignored entirely or mangled severely. Tables may have been misaligned. Paragraph tags may have been placed completely incorrectly. It now becomes almost a line-by-line check of the coded page against the original text. It can easily take longer to correct the converted text than to code the document manually.

▶ **NOTE** In one instance, while I was training a staff member who was using one of the better converters (at that time), a directory listing of the 20 or so documents he'd been working on displayed quite erratically, with pieces of the HTML code appearing in the browser. I suggested that he take a look at the code in a text editor, because I suspected that an ending tag had been omitted somewhere in at least one of the documents. He spent more than an hour in search of the offending code, to no avail. I looked at the code briefly and didn't see any apparent mistakes, but told him I'd check it more carefully while he went to lunch. By the time he returned, I was almost ready to give up myself, because I simply couldn't find any errors.

The conversion software certainly appeared to have done exactly what it should have done. Simply out of sheer desperation, I removed an angle bracket (>) in the code, at the point where the text began to appear incorrectly in the browser. Because the following pieces of the HTML code simply couldn't work without that angle bracket, I reinserted it manually. Voilà. For reasons I will never understand, that cleaned up about five lines of garbage.

I explained exactly what I had done and suggested that he try the same thing in the other documents that displayed incorrectly. He was able to correct the document completely, simply by deleting and reinserting each angle bracket that was apparently not being recognized by any of the three browsers we were using. Time involved in finding the problem—approximately 2.5 hours; time spent correcting the problem—approximately 3 hours, because the problem had to be corrected in each of those 20 or so documents that made up the list. Time spent originally running the documents through the converter—2 hours. Those documents could have easily been coded manually in 5 hours or less.

continues

continued

And, no, a global search-and-replace of the offending angle brackets wouldn't work. The converter wouldn't allow search-and-replace in the codes (though it would in the text). The solution required saving all the documents, bringing them into an editor, and then making the changes—an additional step that should have been unnecessary. ◄

STAYING CURRENT—
THE TIME-CONSUMING NECESSITY

Keeping abreast of all the developments that can affect your Web site can consume huge chunks of time. The single best place for your development staff to research those developments is on the Web. Tips from other developers about new software applications they're using, or in many cases developing themselves, require time to find, study, and try.

Surfing the Web for new ideas for coding and design may sound like tremendous fun to those who don't do it. Don't let the secret out—it's extremely well-guarded—but it *is* tremendous fun sometimes. Stumbling across some completely well-thought-out site is an absolute joy. That's primarily because so many are done so very poorly. You have to kiss (or at least look at) an inordinate number of frogs in this business before you find a prince. But every once in a rare while the frogs are forgotten because someone approached a design very originally or has used a coding trick to good advantage. Surprises keep the hunt for new ideas exciting.

SOMETIMES SURFING IS JUST FOR FUN

You're right, of course, in thinking that not all of that Web surfing is strictly business. It's not. Your developers are human, one would hope, and they're likely to be sidetracked just because something interested them that has absolutely nothing to do with their work. The fascinating thing about that is that

216

somewhere in the recesses of their brains, a note is being made that reminds them why those pages drew them. Something about the site beckoned.

Perhaps it was only that the subject has always been of interest, but developers tend to be just a bit more discerning than most. If those pages don't deliver what's expected in short order, your developer is there and gone—and they remember that as well as the pages that seemingly glue their mice to pads that didn't seem at all sticky before.

Two Web sites in particular are nemeses for me. I simply can't allow myself to visit them on any but personal time. Both *Salon* (**http://www.salon 1999.com**) and *Feed* (**http://www.feedmag.com**), electronic magazines, can bring me to a dead stop for hours of reading. Why? Content. The information contained in their pages is literate, compelling, provoking, and often witty. I don't care for *Feed*'s design at all, because I often don't load graphics and that makes the text on their site less easy to read. *Salon* does a better job with design, but I'm reading these magazines on my personal time, remember? I'm loading pages from home over a 28.8 modem with sometimes less-than-desirable phone connections. The graphics are completely secondary to me when I'm on my own time. I'm simply a sucker for good content.

TESTING THE TOOLS

The trade magazines add some level of assistance in their reviews of applications and advancements, but only hands-on evaluations of most products can give your development staff the truth about the products. It's certainly easy to acquire the products for testing. Most companies offer evaluation software on the Web; others prefer to ship evaluation products.

In this early stage of the Web, your developers are as likely as not to be the *alpha testers* for products that are at the crawling, not walking, stage of development. They may be included in *beta testing* for those products that are almost but not quite ready for prime time. It takes time to participate in the development of applications software, because the developers want the products beat up and thoroughly tested. The advantage of participating in these tests, though, is that your developers may very well convince the software developers to add specific features that you need. Custom-designed software is not to be disdained.

Alpha and Beta Testing

Every software application needs to be tested before it's distributed for sale. Alpha tests (named for the first letter in the Greek alphabet) are the first tests of those products. They're generally limited to a few users who'll find the most obvious problems associated with the product. Beta testing (named for the second letter in the Greek alphabet) is the second level of testing of the product—by a larger number of people, with a wider range of use of the product. It's a much more rigorous test of the product than can be performed by the manufacturer, thus helping the software developers to find flaws that might otherwise be overlooked.

Evaluating software, whether in the testing stages or at the commercial level, is more than installing it and trying a couple of its advertised features. Your staff should be considering applications on at least two or three levels:

- Will this product be easy for your staff to learn to use? We're not talking about just your development staff, but about people throughout your company.

- What functionality will it add to your site, if any, and do you need it? If the need exists, consider whether the application appears to be stable. If you may need it later, are there indications that the company that developed it is stable? (Who needs software that won't be supported or upgraded in the future?)

◆ Is it easy enough to maintain that if your Webmaster gets hit by a truck (the deities forbid!) or defects elsewhere (ditto) that you won't have to spend a fortune on consultants to keep it working smoothly?

HOLDING FIRM

You did think to hire a Webmaster with some element of stubborn recalcitrance, right? That was an excellent move on your part, because people within your company who want specific features added to your Web site aren't likely to care whether the software is easy to install or maintain. They simply want it now, and few other considerations are given.

And you certainly know how pushy salespeople can be! They want your Webmaster to install the software, give it a 10-minute evaluation, and issue a check, now. As if your Webmaster had no other considerations beyond how easily the application installs and how interesting the tutorial is.

Stubborn resistance to being pushed into a quick decision, no matter how frustrating that facet may be to some staff or to the vendors, can be a very good thing. Granted, for some applications (for example, for a forms interface that calls e-mail), the cost of a mistake may not be critical at all. If the initial cost is minimal, the software can be replaced easily and transparently, for the most part. Software that accesses your databases for specialized information to present customized pages is another matter entirely. In addition to the expense involved (which may or may not be minimal), an unwise decision in that regard could result in a mangled database. It's far better to insist on taking the time for a solid evaluation of the product than to be rushed into what could be a very bad decision.

WHAT IF THE WORK'S NOT GETTING DONE?

The questions, the e-mail, the scheduled maintenance, and the evaluations all take time that must be factored into any equation you use to judge the work your staff is doing. Everyone has that occasional day that isn't jammed with priorities; your development staff will have them, too—otherwise you're going to have one very burned-out staff in about 18 months, or maybe sooner.

We all know the dreadful truth, though, and that is that not every person is willing to work at a breakneck pace for extended periods of time. Some aren't willing to work at that pace for more than about 10 minutes at a stretch.

If the work that you expect to have done on your Web site isn't getting done, you need to know why. Like any other project, certain tasks should be scheduled and priorities assigned, not just for the original site but for the ongoing tasks and the new ones as they're added. Constant cries of "other priorities" may be valid, but in that case, what are those priorities, and how do you rank them in the overall scheme of things?

Does work need to be reassigned, or is this simply a delaying tactic? Worse, are the actual priorities nothing more than a fundamental desire to work at a lackadaisical pace? That's quite simply unacceptable for those who work in Web development.

Half-coded Web pages are better than uncoded Web pages, but only by a small degree. If the people who are coding are consistently doing it by halves, they're not doing their homework or their jobs, as far as your Web site is concerned. The same thing applies to graphics that are consistently not delivered, delivered unformatted for the Web, or delivered with content that wasn't developed with your Web audience in mind.

The effect of each minor transgression is cumulative. Content that isn't checked and rechecked, or is delivered without understanding of the market it addresses, still may not be completely without worth. But combine that with incomplete coding and graphics delivered to your development staff, and a considerable amount of time has been wasted. Your staff will either have to send it all back and hope it's complete the next time, or invest their own time in trying to repair the damage.

MANAGEMENT WANTS IT NOW, AND WE'RE NOT READY!

When you begin your Web project, there may be only a handful of people in your company who have more than the most superficial understanding of the Web and its workings. Count on that situation to change. The trade press is focused toward intranets this year, but it's all the same technology, no matter what name you give it. The rest of the media is hardly ignoring the Web. They can't afford to do that, and neither can your shareholders or Board of Directors or CEO. So they're reading about this work in which you and your developers are engaged, and they're learning—not at the same pace, but they are learning. It's a blessing and a curse.

You absolutely need for them to see the value of your Web site. They can hardly do that if they don't have some understanding of the technology and its applications. They may not be 100 percent sold on its usefulness for your business, but they're not so blind as to rule out its possibilities.

It's your job as manager of this project to turn the possibilities to probabilities and then to realities. That means that *you* can't be behind the curve in learning, either. Now there's a curse if there ever was one. It's not like you didn't have enough work to do already, right? But it's important.

Before you know it, some member of senior management is going to insist that a technology be employed on your Web site that isn't in your immediate plan, and may not be in your plan at all. He's read about it, and his nephew (the computer genius) has assured him that it's absolutely the one thing that your Web site must have. And not three months from now, thank you very much—next week would be good, though this afternoon would, of course, be better.

Homework—you didn't really think your developers were the only ones who needed to do it, did you? You can hardly commit your staff to a technology that you know little or nothing about. You certainly don't want to commit them to anything until you know what other priorities are on their schedules right now. That's probably your best dodge for the moment, but don't expect this issue to go away—not for long, anyway.

There are probably some very good reasons that any number of technologies aren't being employed on your Web site. It's quite likely that the senior managers are far less cognizant of the issues surrounding the technology than you are. Generally, they'll happily take "no" for an answer if the accompanying explanation is rational and pragmatic.

Take the old standard "I'll get back to you on that" approach, and then have a talk with your developers. Listen to them carefully. If they give you good reasons for delaying or simply not implementing a technology, and you later mangle that reasoning in your explanation, you're going to have to do it all again, because that senior manager is going to talk to his nephew again.

How to Communicate What You Can Do and What You Can't

One of the most important things for you to remember is that the Web is very much in the early stages of its evolution. Much of that evolution has, until very recently, been driven by some extremely bright and talented young people who had very little experience in the business world. They not only didn't much care whether your business could use the vast potential of the Web; more than a few of them didn't want you there at all. Many still aren't particularly sold on the idea, but have grudgingly accepted your presence in "their" territory.

As luck would have it, many of them are now in the world of business themselves—to some of them, that's more than a little surprising. The technologies they developed were not developed for business. They were developed to show off the capabilities of the Web, and that's what they do—quite well. The technologies that will be developed in the immediate future are ones that are much more likely to meet your needs, thanks in great part to the fact that those early developers now need the same tools you do.

222

The major software developers are fully involved with the technologies now, too, which is something that couldn't have been said as recently as the fall of 1995. That fact necessarily means better tools for businesses. Integrating those tools into other, more familiar products is a given.

▶ **NOTE**   Interestingly, that doesn't mean that the major developers will provide better tools than some of the newcomers to the field. Those companies are rushing to catch up with the hotshots who've been working on the Web and developing for it for several years.

Your Web developers can't yet depend on the standard software companies to sell them everything they need. Why should they, when they can as easily get products that are as good or better on the Web, at less cost to you? ◀

As you consult with your developers, keep those things in mind. This is all going to get easier, and the more carefully you listen, the easier it will be for you. Most Webmasters love expounding on their theories about the latest technologies, and so, in general, do other members of Web development staffs.

Of course, you want more than theories—you need specifics. It's all but impossible to guess what technologies or applications will be new and exciting when you're faced with choices for implementation, but it's quite unlikely that the reasons given for not using them, or delaying their uses, will change very much.

Cost Issues

Some products that enter the market are simply cost-prohibitive, depending on your budget constraints. While it might be a status symbol to install the most expensive Web server software on your site (which presently lists in the $1,300 range), do you really need the features it offers? Can you get those same features for less in another product?

Other types of products, from database management solutions to conferencing software, are as likely to be expensive to add to your site. Not all of them are, of course, and your development staff should have a general idea of what's available and the cost of implementation. Each piece adds to the overall cost of the whole, though, and you may be budgeting for specific solution software that you know you need. If cost is the primary reason for avoiding a technology (of any sort), and you simply don't have the budget necessary to cover the cost, perhaps that senior manager would be interested in footing the bill.

PLATFORM ISSUES

While there is indeed Web server software for all the major operating systems, new technologies and applications aren't always immediately available for all of those platforms. The application was developed on one or two particular platforms, and the initial release of the product is usually strictly for those development platforms. There may be several months' delay before the product is available for other platforms. It may *never* be available for all of them. There would hardly be any logic in changing your basic platform, simply to add a new technology.

SECURITY ISSUES

It's true that nothing on the Web is ever going to be 100 percent secure. *Someone* is smart enough and determined enough to punch holes in the most secure system and take full advantage of those holes. The very nature of a Web server makes it more vulnerable than some other computers on the Internet. New technologies absolutely must be considered with that fact in mind. Your developers and your system administrator's goal is to make the information that you deliver on the Web as secure as they can make it. They can't offer you absolute guarantees.

224

Your developers will be reading the security information that's available to them, keeping tabs on any issues that might make implementing a technology on your site a liability rather than an asset. Is it likely to open some security hole that would be best left closed? Obviously, the answer is sometimes difficult to determine. Java's security features have been touted for quite some time now, but as recently as June, 1996, one very bright Java researcher in the UK reported a security flaw that sent Sun Microsystem's best and brightest to work to patch.

The security issues should never be ignored. And they shouldn't be allowed to frighten you into not trying applications at all. So long as your developers are keeping an eye on your Web site and an ear to the security rumor mill, you and they will be able to weigh the risks against the benefits.

STAFFING ISSUES

There are only 24 hours in each day. Even Web developers—strange lot though they may be—require food and sleep occasionally. They'll be more than happy to give you a list of the projects they're juggling. They may be more than happy to add the needed technology or application, if other priorities can be rearranged or staff added.

If you choose to rearrange those priorities, however, it's your responsibility to notify those people who may be affected by the changes—not your developers' responsibility. You may rest completely assured that they're taking more than their fair share of flack from all sides. Perhaps that senior manager would care to explain the rearrangements—especially those that may affect projects required by other senior managers?

If the priorities simply can't be shifted, additional staff might be added. Can your budget accommodate that change? Is the senior manager so committed to the technology that he'd be willing to cover the cost of a consultant to install the necessary software and train your staff in its use?

Only after you've talked with your developers can you appropriately respond to issues that involve Web technologies (unless you fully understand them already). If, after talking with your development staff, you still feel unqualified to address certain questions (whether they deal with specific technologies or with other technical issues), ask your Web staff to answer those questions in writing for you. Not only will that technique allow you to consider the issue at length—it may even help you find ways to circumvent any objections that your staff may have. Web developers aren't always correct in their assessments, any more than anyone else is.

Your staff should, however, be able to give you more than adequate information to answer questions from those who will be expecting answers from *you*. The bottom line, many times, is that senior management is at least as interested in the bottom line as you are.

You are responsible for selling functionality over features. That isn't likely to be a very difficult sale. Senior management is probably much more likely to expect your developers to be constantly requesting more—and more expensive—features. It's all too easy, not only for your Web developers but for others on your staff, to be carried away by the hype surrounding some new idea, feature, or technology. It's not always easy to maintain a balanced perspective (and it may not make you exceedingly popular in some quarters to do that), but it's by far the wiser course of action for your Web site's future.

You can bet that your senior staff will appreciate a "flashy is fine, but functional is better" approach. They surely have a high regard for fiscally responsible projects. At some point, you're seriously going to need to install more expensive technologies on your site, or add staff in order to distribute the workload. As long as it's apparent to those who can ultimately make decisions about your budget that you are intent on delivering the best possible Web site with the resources they've chosen to give you, you're on reasonably high ground.

EDUCATING YOUR
MANAGEMENT ABOUT YOUR JOB

It's not enough to repeat your Web developers' specialized jargon to your management. They honestly need to be educated to the realities of a Web site. You should make sure that you communicate the ways your site is being used. They may not choose to support the project unless they can be convinced of its worth. No company has endless resources to throw at a project that doesn't deliver some measure of return.

Your reports should include general information about the types of inquiries your Web site generates:

◆ Are you receiving many inquiries about job openings, and is your Human Resources staff happy with the quality of the inquiries?

◆ Has your technical support staff had many people refer to the fact that they checked your Web pages and couldn't find the answers they needed there, or simply wanted more detailed answers?

◆ Are leads for your sales staff being generated from the Web? How many? What's their estimation of the quality of those leads?

◆ If your site is primarily a soft marketing tool, is your site generating other inquiries that lead you to believe that you're offering information that's valuable to those who visit?

The information that you report to your management will help you (and them) to determine how to evaluate the site's value to your company. You want them to visit your Web site and view it with a critical eye. They're in a position to offer you some of the best ideas and help you can find. They understand your market, and, while they may not completely understand the Web market (and who does, really?), they may very well see areas that you've overlooked that could be displaced to your Web site.

They aren't likely to have an overabundance of time to concentrate their efforts on studying your Web site, so advise them of your schedules for regular updates. Let them know what areas of your business are being marketed and why. The more information you can give them to make it easy for them to help you, the better.

You would be well advised to keep them informed of the projects your staff is involved in bringing onto your Web site. Those projects may very well be coming from any number of departments. At some point, decisions about how to share the cost of your development staff's time may not be a small issue.

In addition, keeping them informed about the project will mean that they aren't completely surprised when you request additional staff or equipment for your Web site. Unless you have a magic formula for extending the numbers of hours in the day, your staff will eventually run out of hours that they can give to this project. Web developers tend to be a pretty devoted lot, but some few of them actually have real lives beyond the confines of your office. Honest.

Computers aren't yet capable of physically extending themselves, more's the pity, and somewhere along the way you're going to need bigger and faster. Most managers, at all levels, hate surprises—especially when those surprises involve spending money. Keep them informed as necessary to avoid those surprises. But keep yourself honest—always claiming you need more and better is no different from crying wolf. They'll stop listening.

The issue of sharing costs may also apply to specialized technologies that specific departments may need in the future. You may want your senior staff to be considering now what they deem to be the core corporate use for your site (and will thus support administratively) and what should be deemed too specialized to fund. While a corporate Web site may be a marketing tool across the board, it's highly likely that certain costs should be shared by the individual departments that require them, while general marketing efforts are used by all departments.

Certain issues may be very different from one business to another, but when it comes to budgets, every business today is interested in controlling costs. You want your management to know that you're planning your Web site with an eye to that very important consideration.

Learning What You Need to Know to Make It Work

Your first and best resource may be your Web development staff. If you treat them well, they'll be more than happy to teach you what they're learning—or better, distill what they know into nontechnical education for you. Most are more than happy to explain technical issues in ways that you can understand without being forced to go back to college for a degree in computer science (they aren't really teaching too much of this stuff yet, anyway, so don't waste your time). If you listen to your Web staff and are willing to learn, they'll probably give you as much time as they can. If you aren't willing to learn, but only want quick jargon-laden answers that you can pass along, they'll soon enough tire of you, and you'll be on your own (for the most part), to learn it by yourself.

Even the most patient and helpful staff can't be your only resource, though. You should take advantage of the help and advice that skilled technical managers in your business can offer. They know the ropes when it comes to handling technical projects. There's one caveat in that approach, however—technical managers are many times the early adopters. They love to dabble in the new leading-edge technologies and may encourage you to move forward with those technologies simply because they themselves are interested in them. They can be every bit as persuasive in their rhetoric about the latest, greatest gadget as your very best salesperson is about your product. Beware the technical manager touting technologies. She's quite likely more interested in features than functions.

Read the trade magazines and read as much as you can about the Web and its markets. It's growing and changing on a daily basis. Depending on anyone else to study and predict the trends (unless they're completely enmeshed in that study) is folly. And read on *both* sides of any issue whenever possible. You'll draw your own conclusions, based on your study. Your developers may draw entirely different conclusions, but at the very least it will make for some fascinating discussions.

▶ **NOTE** Precisely what issues you'll be pondering may be very different in six months, but at this very instant I could easily point you to six articles that tout network computers as the greatest thing since sliced bread and another six that might convince you they're worthless. ◀

Surf the Web, but don't simply surf. Read and study. Excellent information is out there. Your developers should send along to you any URLs they find that address issues of which you should be aware. They should also send along URLs of Web sites they find that employ particularly interesting or potentially useful ways to make a Web site work.

Sorry, you can't just set aside two days now to read and study and then never think about it again. The Web is too new and too quicksilver for that. You're going to have to keep learning and growing. It'll keep you young. Promise.

When All Else Fails, Vent!

Primal screams are acceptable among Web developers and managers. They're best done in the company of other Web developers and managers rather than in the middle of a meeting with those you will at some point deem completely clueless. You will be tempted to carry tokens for the Clue Bus around in your pocket to distribute freely.

Your best efforts at educating others will fail miserably in some cases, and some of those cases will have a direct bearing on your Web site. Your efforts and those of your staff to train people who could be of help will sometimes be not much more than wasted effort. Thankfully, there will be successes to balance the failures, so you'll all keep trying.

You'll get a call at 5:30 p.m. that documents are being delivered to your staff that have to be in place on your Web site at 8 a.m. the following day because Marsha, in Engineering, intends to use them in a presentation. She sent them to someone to revise specifically for the Web, who assured her they'd be ready by that time. By the time you see them, your developers will be gathering their coats and purses and preparing to go home, and those documents will not be at all what you want—or what you think Marsha probably expects—and what's more, they won't be coded. They really need to be rewritten, but there's hardly time for that. They have to be coded, at least. This may not seem to be much of a problem for you, but your staff is ready to leave, and they aren't going to be happy at all about this last-minute disruption, especially as it's probably not the first time. They may be ready to kill the messenger—you. Ouch. Expect primal scream, at the least. Ask them to put down any umbrellas they may be carrying before you make the announcement.

You'll understand their frustrations entirely, the day Ernst over in the Design department shows you the absolutely wonderful site he's designed just for the fun of it. As he shows it, he'll make nice-but-cutting remarks about your developers' talents. The fact that he has spent many hours on this masterpiece while the company paid his salary will mean nothing to him. He's an artist! (He certainly is.) You may have wondered what he was doing when you requested his help several weeks earlier because your staff was completely swamped—now you know.

It's perfectly acceptable to visualize wringing his scrawny little neck, but it's simply not politically correct to do it, and it's entirely too good for him. Smile nicely, compliment his talent, leave quickly. Try your very best not to scream before you are safely back on home ground.

There will be more than enough of these frustrations to make you consider the possibility of taking your staff and opening your own Web service business. Don't be hasty. It's not a bit better out *there*. Better the devil you know than the witch you don't.

Besides, the triumphs will at some point far outweigh the frustrations. People you didn't expect to be of any help will be. An idea that's floated nebulously around your staff will suddenly gel, and what seemed bogged down in endless mire will take flight instead. It's just like any other project, but the possibilities for this one—the creativity that can be applied to it—give it excitement that even several days of screams won't damage too severely. You did pack your sense of humor for this trip, right?

◀ **7** ▶

WEBMASTERY IS NOT
FOR THE FAINT OF HEART

YOU REALLY *CAN'T* PLEASE EVERY-
ONE, NO MATTER HOW YOU TRY.

◆

YOUR STAFF NEVER EXPECTED
GURU STATUS AND STILL DON'T
THINK THEY'VE MADE IT.

◆

OTHER EXPERTS ARE EMERGING
FROM THE WOODWORK DAILY. BE
READY FOR THEM!

◆

DO YOU UNDERSTAND YOUR
LIABILITIES? THEY'RE THERE—
WHETHER ANYONE IS PAYING
ATTENTION OR NOT.

Y ou've heard of slings and arrows, no doubt. Odds are you've been on the receiving end of at least one or the other in your time. Webmasters are frequent targets—not only from outside the organization but inside as well. Good Webmasters are diplomatic in the extreme because they have to be. The Web isn't a good business bet for sensitive souls.

If you have a good development staff, they'll make you look good at every opportunity. They have to—you may manage the Web site, but they're identified with it in the most personal of ways. Mail messages, requests, complaints, and, yes, kudos are directed to them. All of those, and the phone calls they field, may reflect on you, but it's all personal to them.

Once your site is officially on the Web, you and they will be amazed at the interest other staff members will take in it. Not all of that interest is going to be quite what you might have hoped, however. A Web site is quite visible, and being responsible for one puts you squarely in the line of fire for anyone who has reasons to take shots at you. The same fate applies to your development staff. That self-confidence that you considered in your choices for your staff will become more, not less, important. Web managers and developers who can't take the heat, or those who are too easily swayed by the opinions of others, will find this project rather difficult. What are you—and they—going to face in the way of challenges? Fasten your seat belt. The ride is likely to be exhilarating, if a bit bumpy in places.

The "experts" all agree that the Web is the future of communication—the software developers, the media, the politicos are all placing their bets on it and you're doing the same. Odds are that you've placed your bets on a technology that will work. Bill Gates is no dummy, after all. He's committed Microsoft to a future on the Web. You're not exactly going to be leaping off the deep end by following his lead—and the lead of many others who are also incorporating the Web into their greater schemes. Digital, Novell, Sun, SGI, and the crowd of other hardware and software developers have already placed their bets. You have little to lose by following their lead, and much more to gain. In fact, you may look very good because you took a chance on a technology that wasn't really very risky, but seemed that way in the short term.

WHAT TO EXPECT

Ha! Expect the completely unexpected. "Two-to-five-years" is still two to five years away! You and your developers are writing the rules, not playing by them at this point. Your most conservative approach isn't conservative by a long shot, when you consider that there are more than a few businesses and people that aren't on the Web yet. The rest are waiting for you to make some really serious blunders, so they'll know what not to do.

You may never have really thought of being a leading-edge kind of company, but—guess what?—here you are. And guess what else? You can make a couple of mistakes. You *will* make mistakes. As luck would have it, you have the luxury of a mistake or two (so long as they're not completely offensive to the Web community). In a year or less, you'll look back on some of the things that you've done, and cringe. Count on it.

Typically, new businesses on the Web offer sites that are far too graphically-intense to offer much functionality. Some go to extremes with content— offering pages that are too long and too confusing to be useful to their visitors. Most don't take the time to understand their Web audience and tailor the site for them. The smart ones learn fast—the graphics or cumbersome text elements are redesigned or compressed, the content redirected to this new market. Others are a little slow on the uptake. Remember that distributor of high-tech wiring components I mentioned in Chapter 3—the one that should (definitely) have hired a consultant? It's been close to three months since their Web site debuted. There's still not a single product specification, not one e-mail address (not even for their Webmaster), and not a single page has changed in that time.

If you're very lucky, no one else will have noticed your mistakes—or at least they won't have remarked on them. Don't expect that luxury from your co-horts in your company, though. They're watching—some very closely. Luck-ily, in most cases they know less than you do—in spite of the fact that some may they think they know more—assuming that you're doing your home-work (and we are making that assumption). You wouldn't have gotten this far if you weren't, after all.

They'll love you. They'll hate you. Your best will be just what they want or not good enough. Live with it.

Marvelous, Simply Marvelous!

Life on the Web is a crap shoot. There will be those who think you're perfect just because you've managed to accomplish a Web site. No offense, but ac-complishing a Web site isn't a big deal. More than a few people manage to do that every day. Two pages, a couple of graphics, a few links—nothing to it. Your 14-year-old niece could do it in her sleep—and may have. If it were hard, there simply wouldn't be as many personal pages as there are on the Web.

It's not easy, however, to bring a *business* onto the Web. That takes a bit more talent and quite a bit more finesse (if you do it well). It also takes a great deal of patience once it's accomplished, and it will take some time to train your employees and associates in using your Web site to its best advantage.

You and your staff will be praised to the skies by some. There are more than enough people who have absolutely no idea how a Web site is built that they will be dazzled by its mere existence. They'll be absolutely sincere in their praise. It's a technical miracle as far as they're concerned, and you're obvi-ously a genius.

Thank them. Then tell them the truth. It's not a miracle. While building your Web site may not have been the easiest project you've ever undertaken, it's not likely to have been the most difficult either. If you're thinking about allowing them to assume that all this Web stuff is actually magic, and you're the head magician, you'll be very sorry at some point.

TELL THEM HOW EASY IT IS…

In the first place, a Web site can expand exponentially, and with that expansion comes one huge amount of work. You want these people to know that it really isn't so terribly hard to produce pages for your Web site. You'll likely be considered rather self-effacing by some, and that's not entirely bad. Some will take you at your word and, with luck, begin their own tentative explorations into discovering how it's done. And, let's just be completely realistic—there will also be those who assume that if *you* can do it, *anyone* can. They'll set out to prove that they can do it, too, whether you encourage them or not. At least you'll be entitled to say, "I told you so," when they code their first pages and announce how easy it is.

Taking any other tack, you simply make extra work for yourself and your developers. You also leave yourself open for unnecessary criticism when, little by little, others learn the workings of the Web—and they will. They're going to be forced to do so, in many cases, to survive in a market that incorporates the technology of the Web. It's coming to an office, and it's not one that's just *near* theirs—it *is* theirs.

By the time your biggest technophobes are forced to learn it, the tools will be in place to make it easier for them, but it's unlikely that you'll be able to spare them entirely from some of the growing pains. Don't scare them inordinately with allusions to magic at this point. Assure them that it's far from magic, and that you and your development staff are more than eager to teach them how to do it themselves. Of course, most won't take you up on the offer, but it's a smart move on your part, nonetheless.

...It's Getting Even Easier!

This new technology will conspire to make you look pretty silly if you attempt to make it appear difficult now. The tools are getting better. Within six months of the time your Web site appears, they'll be much better. Anyone you managed to convince of the difficulty factor is going to decide you're either an idiot or a control freak, when they use some conversion tool that codes their 30-page document for the Web in two minutes or less.

Those of us who've been at Web development since before the media discovered it have watched the tools grow from a very few homegrown converters that might—on a very good day—convert a document accurately to HTML, to an amazing number that do the job pretty well most of the time. They're not completely reliable yet, but they're reliable enough that beginners can turn out a few basic pages fairly quickly.

We've been telling those beginners how easy it is. Now they're beginning to believe us, and we're not going to make noises about not having the tools when *we* started. Serious Web developers are evangelists for the technology—in spite of the fact that the majority of us still insist that the most reliable HTML code is developed manually in some primitive text editor. It's what we use because we trust ourselves more than the software. It can make us sound like a bunch of dinosaurs sometimes, but we don't really care. In many cases, those text editors do what we need done more quickly than the tools that have been developed to do our jobs.

▶ **NOTE**   This principle was brought home to me all too clearly in the recent past. Our graphics designer coded a new page, and, as we talked on the phone, I brought the page into several browsers. Netscape, Internet Explorer, Lynx—looked great. Browser #4, however (Mosaic), displayed nothing but the top three lines of the document. It looked very nice, but we decided that a white page with no links and nothing beyond our logo and one short phrase might be a bit more conceptual than we had intended. The afternoon was spent looking for the offending code.

We called in reinforcements before we went blind. She noticed a space in a comment. When it was removed, the next section magically appeared. Success! She mailed a note to the designer, who then looked at the fixed pages in Netscape—and, oh *&^*$, now they didn't work. The evening was spent looking for the offending code.

The middle-of-the-night revelation that finally fixed the pages? She had coded them in Microsoft Word, which automatically translated two hyphens followed by an angle bracket (-->) to a right arrow; the browser simply didn't know what to make of that particular code. In a text editor, the difference was barely noticeable to us. Because we operate separated by thousands of miles, neither she nor we had the slightest notion of the translations that were happening.

A text editor is an HTML coder's best friend when something doesn't work the way it should. ◀

You want to convince as many people as possible that they can do what your staff does. It's absolutely true that most of them will never learn how to install and administer a Web server, or understand all the work that goes into planning and maintaining a full Web site. They don't need to know about all of it unless they simply want to. Your development staff can take care of those details for them. Preparing and revising pages, however, is another ball game; you're going to need all the help you can get in that department.

Is All That Praise Sincere?

Besides those who are sincerely amazed by your achievement, there will of course be those who will tell you how completely wonderful the Web site is, even as they tell others how very lame it is. You already know these people, and expected nothing else, right? If you didn't, you are a serious candidate to retake Project Management 101.

This particular group refuses to criticize the Web site to you, but rather couches every criticism as a suggestion. It's similar to learning a new language; there should be phrase books that Web developers could use. For instance, "Maybe we should consider a different background that's easy to distinguish from the text?" (Translation: "These pages are impossible to read.") In spite of the transparency of their approach, some of their suggestions may very well be good ones. Your developers will learn to listen for the stray reasonable and functional idea, without regard to the source—at least they *should* learn that. Otherwise, these people will keep them entirely too busy making changes that are unlikely to be more than busy work, without adding any functionality to the site. Unless you have a large development staff that has hours to devote to nonessential tasks, they must learn to set realistic priorities rather than spending time on smoke and mirrors. You want them spending hours adding useful pages on your Web site, not recoding every page because a senior manager insists that each page needs a customized graphic (that someone in her department will produce, of course).

AWFUL, SIMPLY AWFUL!

Those who deplore your Web site—and some will—in very straightforward ways are likely to fall into several camps:

- Those who want it to do something it doesn't yet do—addressing their perceived needs
- The technology mavens, never satisfied until every page dances, sings, and generally sports every gadget that exists (and two more, if that's possible)
- The group that hates anything that's visible and works—at whatever level—simply because they're not in charge of it or they're afraid of it

It's all simple real-world business, translated to the Web. In each of their seemingly perverse (or at least obstinate) ways, these groups are good news for

240

your Web site. Some days you'll question that appraisal quite seriously, but at those times when you can take a minute for rational reflection (they happen once every three or four months), you'll see that each group offers a unique challenge and an opportunity to make your Web site better.

WHAT ABOUT US?!

The group that honestly wants the site to work—but for some purpose other than the ones for which it was designed—is likely to improve the site more quickly than the rest, because they see the need as a business application. You'll bring your site online with the express purpose of marketing a new line of audio speakers, but the people over in Technical Support want to have information on the site that will relieve them of some of the phone calls they take every day. That's wonderful—encourage them to do something about it. If your development staff is typical, they simply don't have time to develop every area of your business simultaneously.

The site will grow as more staff become involved in developing good content and design. It's quite literally a building process, with each piece contributing to the whole. It's a building process with a learning curve, though, and your developers can't be the only ones doing the learning.

To address the needs of those who want the site to work for them, encourage them to begin to think about those needs in relation to your Web audience. Remind them that the Web is a new medium, and urge them to think of ways to approach a Web audience that address that audience. It's very difficult for most people to look at their ideas from the other side of the table, but it's even more important to do that in this medium. You won't convince them overnight. Some will try, but most are so much more comfortable with traditional marketing (that one-to-many approach) that it will take time and patience—and maybe allowing them to make a few mistakes—to educate them.

Hang in there. You'll be so frustrated with it some days that the idea of simply pulling the plug on your Web server will be very attractive. (You'll get over it. Some tiny piece of proof that you've lifted the veil of ignorance even so much as $1/8$ inch will be more reward than you expected in your wildest dreams.)

You'll have days of total despair. You'll be sure that no one is listening to anything you say. The truth is that some people aren't listening and never will, which doesn't make the business of the Web one whit different from any other. Small triumphs are still triumphs. You'll come to appreciate them greatly.

IT SHOULD DO SOMETHING ELSE—*ANYTHING* ELSE

The technology mavens will make your life miserable—and more so because your developers would, in all likelihood, love nothing better than to concentrate on the technologies to the exclusion of other work. They can't, though, if your site is going to work for you; at least, they can't if you don't have people and money to devote to the technologies.

Your Webmaster, especially, might consider the idea of being allowed to add gadgets and gizmos to your Web site at will little less than nirvana. Webmasters come to love those times when they can sequester themselves with a Web server and play to their heart's content with the latest technology. It just doesn't happen often in the real world. A good Webmaster will content himself with the occasional dip into the technological pool, and finally decide that animating your logo is completely cool but just a bit lacking in the functionality department. Oh well. He'll have had fun trying it.

The technology mavens, though, really want your Web site to have cool pages. You and your staff need perspective, even if this group doesn't have any. Is your corporate culture such that you can carry off "cool" with aplomb? It's not easy, and it has to be done very well. Advertising and design agencies, artists, the developers of the technologies, and certain other businesses may manage it well. Most won't—simply because, without a thorough

242

understanding of the technology and the audience of the Web, most of the technologies can't be employed practically without being obviously used only for the sake of using them. A book publisher could very well use audio capabilities on its Web site to demonstrate its audio books, but book covers that dance across the pages, while no doubt interesting, would add little to the functionality of the site.

You'll never convince the mavens of that, though. Instead, encourage them to offer practical applications for the technologies. You may be overlooking ways to use them that will be perfect for some portion of your Web site. This group can be very creative. They're not always very practical, but you'll have some fun with their ideas—and your Webmaster may get lucky and have a good reason to play.

LET *ME* TELL YOU HOW TO DO IT

The group that would like to control your Web site, now that it's working, is a wonderful challenge—and will drive you to both homicidal and suicidal thoughts from time to time. For the most part, they won't really be willing to take the time to learn what they would have to learn to manage your Web site (though they will assume they can, without much effort). However, they'll tell you, at length, what you should do to make it perfect. They'll generally base their opinions on a few cursory looks at your competitors' sites—that's good and can be helpful—and some of the most popular sites on the Web. That's good too, but if you don't happen to be in the Web service business—producing browsers, servers, Web sites, reviews, indexes—those may not be quite the models you would choose to emulate.

Your mission is still education, and it's not likely to be easy. They'll learn just enough of the jargon to impress only those who have no idea what they're talking about anyway. There are only so many ways you can explain the difference between a Web server and a Web browser—be creative. Be patient.

THE FEARFUL

There are two distinct subsets to this "We hate your Web site" group, but each wants, in its own strange way, to be part of something that looks like it might have an exciting future. The first group is actually afraid of it, in spite of the fact that they can see it does have a future. They're afraid not just of Web technology but of any technology that even hints at either replacing or changing their jobs. Status quo is a good thing—your Web site therefore is not. If they can convince enough people that your Web site is bad, maybe it will go away, right? That's hardly a realistic attitude, but it's the best they can do for now.

They'll ask some of the funniest questions you will ever hope to hear—at first:

- After conscientiously announcing to all and sundry that your Internet connection will be down for some type of maintenance or upgrade on Sunday from 9 a.m. to noon, on Monday morning you'll hear, "The Web wasn't working yesterday." Well, the *Web* was, but your piece of it wasn't, and they won't have understood that their connection to it is accomplished through the Internet.

- "Can you activate my TCP/IP account?" Well, no. TCP/IP is a protocol that must run on their computer in order to use the Web, not some computer "out there in the great ether" that they can log into.

- "Why can't I search our site? That button on the browser says 'Search,' but I can't search our pages with it." That button is an icon on the browser that searches the Web, not your site specifically.

You'll tire mightily of trying to find new ways to answer those same questions after a year or so. Some of them will be so intimidated by the technology, or by your knowledge of it, or even by their own superiors who fear the technology, that they won't even bother to ask questions. There's little you can do except be available to answer their questions repeatedly (on the rare occasions when they summon the courage to tender the questions).

Webmastery Is Not for the Faint of Heart

Web technology may make their jobs easier at some point, or at least make them different. Forcing them into it prematurely will only complicate your life and theirs. Educate when you can and bite your tongue when you can't.

AND THE FEARLESS

The other subset of this group is the instant experts. How they became "expert" may forever remain a mystery to you. Perhaps they once coded a Web page—or knew someone who did. (It's a new medium, after all. It can't take much to be an expert at it.) These folks don't need to ask questions because they already know it all.

They're ever so helpful. They'll be more than willing to tell you and your developers exactly what's wrong with your Web site. The graphics aren't good enough; the content is terrible; there's not one single instance of a dancing anything anywhere! They won't do anything about it, of course. That's *your* job, not theirs. You've got to love this bunch—or shoot them. Your choice. If you decide to keep them around—or if you have a company policy that forbids you to carry weapons—you're going to need established guidelines for who vents where and to whom. Scarlet faces (from anger) and lips that have been chewed raw (from refraining to give the retort that was so close to the surface) are occupational hazards for Web developers who deal with these people.

Believe it or not, they actually do have something to offer. They'll certainly keep you posted about what your competition is doing on the Web. Occasionally they'll have a valuable idea. And you can always count on them to find any link on your site that doesn't work, no matter how obscure it may be.

If they realized they were doing things that were actually helpful, they'd stop, so it's necessary to thank them in ways that acknowledge their expert status—something similar to, "Only someone with your experience would have found that so easily!" (Translation: "Wow! You really must have some time on your hands to have noticed that the word *inturgescence* is misspelled on a page buried that deep!")

A few of this group will mellow over time. It's grudging when it happens but still a triumph of your patience—and your company policy regarding weapons.

Your Web Audience—Remember Them?

Unlike the people who work in your business, your Web audience will take a look and you'll get their attention—or not. If you've offered them quality information presented well and uniquely, they'll bookmark your site and they'll tell their friends. They may not love you, but they're unlikely to hate you. They may be indifferent. Indifference is actually the worst that can happen. If they hated your site, they'd still tell their friends, and some of those friends might appreciate your site.

If you've done the very best you can at addressing the needs of your audience, your site will work. It may not be as wildly successful in the beginning as you might like. You had to build your business in the real world, and you're going to have to build your business on the Web. It's truly not magic and there are no magic formulas. If you offer a product or service on the Web that fills a need, you will not lack for visitors. If you deliver what you promise, your Web business will grow.

There are no easy answers for businesses on the Web. There are those who would like to sell you the service of listing your pages on the various index sites and assure you of hits on your site. They can probably deliver precisely that, for what those hits are worth, and for instant gratification based on the numbers. It's not terribly difficult to deliver numbers on the Web—any more than it's difficult to deliver numbers in the real world.

▶ **NOTE**   Because very few people in our company spend any time looking at the source code in our pages, it would be a simple matter for me to increase the number of visitors to specific areas of our site. Simply by inserting a `meta` tag (it's a real, bona fide HTML tag that goes in the `<head>` information) and associating that tag with the word *sex*, I'd increase the number of hits. Search engines use the words found in the `meta` tag to determine key words when people are searching their indexes. The likelihood that the resultant hits on our site would be of a quality that our senior management would approve would be slim to none, and Slim's out of town. If you don't understand the "tricks," however, *you* can be tricked. Numbers just don't always mean very much. ◀

The Web is so new and such a mystery to so many people in business that they don't see the obvious problems they would instantly recognize otherwise. A service provider or a company might offer to list your Web site on a certain number of the index sites for a fee. Of course, they're probably not going to do much in the way of customizing your listing, so you might end up in questionable company on that index. That's not their problem. They promised to register your site and that's what they did. While some providers who offer this type of service *do* customize the listings for you, it's likely to be a rather expensive process.

Your most reliable registrations are those you do yourself. In addition, if you make your URL known, and you have return links from other companies that have been on the Web for a while, your site will be indexed without any effort on your part. The index sites send out what are known as *robots*. They traverse and index any pages they find. A look at your server logs can generally tell you whether your site has been indexed. One of the first things the robot will look for is a file on your site called **robots.txt**. People who develop sites they don't want indexed include that information in a file named **robots.txt**, and the search engines generally respect the wishes of the site owner.

Once your site is registered, your traffic will increase. Still, you're responsible for offering your visitors full value for the time they invest in learning about your business. Without that value added, you can hardly expect rave reviews. That necessarily means that you must consider your Web site from the perspective of your audience.

SHOULD WE ADVERTISE?

Of course you should advertise to the extent of adding your URL to business cards, letterhead, your e-mail signature line, and your traditional media pieces. The usefulness of buying advertising space on one of the major Web sites that sell advertising banners is subject to debate (and any number of magazine articles). You've probably seen them—those generally rectangular mysterious boxes (about 4 inches by 1 inch) that have cryptic messages like "Lost? Click here" or "Win a Pentium." If you've got a few thousand dollars and no place to spend it, advertising that way might be reasonable. Certainly the larger sites—Yahoo, Netscape, the Wall Street Journal, c|net, and dozens of others—are visited by large numbers of people daily. In some cases, they can offer you a targeted audience. Your ad for your jewelry stores might appear on the results page of a search for gifts or jewelry, for instance.

Banner advertising on Web sites is becoming big business. A great deal of money is invested in just such advertising. But when was the last time you sat and really paid attention to an ad on TV or fully read a newspaper ad? You paid attention to those ads because you had an interest in the product or service offered. Advertising on other Web sites may increase the number of visitors to your site, but those visitors won't stay or come back if you don't offer them something they need or want.

You might entice visitors with a mysterious banner ad alluding to fame and riches, but if your Web site is nothing more than a self-aggrandizing advertisement at the end of that link, you'll have wasted your money and your visitors' time. They're going to be very annoyed if the banner ad that originally captured their attention misled them.

▶ **NOTE**   Personally, I refuse to explore advertising banner links. The companies that generally buy them are companies I could find quite easily on my own if I were interested. In addition, it's very much like being forced to page through four pages of advertising before getting to the table of contents in a magazine—but a great deal more annoying. The Web banner ads use screen real estate and take time to load. At least with a magazine I can quickly skim past the ads. ◀

Your much better bet would be to build a Web site that's so good it attracts hundreds of thousands of visitors each day. Then you can sell ads on *your* pages. Yes, you'll have to work very hard to achieve that—offering fantastic content or using the new technologies to their fullest advantage. The simple fact is that word travels very fast in the electronic community. The URL for a good Web site that one person finds and shares with six people can easily be shared with hundreds of people in a matter of minutes. Word of mouth— or, in this case, word of e-mail—is the best advertising you can get.

AT SOME POINT YOU'LL KNOW MORE THAN MOST—ENJOY IT

You and your development staff will be dealing with your own associates as well as dealing with the inquiries your site generates. You'll be trying to concentrate on making your Web site work and then work better. In the meantime, you'll be educating your employees and senior management about the Web and specifically about using your site in ways that will make it more valuable.

None of those are small tasks. Depending on the size of your development staff, you may be able to assign specific duties to specific people. If your staff is small, each of them—and you—will have to respond to both the Web public and your business compatriots in each of your own areas of expertise. Each of you must understand your own limitations and defer to the others in those areas.

You Can't Stop Teaching

A small, specialized Web site might easily be handled by one person—if that person is talented with words and graphics and has the necessary technical capabilities or support. Large sites, and especially those that are designed to be serious marketing tools, need more people who can contribute to that effort. Those people don't need to be strictly devoted to working on the Web site. They may be involved in very peripheral ways—from offering ideas to writing content to preparing graphics. They require education in order to do those things. Your development staff, whether 2 people or 200, must continue to study and learn while teaching others.

You Are the Experts

Your staff will find that teaching is the very best way to reinforce their own studies. A question they're asked will require more research on their part. They'll learn in the process. The Web is vast, and though they're never likely to learn everything there is to know about it, they'll acquire a level of knowledge that's far beyond that of most people.

If you've chosen well, they'll gladly share what they learn. They may grouse and complain about the amount of time required to explain things to those who, in many cases, have even less than a basic understanding of the Web. That does take a great deal of time, in fact, and a considerable amount of patience. They may not admit that they're actually having fun in the process. Work isn't generally considered fun, and they do want you to continue to pay them.

Assuming that you've assembled a Web development staff that's intent on building a Web site that benefits your company, and that they're willing and able to teach others, you and they should enjoy this project immensely. You'll become the acknowledged experts, in your own company at least, whether or not you intend for that to happen.

Consulting, Perhaps?

In the process of learning and teaching, you may even find that you've become skilled enough to offer your expertise to people or companies outside of your own. If you have time to consult in the field, you may even produce some unexpected returns on the investment your business has made in your Web site. If your skills are in demand, your company can market your services and perhaps recoup some of the investment they've made in your Web site. That won't happen overnight, and it certainly won't happen unless you and your staff continue to hone your own skills.

There are many Web service providers who know the Web. There are very few Web service providers who truly understand the needs of business. You and your staff may very well be a resource that others need. You're not likely to have time to fill that need until you manage to train enough people within your own business, however, so get busy with that piece of this project as quickly as you can.

Stop Laughing!

You absolutely can expect tremendous frustration as a direct result of taking on a Web site project. Even the frustrations are fantastic fodder for inside jokes, after the fact. Some require great levels of self-control. Those who refuse to listen long enough to understand some technical aspect of the site will explain it in a meeting as though they are thoroughly conversant with it, and mangle it beyond all recognition. Remaining quietly in your chair rather than hooting with laughter is the prudent though much more difficult choice.

▶ **TIP** Invest in a pager and carry it at all times. On those occasions when hysterical laughter or homicidal inclinations are overwhelming, you can make quick apologies and dodge for the nearest exit because "There's a technical problem that must be addressed." Have a well-rehearsed list of plausible excuses. Even if you only need them once or twice, you're going to need them. Rolling on the floor laughing isn't generally considered professional behavior, after all. ◀

MINGLE—IT'S FUN AND INTERESTING

In spite of the frustrations, you'll still have fun with the project. It's work, but it's a field that requires a level of technical ability combined with artistic and social skills that draws a wide range of very interesting people. Attend meetings with other Web developers, and you'll find yourself among people who combine awesome technical skills with literacy in any number of areas.

They're curious, they're bright, and they can be very, very funny. They're simply not what you might expect in a group of people considered computer nerds. Leave behind any preconceived notions about serious computer types. Web developers come in all ages, races, genders, and levels of experience. If you don't enjoy a meeting with these people, you don't have the sense of humor necessary for Web site development.

WHEN TO REFUSE PAGES

The Web is serious business, but it's a fun place to work. Any number of people will see no reason for you and your staff to be the only ones having fun. They'll begin to develop pages for themselves that they'll want displayed on your site. That's exactly what you've been encouraging them to do, so this is very good news.

Well, maybe.

If you've really planned for this eventuality, it may *be* very good news. If you haven't taken the time to adequately educate people about the Web, it may *not* be. It's no secret that every department or division manager within your company is quite knowledgeable about his or her group. That doesn't make him or her knowledgeable about the Web and its audience. Nor does it make him or her an expert at design or document preparation for the Web.

The time will come when you or someone on your development staff will be forced to, at best, return pages to be reworked or, at worst, refuse to use them. If your company allows multiple Web servers, you may even find it necessary at some point to demand that pages be removed from your site.

They Wrote It; They Designed It; It Isn't Up to Your Standards. Now What?

Unless you can find something seriously wrong with it, you may be stuck with it. Some battles aren't worth waging. That's one reason you should create specific guidelines for your overall site early in its development. If you haven't developed those guidelines, you can hardly expect people within your company to read your mind. They may very well think that *your* attempt at design is absolutely terrible, and see no reason to incorporate any piece of it into their own work. You need, at a minimum, a policy that addresses your core site. You may also need a policy that addresses peripheral pages that will be a reflection on your company simply because they carry your domain name.

What Guidelines?

Consider your basic design first. Are there pieces of that design that you want carried through all the pages of your core site? Navigational devices, for example, are especially important (as described in the next section). If they're not consistent throughout your site, your visitors will become confused and lost. That's very frustrating and certainly not what you want.

Navigational Consistency (Where Am I?)

A Web site is very much like the physical reality of a university campus. People who live and work there know which departments are housed in which building and how to go from one place to another without endless backtracking. Newcomers may be completely at a loss. They need signs and maps to get them to their destinations.

Your navigational tools are the signs and maps your visitors will use to find their way around your site. That may be something as fundamental and simple as a hypertext link. As you've done your own looking around on the Web, you probably noticed that links you hadn't yet tried were blue and those you had already followed were purple. Whoever chose those particular colors as the default choice for browsers probably wasn't a designer, but did have a fundamental grasp of the importance of visual clues for Web site navigation.

Remember the first time you visited a site where the designer had changed the default colors for those links? You were probably a bit disoriented by that change, at least temporarily. You had to stop and consider which color indicated that you had seen the page and which meant you hadn't. If people throughout your company are allowed to change those link colors at will, your site will be one very confusing place.

That doesn't mean that you absolutely must use the default colors on your site, but it does mean that, at a minimum, the link colors should be consistent throughout. On our site, we chose to retain the browser default colors, not because they work with our design—they don't—but because we decided that we didn't want our visitors to be bothered by that most simple piece of navigation.

Red is stop and green is go in stoplights everywhere. They may not be the colors that city designers would choose for their streets, but it makes for fewer accidents and less frustration in navigation.

Your navigational tools are essential to the overall usefulness of your site. Whether those are beautifully designed graphics that indicate your present location and other areas for exploration, or just simple links, they need consistency.

GRAPHICAL CONSISTENCY

There may be other pieces of your site's design that you want to be consistent throughout. Certain graphics may change regularly and require changing at all levels. In order to make those changes without resorting to recoding (or at least checking the coding) on every single page, you may want to require that those graphics always be addressed in one central location. As long as the name of the graphic doesn't change, the graphic itself can change many times—and be changed at the same time on every page it affects.

Granted, it may look a little funny to those who view your HTML source code and find a reference to **flowers.gif** when they're sure they saw a picture of a polar bear in that location, but people who view source code are learning the ropes, or would like to employ some trick you've incorporated—or they've found an error on your site and want to tell you how to correct it. None of them are going to care much what the graphic is named.

▶ **NOTE**   You can view the *source code* (the HTML commands that create your pages) within your browser—generally by choosing a menu item like View Source or View Document Source. ◀

They Wouldn't Really Change Our Logo, Would They?

Something you consider as basic as your company logo can be made into
something you never wanted on your Web pages, if you don't specify in your
guidelines that tampering with the logo is not permitted. Your logo may be
blue-on-gold. Count on there being people in your company who really
think it would look much better on their pages as green-on-gold or pink-on-
purple. If you don't issue the guidelines, you're likely to find out just how
creative people can be.

A 3MB Graphic File Is Just a Tad Large

What's the largest graphic you'll allow? Can it be as large as they like—in
spite of the fact that anyone who views it is going to have to scroll up, down,
and sideways to see it, and once she scrolls beyond the first screen she's unlikely to remember how this piece fits with the rest? Are you designing for
17-inch monitors or the far more common 14-inch ones?

And that only addresses the physical size of the graphic. Do you perhaps want
to limit the size of the file itself? It's actually self-defeating to attempt to serve
a page that will take so long to load that only diehards will wait for it. You
may decide that guidelines in that case are unnecessary. They may not be necessary, but at least give people an idea about the time required to load those
large files. They may be completely unaware of the ramifications. If you put it
in writing, no one can be personally offended or feel that you have issued
guidelines simply to thwart them.

It Says *What*??

What about content? Who has the ultimate authority over it? Should that be
centralized or distributed? Your corporate culture is likely to dictate in this
instance. The authority may be one person or department or it may be each
manager or project director. Who has the authority isn't as important as the
fact that *someone* must have authority—and everyone must know who that is.

Webmastery Is Not for the Faint of Heart

Your Web development staff may be the central authority in the end, but it would be wiser to require that pages that are delivered to them already have been approved by managers in the affected departments.

Your content guidelines should cover the quality you expect from your Web pages (probably a reference to your Policy and Procedures Manual that covers authorship). You might also want your Web pages to be gender-neutral. The guidelines should definitely require that the pages be proofread for grammar and spelling.

If the authority for issues of content is decentralized, ideally your development staff shouldn't have to be concerned with it, but we're talking about a new medium that few people understand. At the least, your staff should help others within your business understand how best to direct their pages to their Web audience. There may very well be times when you will be more than a little surprised at what some people deem proper to serve to the world.

They may not get it right the first time, or the third, or even the sixth. That doesn't mean that their efforts are completely unacceptable for your Web site. Each of us who works in this business is learning from the rest. Unless the content is patently unacceptable, allow them to make their own mistakes.

The style may not please you, and the pages may be essentially useless for your site. In that case, they're likely to be ignored by visitors for the most part. It may not be the best possible way to deal with content issues, but it will lower frustration levels among your development staff. The excuse that they're only following orders will be little more than a salve to them when others in the Web business point out glaring problems—and they will—but it's a salve, nonetheless.

DESIGNING FOR THE SUPERCYBERBROWSER 5000

What about technical issues? What standard will you accept for your pages? Is it perfectly acceptable to design them for one specific browser, or should you insist that pages be designed to be accessible and acceptable on a wide range of browsers? Your guidelines should be reasonably specific in this regard. If you sincerely believe it's acceptable to code pages without regard to those people who might view them from a text browser or older versions of some graphical browsers, it will certainly make the job of coding less complicated. But it also may seriously affect the usefulness of your Web site for a significant number of people.

But Our Server *Can't* Serve Your Cool Gizmo!

Will you accept pages that require specific technologies without regard to your present capabilities? If someone designs pages that require you to add those technologies, who's going to be responsible for the cost? And if that means that your Web server, which runs on XYZ platform, can't adequately handle the load or doesn't support the technology, are you willing to add another server on another platform? It's decidedly better to have established policies about such issues than to be caught short at some point.

It Did *What*??

If one of your departments decides to outsource specialized coding, are you willing to serve it? Suppose, for instance, that they have applets programmed in Java or Visual Basic or any one of the other languages being used to make pages more animated. Do you have someone on your staff who can verify that the code does precisely what it's supposed to do and nothing more? If code that accomplishes some malicious purpose is generated from your Web site, there's no way for your Web audience to know that no one on your staff wrote it. Being told that you have managed to transmit a virus that wiped out hard drives across the Web would not be what you'd need to hear—at all! Your guidelines should reflect your concern with this issue and perhaps suggest specific companies with which you are familiar that are acceptable for the work that will be needed.

Who Do They Call for Help?

What's the chain of command? How do people in the various departments go about scheduling new pages to be added to your Web site? Your developers can hardly be expected to simply drop any other work they may be doing in order to add pages overnight with no prior notice. Those pages will have to be tested, after all, if only to ensure their link integrity—and without regard to design and content issues. How much advance notice do your developers realistically need to meet a specific deadline for making those pages available on your Web site? Who should be notified of the deadline and who needs to be involved in the content and design issues in the meantime?

For example, your guidelines might specify that your Webmaster be notified of pending projects at least a week before they're expected to be put into production on your site. It's a simple matter to add a page or two, but ten or more pages can take much more testing. As with any other project, the longer the lead time, the better, but you and your development staff will have to weigh the amount of regularly scheduled work and determine how much time is necessary, given your own unique constraints. If your Webmaster is budgeted to work only two hours a day on the project, it may be completely impossible to test all the new pages in a week.

Document It

Decide on specific elements that are important to you and craft guidelines around those elements. But be careful. If you're too restrictive, you'll take the fun out of it for everyone. If you're not restrictive enough, your site will suffer for it. Try to issue general guidelines that allow people to experiment to some extent with their own creativity. You may find some very talented people in unexpected places if you do.

There are so many things that your Web developers will discover over the course of time that it will be difficult for you to keep your guidelines up to date. It's difficult for you to remember to keep one another informed, let alone write it down for everyone else, but your guidelines are critically important. They can make your life much easier in the long run.

Dodge Where Possible

Until you have policy guidelines in place, it will be very difficult to refuse to serve pages on your Web site unless they're simply unacceptable to the manager responsible for the department they address. If that manager finds them acceptable—whether or not you or your developers agree—you may very well be in no position to refuse to serve them.

If you're lucky, you may find technical issues that need to be addressed that can buy you some small amount of time, which may be enough for you to do some quick education. It's going to need to be done very diplomatically, however.

Webmasters must think on their feet—sometimes at a dead run. More than a few have been known to plead a lack of server space, rather than include pages that are seriously out of sync with the rest of the site. Those pleas tend to be couched in terms similar to this: "I'd love to add your pages. Which other pages do you think we should delete, in order to do that?" Combine that with placing the responsibility for persuading someone else to remove their pages squarely in the lap of the requester. It's an effective though generally temporary dodge, assuming that the requester has no knowledge of the size of your server, or your server is really very small.

Praise Pays—Use It!

Unfortunately, it's quite likely that no small amount of effort has been invested in the finished product that you have been asked to serve. It may have involved quite a lot of effort on the part of several people. Apply praise. In spite of the fact that the pages may not be what you would choose, you have people who have taken the initiative to learn new skills and apply them in this new medium. That alone is worthy of your sincere compliments. In all probability, they will be more than happy for your help and guidance in the future if you acknowledge their efforts on this project. If you sneer or are condescending, you can expect very little in the way of future cooperation (hardly a new concept).

It Works; It Fits Your Design; It Links to sex.toys.com

Oh, dear. If your business doesn't happen to be one that manufactures, sells, or distributes sexual material or devices, this may not be the best choice to provide a link from your site. Common sense dictates that any site you link to is essentially an endorsement by your business of that site. In fact, it may simply be that whoever was responsible for preparing the pages likes that site. That doesn't mean they're responsible for whatever ramifications may occur if you allow that link.

Your company is responsible for primary links to other sites. Not only are you responsible for them simply from a common sense, basic business aspect, but legally. You could incur legal liabilities based on those links.

▶ **CAUTION** If you have any doubts about primary links from your site, consult a lawyer who's conversant with the Web. We took our initial approach to primary links from our site based simply on common sense, and the desire to be viewed seriously. Your mileage may vary, as they say on the Internet. ◀

Don't Forget About the CDA

When the Telecommunications Bill and its attached Communications Decency Amendment (CDA) were signed into law in February, 1995, the stakes for individuals and companies on the Web were raised. The CDA would essentially make it illegal to transmit to minors any "indecent" material or "any comment, request, suggestion, proposal, image, or other communication that, in context, depicts or describes, in terms patently offensive as measured by contemporary community standards, sexual or excretory activities or organs." A lawsuit challenging the constitutionality of the CDA was filed immediately and was upheld in June, 1996. It's likely to be taken to the U.S. Supreme Court, however, before the issue is settled.

The CDA, on its face, would appear to be reasonable. Certainly your company has no intention of transmitting indecent material to minors. The problem is that the word "indecent" has never been legally defined. You may develop your own terrifying scenarios for who might find what link on your site "indecent." If your company links to valuable information about AIDS research and education, is that indecent? It may be considered so by some people, if it's available to minors.

The CDA could be a serious quagmire for businesses on the Web if it's allowed to stand as written. By the time you read this, the U.S. Supreme Court may have ruled that it's unconstitutional. If it doesn't, you may want to give some serious consideration to adding a lawyer to your Web development staff. We live in litigious times; businesses would be prime targets for lawsuits on this issue, since we all know they're rich and might be willing to settle quietly, right?

IS THE LINK A GOOD ONE?

Since the first stage has been passed and the CDA deemed unconstitutional by one court, you may have no need to concern yourself with it. But that doesn't mean that you won't be legally liable for primary links in all cases. (As I said, when in doubt, talk to a lawyer.)

Beyond any issues of legality, you surely want the sites to which your company links to be good quality sites. After all, a link is an endorsement, in a way. You give credence to the information contained on the page to which you link, simply by pointing to the information.

262

Encourage people within your business to take time to investigate the information contained in any page to which you provide a link. Is the content valuable, and does it add depth to the information you provide? Your developers should also check those primary links to verify their suitability. Any questions that arise should be carefully considered.

Your developers should also check those links regularly. A Web page can change quickly. What was entirely suitable one week may be completely unsuitable the next. It might not even be there, in fact. It's not uncommon for a page to be removed entirely, or for a business to change providers and have a completely different domain name.

Blatantly offensive links can easily be removed. It's doubtful that anyone in your company is going to be upset if you point out the problems and possible pitfalls. The quality issues may be more difficult to address, and some are likely to be nothing more than judgment calls on your part. Unless you're completely arbitrary in your judgments, serious problems or disputes are unlikely to arise. Your basic approach to primary links should, of course, be included in your guidelines.

OTHER WEB SERVERS? ON OUR SITE? REALLY?

All of the foregoing assumes that you have a centralized mechanism for adding Web pages on your site. That's fine, as far as it goes, but it doesn't go quite far enough. (You thought this was going to be easy??) It's entirely possible that there are Web servers operating on your site of which you have no clue. That new kid in the mailroom may very well be running his own Web server, and heaven only knows what he's serving to the world at large, using your company's domain name. You're responsible for his pages, too, whether or not he knows it, and whether or not you're aware of his Web server.

You Need Security

If your company has a large computing network, you probably are located behind a firewall, so it's entirely possible for you to block incoming requests for Web pages to machines other than those that are specifically designated to serve your "official" site. If you don't have the capacity to segment your incoming traffic that way, you should consider it. Security of the data on your network can be seriously jeopardized if incoming Internet traffic isn't monitored.

Talk with your network administrators and determine your capabilities and your liabilities. Determine what you need and what you can do. If your computers have Internet access and you haven't considered protecting the data on that network, you are remiss. It may be unlikely that someone is interested in stealing the information, but that doesn't mean someone won't—or that someone can't do enough damage to it to make your life very difficult for a while. How long would it take for you to completely rebuild your employee databases? It's not worth taking the risk. And that applies whether or not you have a Web server.

Track Down Those Servers

You can install software packages on your computer that detect other Web servers on your network of which you may be unaware. Because most people are excited about serving their pages on the Web, even those that are essentially unauthorized, they tend to register them with the index sites. Your developers should at least be doing regular searches on those sites for occurrences of your domain name. They may be surprised at the results.

▶ **NOTE**   In one instance, a regular search turned up some personal Web pages on our site that were far from what most of us would consider professional. The offending party was asked to remove the pages and agreed to do so. He did, however, leave a link to his new site on a machine bearing our domain name. Because the pages weren't overly offensive, only unprofessional and decidedly juvenile, we decided not to pursue the matter. The link was later removed without our intervention.

We did get quite a few good laughs over his rant to the world that he'd been asked to remove them and why he determined that we were perfectly within our rights to do so. One paragraph would have been more than sufficient. He went on at great length. ◀

What's on This Web Server, Anyway?

You may find an unknown Web server on your site that's *password-protected*—you can't see the information on the server without a user name and password. That may be fine, if the server is being used to share project information that needs added security. Are you sure that's the case?

You're responsible for any pages bearing your domain name. Who has the authority to determine exactly what's being offered from that site? Someone needs to be able to verify that the pages that are served from your site—from any Web server—are professional and in keeping with the standards of quality your company maintains.

But We *Want* Them to Have Their Own Pages!

Many companies allow their employees to have personal pages on their company Web server. They put a personal face on the business, and that can be a very good thing. Your employees may make some very good friends for your business if you allow them to tell the world about themselves and their interests. It's simply in your best interests to know what's contained in those pages.

If you have a central repository that's made available for personal pages, they can be subjected to the same standards as other pages. Consider having a separate set of guidelines that govern them, allowing for more creativity but still reflecting your essential goals for your site.

If fact, nothing is more likely to replace the previous yawns or objections about your Web site quite so quickly as publishing a picture or information about those who yawn or object. The Web site that was too boring for words or simply unacceptable as a whole suddenly takes on much more interest for them. Human nature—isn't it great?

It Only *Sounds* Hard

A Web site is no small project, even when it's a small project. There are simply so many things to consider and so many things you need to do to make even a small site a working site. Educating your own employees and others in your business is far from the smallest piece. Your guidelines can help you do that, and they can prevent frustrations—not only for you and your development staff, but for everyone else who has a need to use your site.

Remember that any guidelines you create in the early stages of developing your site will change—almost as fast as the Web itself. Things that couldn't have been done in the beginning may be done—may even be the preferred method—in six months or a year. Try to keep the guidelines current. That in itself is a major challenge. Web developers become so busy working on pages for other people that they have little time to work on their own. Making time to do it is difficult, but it's important.

You've done almost all of these same things with virtually every project you've ever undertaken. Those projects may not have been as technical but the fact of the matter is that, though the technical aspects of this one can make your life a bit more interesting, the actual complications you're most likely to encounter are ones that are going to have absolutely nothing to do with the technical aspects. They'll be people problems and scheduling problems and not enough help—or too much help—problems, for the most part. Personalities won't go missing from this project just like they don't disappear from others. Politics, the same. But they're very little different here than they would be anywhere else.

Webmastery Is Not for the Faint of Heart

Technical issues are quite likely to be the very least of your worries. Oh, they'll crop up. Some piece of software won't work with some other piece of software, just when both of them are most needed. The server will take a nose dive at 3 a.m. and your Webmaster will be one very unhappy camper because she had to drive into the office at that positively ungodly hour— through the snow, no less—because it didn't come back online like it should have, and one of the busiest times on your Web site is 5 a.m. to 6 a.m.

It happens. You'll get used to it and so will your development staff. None of you are going to like it, but it's life on the Web. That won't make it less fun and it won't make it any less a job that you all enjoy. It'll make for some great war stories when you meet with other developers. There are a certain number of dues to be paid in any job. Your Web site is no different. It's still a job. It makes demands. It takes some stamina to work in a medium that's new. It's not the kind of stamina that only a 20-year-old can have. It's the kind of stamina that any person who loves a challenge has and loves to put to use. It might as well be you as that other guy, right?

◀ **8** ▶

WE'RE ON THE WEB!
CAN WE QUIT NOW?

WHAT DO YOU NEED TO DO
NOW AND FOR THE FUTURE?

◆

THE NEXT NEW TECHNOLOGY IS
ONLY MINUTES AWAY; ARE YOU
READY FOR IT?

◆

YOUR FUTURE IS BEING WRITTEN
ON THE WEB—
IF YOU WANT IT TO BE

◆

WEB DEVELOPERS AREN'T
MUSHROOMS; TREAT THEM WELL

Web Site Management Excellence

Just a wee bit tired of looking at your own Web site, are you? Well, maybe not—yet. Your development staff is no doubt sick to death of touching those pages to make minor revisions in coding and content, however. They probably didn't stop until hours after that arbitrary deadline was past that you set for putting your Web site into production. They're still not convinced that it's working, in spite of the fact that it's obviously working.

They'll suffer from a serious drop in adrenaline levels for the first few days—major crash. Odds are they've been running full speed ahead for a couple of weeks at least. Not only have they been fighting a deadline, they're probably still living in terror that someone, anyone, will rip the whole thing to shreds—find that one fatal flaw that will make this carefully crafted house of cards collapse. That's not likely to happen, because you've all tested and retested and tested again, but they're still waiting for it just the same.

They'll suddenly find themselves with nothing to do, relatively speaking. It's just like every other project deadline. When you've been functioning at high speed on little more than adrenaline for any length of time, adjusting back to something even vaguely resembling normal is tough.

You realize, of course, that none of you can really stop now. You may get a breather, but that's the extent of it. The Web as a whole hasn't stopped growing and changing, and your Web site can't either. You'll find several things to be absolutely true:

- ◆ Working Web sites take on a life of their own.
- ◆ Working Web developers' lives can be co-opted by a Web site.
- ◆ You don't have to be crazy to manage a Web site, but it certainly helps.
- ◆ You should take a vacation now. You may not get another for a while.

THE REAL RULES OF THE WEB

For a month or two, you may think that you manage a Web site. Enjoy that little fiction while you can. Before you know it, and probably gradually enough that you won't notice it at first, your Web site will be managing you and your development staff.

Whatever amount of time you budgeted for revisions and maintenance will double, then triple. The only possible way to prevent that occurrence is not to allow the site to grow—virtually impossible, unless you have a very small business and never intend for the business to grow. If that's the case, why in the world did you put yourself and your development staff through this ordeal?

No business funds even a small Web site without some hope that it will increase the business, at least in some small way. After you've spent all that time planning and implementing what you hope will be a functional site that will eventually support itself, you can't seriously think that you can easily contain it. Nor should you want to, beyond the point of making sure that anything added to it, or changed about it, adds to its functionality.

IT'S NEVER COMPLETE—NEVER

You and your staff still have a lot of work to do, and more after that. Within a month of putting your Web site into actual production, your developers will be redesigning it, mentally anyway. They'll see its every flaw and decide that they might as well just start over. By that time, they'll have forgotten how completely exhausted they were when they finished their first effort. It may be tempting to let them fix the flaws, as you've also noticed them, but you should steer in other directions. This isn't the time for a redesign. Adjustments, yes. Redesign, no.

Give the site some time to settle. Give your visitors some time to comment and critique. Don't accept the first compliments or criticisms as gospel.

(A preponderance of one or the other is a different story, obviously.) The criticisms may give you ideas for adjustments that are worth pursuing, but if you did your homework, you produced a Web site that functions and is visually appealing. Consider the comments, and unless they're by far over-whelming on the side of critical, wait.

Let your visitors tell you what works and what doesn't. You will eventually redesign the site, and that's likely to happen within three to six months. In the meantime, you and your developers have a gracious plenty to do. Thumb-twiddling isn't in your immediate future.

Start the Education Process Now

You've got all that in-house training to start, in the first place. Whether you believe it or not, it's going to be one of the biggest challenges you've ever faced. If your company is at all typical, you have employees who have never used a Web browser. Some of them are going to be so frightened of the tech-nology that they'll assume they can kill your network and the entire World Wide Web by themselves. They can't, of course, but that's beside the point entirely, as far as they're concerned.

Patience, remember? Don't laugh at them. You can make fun of your own first stumbling efforts with the technology all you like. They'll appreciate not feeling as though they are the first to be a bit hesitant about it. The future is happening all around them. They don't understand it, but they sure don't want to break it. (Whatever would they tell their children? "Sorry, kids, no surfing this weekend. I broke the Web." And they definitely don't want to have to explain it to all those reporters who've been saying how great the Web is. That's not a major exaggeration of the very real fears some have of the technology.)

This is in complete opposition to those who love the technology and use it at privilege levels just barely below deity status. They delight in retelling tales of the day they successfully killed the network—after the fact and assuming that they still have their jobs. They understand that they'd make a fortune telling the story (to those same reporters) of how they managed—inadvertently, of course—to bring the Web to its knees.

A Web Site Is Not About Vanity

You've also got an immediate training challenge for those within your company who will see your Web site as a golden opportunity to produce some *vanity pages*. They have absolutely no understanding that a Web audience isn't the least bit interested in learning how wonderful they are—either personally or as a division of your company. Your Web site can't be about vanity. It simply won't work on the Web. You can serve Web pages that tell your audience about the things your business does very well, but those pages must be in the context of offering your audience what *the audience* wants. That lesson can be more difficult to teach than you may imagine.

There will be those who grasp the concept quickly and work to achieve that very fine line between "Here we are—aren't we great?" and "Here we are—how can we help you?" With others, you'll be forced to take the dripping faucet approach—say it over and over and over until they pay attention. It won't make you popular, but those who really care about your Web site will appreciate your efforts (in time). They're not all being deliberately obstinate. They're simply steeped in traditional marketing, and it takes time to learn how to use a nontraditional one.

Yes, there will be those who will want nothing but vanity pages—some few at least. Dealing with them is a major challenge. You may manage to appease them with some slight nod to their vanity—a photo, an e-mail link, something. Be creative. No, don't register the page containing their information with key words that ensure that anyone who searches on the word *fetish* will find them. That would be wrong—fun, but wrong.

Thankfully, only a very small minority will insist on vanity over function. It's likely to be more difficult to persuade those who have something very useful to offer your Web audience to make themselves available. They're busy people. They don't have time to talk about what they do and how they do it. They can't possibly answer e-mail from people who might bombard them for information. (Groveling is sometimes effective with this group.)

Then there's always the training you need to do so that your development staff can stop coding all those pages. There's another challenge for you. It's really not easy to convince people that it's easy.

Those guidelines for your pages have to be written, too. Don't forget them. That's an especially important project to put at the top of your list. Thinking about them was fine until your site became a reality, but now's the time to get busy. Delay at your own risk.

Keep It Fresh

Oh yes—then there's the updates to your Web site. They have to be planned. You can't let your site get stale while you're attending to other things. Well, you could, but it would be a very bad idea. A Web audience can be very fickle. They may check back once or twice to see what you've changed, but they won't check back often if *something* doesn't change, and soon. You want to develop repeat traffic as soon as possible—visitors who come back often. To do that, you need to be planning revisions and additions regularly. How regularly? As often as possible. Do you have the resources to plan them daily? Weekly? Biweekly? Monthly?

Who's going to be responsible for providing the necessary content, coding, and review? How will they be integrated into the site? It's not enough to add a page. It has to be linked from another page. Who's going to decide where that link goes and who's going to write the text for it? Can the updates be accomplished without special graphics, or are they required? Who's going to provide them, if so?

Your goal must always be to accomplish updates with the least amount of effort. That ensures that they can be effected quickly and on a timely basis. That doesn't mean that the updates can be less than professional, but the fewer people required to be involved in making them, the better.

The channels of communication among those providing the content, coding, and graphics must be open and used. It's not at all acceptable for people to commit to providing some piece of the whole and then not deliver that piece without notifying anyone else. Schedules for Web site revisions are no different from any other project deadline. You can build in some flexibility, but beyond a certain point you chance a serious loss of credibility with your Web audience. Everyone involved with your Web project must understand that fact, and be willing to do what it takes to get the job done.

Of course, there's also the new tools and technologies your developers should be testing and evaluating. New ones arrive on the scene daily. It's not necessary to try every single one of them—no one has that much time—but it's smart to be reading about them and talking with people who are testing them. Some of those tools and technologies are likely to save you time and money in the not-so-distant future.

PLAN FOR NEW ADDITIONS AND PROJECTS

You may have a little time before other large projects need to be added to your site. Get busy with the details of training, educating, writing guidelines, and determining scheduling as soon as you can. Once those other projects begin to make their own demands on your developers' time, it will become increasingly difficult for them to find time for the basic functions.

Set some priorities about future projects, too. Don't naïvely think that they aren't on your horizon. They are. If your Marketing department and your Technical Support department both have projects that require attention simultaneously, how are your developers going to decide which will take priority? That priority can't be set arbitrarily. The fact that you and your developers enjoy working with one group over the other is not a reason to give precedence to the preferred group. Who decides the priority, and based on what criteria?

Obviously, precedence should be given to the group that offers your Web audience something it wants. If both projects do that, which is the most important to the most number of your visitors? By extension, which will be the most compelling—attract the attention of present and prospective customers, the general public, your competitors?

It will be difficult for you and your developers to maintain perspective when the pressure is applied from several sides at once. If you take the time now to determine how you'll make those judgments in the future, you'll be very glad you did. You'll find that if you can make a reasoned case for your decision (and *someone* is going to have to make that decision) it will generally be accepted with good grace.

That makes your guidelines for scheduling even more important. A group that consistently waits to advise you that one of their key people is demonstrating their new Web pages at a conference *tomorrow* holds your site hostage, just as surely as those who don't deliver what they promise, if you allow it to happen regularly. What are the odds that that demonstration wasn't in the planning stages for months?

Of course, there are rare occasions when a previously booked speaker cancels and someone from your business is called in at the last minute. You'll have to make adjustments in those cases, and your developers will understand that need. Constant adjustments for specific individuals or groups, though, are not understandable—to anyone. Instead, it will appear that your guidelines are only for those who are kind enough to play by the rules. It's just another project, after all. Everyone should know the rules, and exceptions should be exceptional.

EVERYONE WANTS REAL ESTATE ON YOUR HOME PAGE

You'll hear this a gazillion times—and that's a lot. No one, ever, wants to have their pages linked from anyplace other than your home page. Well, of course they don't! And of course it's impossible to satisfy them all. There is just so much real estate you can claim for your home page without exhausting your visitor's patience.

Requests for prime real estate range from the subtle to the outright threatening. There's always someone who's sure that if he tells your developers that some very, very senior management type absolutely wants her department's pages featured on your home page, that neither you nor the developers will question it. You've got developers who aren't easily intimidated, right? Good, because a demand of that sort can require a major adjustment to your design. Scurrying to redesign that page for one group is going to mean more scurries later. Count on it.

Even those who understand the amount of work involved aren't above applying a little pressure from time to time. Learn to say "No." It's really not that difficult. Practice. Those who don't understand will assume that your developers are being obstinate just for the sheer pleasure of it. In fact, every good Web developer is sincerely interested in making it as easy as possible for your visitors to find the information they want as quickly as possible. Functionality is always the desired goal. It's not always easy to achieve, but they'll strive for it. They'll keep trying, and each attempt will please some groups better than others. So what else is new?

▶ **NOTE**   My own absolutely wonderful boss appeared on my office doorstep one afternoon after I had gotten our department's pages newly written for our intranet (finally—we are the stepchild, because I seldom have time to devote to my own group), and assured me that he absolutely had to have some of the prime real estate on the home page for that server. I told him (and it was mostly true) that I had no control over that placement. Content for that page resides in other hands. Well, sort of.

continues

277

continued

He allowed as how I had a good deal of pull with that other party, and that was certainly true—we work very closely. I reminded him of all the same pressures I'd had over time. He could hardly argue with that, and in truth his request was mostly in jest. I think he just wanted to see whether I'd make someone else's life as uncomfortable as mine has been at times. I've learned to say "No" in every way possible, from complete misdirection to suggesting that the issue be taken to that very senior manager who could call me with his request (he never did). ◄

The Next "Gee Whiz" Technology Was Announced Today

If this were the Web, and if you had a PC equipped with a browser, some fancy plug-ins for that browser, a sound card, and an hour or so to wait for the sound files, you would see fireworks dancing on your screen—oh, you'd need at least a 17-inch monitor—behind text proclaiming **THE ALL NEW GREAT THING**. It would be accompanied by Dvorak or Handel or maybe both—simultaneously might be an interesting effect.

The next great thing was announced yesterday while you and your developers were doing boring things like adding the latest database required by several projects. What do you mean you missed it? Are you crazy? This is IT! This is the one that you've got to add—tomorrow!

Forget that it would mean trashing your server, redesigning your site, and starting all over. It'll be worth it, don't you know? (You haven't been there yet if you didn't just sigh heavily, and think it would be funny if you weren't so tired.)

The training, the guidelines, the meetings—they just weren't listening. Worse, they were, and you're simply too conservative for words. Boring, boring, boring. Where's your sense of adventure? Why can't you see that this

278

\<expletive>technology\</expletive> is the be-all-end-all? You're quite obviously a brainless idiot.

Keep smiling. It just appeared on the scene yesterday (or last week or last month). Your plan for your Web site, the redesigns, the additional functions you'll have added and are planning to add, are all well-considered. You've been working at them for some time.

This technology may actually be the one that will send you back to square one, but you don't deep-six carefully crafted plans without very good reasons. Assure the "technology evangelist" that you and your developers will take a close look at the new thing, and suggest she take a nap or something. Okay, you should probably be a little more diplomatic than that, but you get the picture.

The truth is that she probably doesn't understand the technology she's touting. She probably saw it in all its glory on the Web site of the company that developed it. She doesn't know how you'd use it or even if you could, but it sure is cool. Probably so.

▶ **NOTE**   As far as some people are concerned, your first and biggest mistake, no matter your reasons, will be your operating system and your choice of server software. These aren't really technology issues; they're more like religious issues. I've been asked twice in just the past week why we chose the server software that we did. We use WebSite by O'Reilly & Associates. "They" want to know why we're not using Netscape's or Microsoft's server.

It's pretty easy to answer, actually. We had already decided that we wanted to use Windows NT as our platform for the simple reason that the operating system would be the most familiar to the people within our company (which would allow more of them to work on their own Web projects). At the time (the spring of 1995), Netscape didn't have a server that operated on Windows NT, and Microsoft didn't have one at all. Additionally, even after the two

continues

continued

giants provided us with servers that we could use, they chose competing security models. We'd already installed our WebSite but we weren't (and still aren't) completely tied to it.

We had to make choices; could we realistically be assured that one model would outpace the other? No, obviously not. With the entrance of VISA and MasterCard and their security plans, we would have simply been taking a chance that was unnecessary at the time. WebSite was scheduled to include both security models in their Pro package (which I will install as soon as I find an hour without other priorities). We determined that serving more people was more important than having the product that had "market share."

Try to avoid these "religious" discussions as often as possible. As in real religious issues, you can't win this kind of argument. Simply agree that the objector may have a point and let it go at that. ◀

Bah, Humbug

By the time you encounter this passion—and it is indeed a passion—for the next cool thing, you're likely to have become just a tiny bit jaded. You'll have seen "cool" come and go. You'll have tried one or two of those cool things— or several—and decided whether they were worthy of your attention. Few will have been worth scrapping your other plans.

Welcome to the real world of the Web. It's not that the technology is any less exciting after you've been in this business for a while—it's not. It's just as exciting and just as challenging, but a healthy layering of pragmatism will armor you against sudden jumps to each new technology. If it's good, it's not going away.

YES, WE KNOW ABOUT IT

If it's really, really good, your developers are likely to have been planning to use it months before the debut was announced on the Web. They may even have been among the beta testers for the product. A new technology seldom arrives on the scene full-blown without plenty of advance notice among those who are working on the Web and studying the trends.

Terrific new technologies that are yet to be seen by the average Web surfer are being discussed and evaluated right now, their pros and cons praised and critiqued for all to see—that is, all who are still learning and studying. That part never loses its challenge or excitement. There's a large community of Web developers watching and talking in their own medium—the Web and the Internet. Only developers who don't plan to be in the business for long ignore those discussions.

Your developers will be paying attention and you won't be caught short by the technologies, if you're listening to them and studying for yourself. Beware the developer who jumps with each new blip on the Web technology front. Encourage consideration of each, but remember that they aren't all equally wonderful or useful. Judicious planning and functional beats cool, hands down.

WE'RE GOOD ENOUGH—THE WEB'S ISN'T, YET

Keep in mind that if your business is based even in part on any of the technologies, if you use those technologies you must use them very well. There are very good reasons not to use them at all, if you can't demonstrate your talents to best advantage.

You might make absolutely stunning videos. The technology exists to demonstrate them on the Web, but they're unlikely to be stunning, given that six to eight frames per second is about the best you can deliver over the lines and equipment in place at present. That video is going to lose a lot in the translation. Better no demonstration than a bad one. You don't really want to shoot yourself in the foot, do you?

▶ **NOTE**   Remember that virtual world I so want to try, as I mentioned in Chapter 5? I'll be forced to grovel to the in-house experts in order to accomplish it (not that I'm completely above that). They do virtual reality at a level of detail that simply can't be demonstrated on the Web at this time and probably for some time to come. I'll keep my options open. Maybe a VR demonstration on our intranet, of a network wiring closet? ◀

WHERE DO THEY FIND THE TIME?

Don't deceive yourself that you won't have a certain number of in-house technology buffs, even if your business is far from high-tech. There will be those who devour the magazines and surf the high-tech sites as though no others existed. Humor them, but only to the extent of acknowledging how very interesting some of those sites can be. If you can't make the technologies work well for your company, your wiser choice is not to use them at all.

Of course, the technology buffs won't all see the sense in that. They aren't likely to understand any hesitation. You might point out the amount of time required to download some of the technologies, but it's as likely to fall on deaf ears as be heard. If you so much as suggest that you're surprised they have time to wait for all that fluff, they'll become defensive, for obvious reasons, so don't bother.

▶ **NOTE**   As I was preparing for work recently, the technology reporter on one of our local channels was reviewing a truly gee-whiz Web site. His remark that "some of these files take hours to load" gave me a very good laugh. It takes a serious technology junkie—or at least someone with lots more time than most of us have—to be willing to wait for those kinds of downloads.

282

Can you honestly imagine one of your clients being willing to wait that long? You'd better be delivering precisely what he or she wants for that kind of time investment. ◀

THE AMAZING SHRINKING WEB PAGE (SERIOUSLY!)

Believe it or not, every now and then a Web site requires a major overhaul and parts are remanded to the bit bucket. It's all too easy to add and add and add until the site becomes all but unmanageable. You can leave this nasty job to your developers. It's much like spring cleaning, in that one family member may hate that old lamp and attempt to slide it quietly into the trash. Another insists it's not only the most beautiful lamp on the face of the earth, but the most functional, too. Your staff will develop methods for dealing with most of these family feuds, though you may occasionally be called on to mediate.

In truth, the Web page equivalent of a truly ugly lamp is not likely to be missed by anyone. If the Web site cleanup is combined with a regular redesign, it may be months before anyone will miss specific pieces that were omitted. Your Web audience will let you know fairly quickly if you happen to omit something they use regularly. Your developers will, of course, be monitoring the site closely enough to know which pages aren't serving any good purpose as far as that audience is concerned, and which are.

COMMITMENT: AN ASYLUM OR YOUR OWN EMPIRE (SORT OF)?

This book has several times mentioned firearms. There's a very good reason for that. Everyone who manages a technical project or works in Web development has, at some point, considered using them. This business is enough to make the most sane and peace-loving among us into raving idiots. If you happen to start the project at that level of insanity, abandon all hope. You're lost. If you don't have one finely honed sense of humor to balance the ravings, you should seriously consider some other line of work.

Working on the Web demands such patience, humor, self-confidence, and willingness to take risks that not everyone is quite ready for it yet. It's not beyond the capabilities of most good managers, but it will test your limits in many areas. Haven't yet bitten your tongue instead of announcing to whomever you are listening to that he quite obviously wouldn't recognize a clue if it were delivered to him, labeled, on a silver platter? You aren't yet managing a Web site. If you are managing one and this hasn't yet happened, you are either so new at it that the rest of us salute you or so clueless yourself that you shouldn't be managing a Web site.

In the former case (you're new at this), you deserve respect for trying. Many people are too fearful or at least too unaware of the potential to make the effort. In the latter case (you're clueless), you aren't likely to be paying your dues. Those required in this particular medium are those paid with serious study. You don't learn the Web by osmosis—not yet. If you expect to get it that way, wait five years. It will be much easier then.

THE PROJECT THAT WON'T DIE

You may dimly recall that Chapter 1 referred to a Web site as being a project that's virtually impossible to kill. It's true. The only way to kill it once it's started is to pull the plug on the Web server, and even that isn't foolproof. A URL is a prize. Your products, projects, departments, or divisions will have their own, and they won't relinquish them with grace or ease. Had Patrick Henry been a Webmaster instead of a patriot, you can imagine how his most famous utterance would translate in this day and age.

You can, however, trust one thing—if your Web developers are serious about your site, they'll gladly pull the plug rather than allow anyone to make it trivial. Having no site is better than having a nonfunctional or stale site. If it's not going to be maintained and kept up to date, they'd prefer that those URLs bite the dust. They don't want to be associated with a site that isn't fresh. It's a personal affront to their professionalism.

THE CARE AND FEEDING OF WEB DEVELOPERS

By the time your site is operational, you'll have staff with skills that are in demand. It's unlikely that you want them to take those skills elsewhere. In two to five years, there will be many people who have basic Web skills, but until then you want to keep your staff reasonably happy. It will cost you considerably more, in all likelihood, to replace those people with others who have comparable skills from outside your business. So how do you keep your developers happy and working at optimum efficiency? It really shouldn't be too terribly difficult:

- ◆ Give them the necessary tools to do the job: the software; the computing power; a work area that can be private, quiet, and ergonomic for the hours of pointing, clicking, and keying that will be necessary to the job; voice mail so the vendors can be avoided at times; subscriptions (not shared) for the trade magazines (so they can take them home for study in those rare spare moments); and books, books, and more books so they can study the technology away from a computer monitor from time to time.

- ◆ Make sure that they have time to continue to study and learn. It's entirely likely that other staff members will resent the time your staff spends surfing the Web to what appears to be no good purpose, and they may very well complain (or at least make note, out loud) of that time. You should be prepared to deal with those complaints. Your staff needs to keep up with what's happening on the Web and they can't do it without surfing.

- Remember that the day-to-day details of Web site development are time-consuming—don't overschedule the work.
- Support them when necessary.
- Thank them for their efforts.

Your development staff must stay one step ahead of the multitudes in their use of the technology. To do that, they need tools, and they need the time to continue studying the Web themselves. The work can become so overwhelming that they hardly have time to accomplish the absolutely essential chores. Ideally, you'll have enough staff to parcel specific duties to specific individuals. In fact, many sites have very small Web development staffs who attempt to handle all the necessary tasks. It can be done, but it's certainly not easy.

▶ **NOTE**   Our staff is quite small. We began with one person budgeted at 25 percent time in 1994, and staff has been added incrementally over the past 2+ years. Four developers now devote the majority of their time to our Web projects. Two work primarily on our intranet and two primarily on our external site, though work is often shared in order to balance the load as much as possible. Creative time management is an absolute necessity; even at that, far too many things go undone for lack of hours in which to accomplish them. ◀

If work is being funneled to your developers from various areas of your business, it's ultimately your responsibility to approve and support the priority levels determined for the various pieces of the project. You'll complicate an already-complex process if you constantly shift and change those priorities or allow someone else to do that.

Your developers will never object to your pride in your Web site if you share credit for it with them. If you don't? At best, you'll lose their respect; at worst, they'll find some other company that values their skills. In all probability, your developers will actually love their work—not precisely a common attitude these days. You want them to appreciate their work environment as well.

Who's Really Doing the Work?

Make it your business to know who's doing the work and who's only claiming responsibility. Wonderful new pages may appear because some group really did take the initiative and develop them, or they may have been dropped in your developers' laps at the last minute. Good developers will cover for even the most inept people, rather than allow a deadline to be missed. You should be aware of the facts in either case.

If your staff is small, it may be very easy to determine who's doing the work and who's not—simply ask. If your staff is not so small, you may need to put into place some tracking of the work that's being done. Have your Webmaster keep a log of each project that's being done, who's scheduled to produce each piece, and when. At the very least, meet with your staff regularly to determine the state of the various projects that are in progress. If your Webmaster were to walk out the door tonight at 5 p.m. and not return, you'd need to know how to proceed.

High praise is always due to groups or departments who are serious about learning the technology and are seriously working and studying to that end. Awarding that same high praise to those who only claim responsibility is a formula guaranteed to make your developers grind their teeth.

Lead or Stand Back

You don't have to know how to administer a Web server to manage Web developers, but you do need to be willing to learn slightly more than most. If you don't, your developers will become quite adept at bypassing you on any technical (and many procedural) issues surrounding your Web site. In truth, if you're not willing to learn more than the very basics, you should hope that they do bypass you. In other words, if you're not going to lead, don't get in their way. If you plan to lead, you've got to learn.

EMPEROR ‹*YOUR NAME HERE*›?

You can make your Web site and those who develop it into your own little empire of sorts. Certainly, managing a group that's technically skilled in this medium isn't a bad position to be in, these days—if you do it well. A Web site is a cooperative effort, however. Your empire exists, such as it is, because your staff has the skills to make it so. And it's only one tool, when all is said and done, among a number of other tools that your company employs in its efforts.

You can't use that tool to leverage power without hurting the site. You can't arbitrarily decide what will or won't be allowed on the site without lessening the functionality and usefulness of it. Basically, as an empire it works only if you can act as benevolent despot—firm but fair. Tyranny seldom plays well with anyone, and it doesn't play at all well with Web developers in the present market. They hardly have to walk across the street or next door to find other positions in the field.

HOW MUCH LIFE BEYOND WORK DO THEY REALLY NEED?

Not much, actually. Web developers have a tendency to immerse themselves in the technology. They really do love it. It's a fascination and a disease. They spend their regular working hours working at it and their personal time studying it. If they're able to access the Web from their homes, you can be sure that they will. And because they're serious about your Web site, you can be sure that the personal time they spend on the Web involves looking at it critically. They may be playing, by their own admission, but that play time will ultimately benefit you.

Web developers are serious about Web development, and though they're as likely as the next person to go in search of sites that are fun—those that may serve no purpose beyond entertainment—they'll learn in the process. If they're social types, and they generally are, they'll search out those sites where they can communicate with other developers. They'll participate in forums that attract not only developers but the surfers you hope to attract to your site. They'll ask, or answer, a question and attach your URL to their message, which is likely to attract more people to your site.

They may seek out interactive sites in order to carry on conversations in real time with other Web surfers. Some of the people they'll meet on those sites will be extremely knowledgeable about the technology. Some will want to learn it. Your developers can learn and they can teach; in either case, if they're sincere in their efforts, they'll make friends for themselves, build a network of people who'll help them when they need help, and increase your Web site's visibility at the same time. All in all, that's not a bad deal for your company—especially considering that they think of it all as "play time."

They Get Paid for This?

Web developers need understanding families. The rest of the world often takes a back seat to the technology. If there isn't one already, there should be a T-shirt that says "So much Web—So little time." They're not, of course, the only ones who develop serious compulsions for this technology. They just happen to be the ones who are lucky enough to get paid for their compulsions.

They use that not-inconsiderable weapon to hold their friends and families at bay while they "work" (when you do it at home, it's work, even if you tell people at work that it's play). Honest, if you get paid for it, you can call it work even when you're playing games. Family members will acquire their own Internet accounts in order to send e-mail to them. They're sure that at least their spouse/mother/father/child will pay attention to *that*.

▶ **NOTE** My sister swears that she learned this technology, which she now teaches occasionally, simply because I either refused—or had forgotten how—to use the telephone. I remember it differently, of course, and contend that I insisted "for her own good." ◀

PAY ATTENTION, EVEN WHEN THEY DON'T RANT

Your Web site will make considerable demands on your developers' time. For the most part, those demands won't seem excessive to them. The joy of learning and the opportunity to use what they learn in practical and exciting ways will make the extra effort more than worthwhile.

However, if they feel that you take advantage of those efforts—if you allow the priorities they have to far exceed the time you budget for their efforts, or if you allow their schedules to be upended for last-minute crises on a regular basis—you're likely to get some serious feedback. They won't bother to send it through that form on your Web site, either. They'll deliver it personally, in the form of a rant or a quiet resignation. You may or may not have the luxury (?) of some number of rants (arbitrary number based on the patience levels of your respective developers). The really patient ones just fume quietly until you push that one button you shouldn't.

▶ **NOTE** Our group has a mutual venting relationship. Any time any one of us is ready to simply walk, and those times definitely do happen, we rant to one another. We each know that if one of us dropped out of the picture, the rest would be even more busy than we already are. Even though we all under-stand that not one of us is indispensable, we each are made to feel indispens-able by the others. We're inordinately lucky to have assembled a staff that's compatible and fiercely loyal, not only to one another but to the company. ◀

SEND THEM AWAY

It's a great job being a Web developer, but they do require food (not always eaten at the keyboard), fresh air (not necessarily during daylight hours, but fresh air nonetheless), sleep (the occasional eight hours in a row will be greatly appreciated), and companionship (they like their coworkers just fine, but enough is enough). Not to worry. They're really not as a rule a demanding lot, except as it regards your Web site and their own view of their work.

Ship them off to a conference of Web developers. They'll learn. They'll come back with some new ideas. Perfect solution (temporarily, at least). They'll love you for it—as long as you don't require that they make a presentation while they're there.

▶ **TIP**   Oh, and don't require that they make a presentation to the rest of the staff when they return, either. In the first place, those little gatherings are boring in the extreme, as a rule, and in the second, you'll never really hear what they learned that way because they just want to get it over with and sit down. Instead, plan a lunch (company paid) and simply ask questions. ◀

MAKE SOME ADJUSTMENTS

For the longer term, you may very well need to budget longer hours for your Web staffers (if they're not already committed to the project on a full-time basis), adjust the workload, or add staff. Those options sound simple, but of course they aren't always. Depending on your resources, adjusting the workload may be your only real option.

Projects may need to wait a little longer for attention, perhaps. Lead times for scheduling projects may need to be extended. In-house training may have to be adjusted to allow adequate time for other duties. There are always things that can be adjusted. The problem is to decide where and how to adjust.

Your Web site audience generally will be your first priority. The revisions and regular maintenance should be at the top of any developer's list. Beyond that, the adjustments depend primarily on your own priorities within your company. There are no hard-and-fast rules. New functionality may be delayed. Projects may be moved up and down in the schedule.

Whatever the case in your particular instance, you shouldn't expect your developers to be the ones on the firing line when the schedules or priorities are adjusted, if the adjustment is your decision—based on your inability to add hours to the schedule or people to the project. Tell your developers to route outside complaints to you, and stand behind your decisions with those who do the complaining. Your developers will appreciate your attempt to take some of the load off of them. They'll take more than their fair share of complaints before kicking them up to you.

DOES THIS JOB HAVE A FUTURE?

You certainly have a window of opportunity, at the very least. For the immediate future, Web developers and managers have skills that aren't yet common. More and more people will develop those skills as the technology matures. Because the major software developers are intent on bringing the Web into your office at some level, learning the basics of the technology now puts you a step or two ahead of those who choose to delay what appears to be the inevitable.

The inevitability of some form of Web presence in your office, though, ensures that the skills for using the technology will be acquired. Fifteen years ago, only a few people were willing and able to put a PC to good use; in the same way, the number who will use Web technology to their advantage now are few. Those numbers will change—if the past year or two are any indication, they'll change very quickly. People are already familiar with their computers, and the technology of the Web will simply be integrated into those computers.

292

There is just as much future in any job in Web development now as there was in any computing environment 15 or 20 years ago. Then, as now, those people who took it upon themselves to learn the technology, and who continued to stay abreast of the changes in it, carved out futures for themselves if they chose. If you expect a future that involves leadership in the Web, and that will evolve, you'll be forced to do some serious studying and learning. This is a new world, and one that can prove enriching, but not without effort on your part.

The ability to organize and present information isn't uncommon. The talent to translate those abilities to the Web is, for now. Your window of opportunity is now, and it closes just a little with each passing day. More and more people are involving themselves in various aspects of the technology. As it happens, though, talent is greatly admired on the Web. If you have the talent for it, the Web has a future for you.

CONSIDER THE FUTURE TODAY

It makes a great deal of business sense to begin planning for the Web now. There are certain basic questions that managers should consider, that may save a great deal of time and frustration later.

A Web site could very well become completely unmanageable unless some guidelines are in place. It's quite likely that departments and divisions may choose to serve their own pages rather than have them served from any central repository. Is that acceptable from the corporate standpoint?

SHARING IS NOT ALWAYS A GOOD THING

Some sites have hundreds of internal Web servers. Some have only one. No matter how many servers or how few, someone has to determine what information will be shared and with whom. Your corporate culture will dictate some of those decisions, but it's important to be giving thought to how those decisions will eventually be made.

There are likely to be some very interesting decisions to be made at corporate levels over the next few years. If anyone can run a Web server from her desktop, who will be charged with protecting information that shouldn't be shared? Personnel and financial records and confidential data will need to be safeguarded, though pieces of that information may need to be shared. Who's going to make those decisions? And how will they be implemented?

Quite obviously, your business has a great deal of information that you have no desire to share with certain people, whether those people are within your company or without. What may seem perfectly obvious to you, however, may not seem so to others. There may be some interesting battles in your future, if you decide that you actually do want a future managing a Web site.

Inadvertent Sharing Is Worrisome

If you have a corporate connection to the Internet now, you may very well have employees running Web servers on their desktops. No computer connected to the Internet can be made 100 percent secure from those who have the time and desire to gain access to it. At this point, a Web server is a fine target that's easier to invade than many, and certainly much easier if the person who operates it isn't fully cognizant of the many ways it can be compromised.

If your company isn't Internet-connected, or if you have good security measures in place, you would still be wise to know where Web servers are located, because the data that resides on those computers could be shared indiscriminately. Most people are extremely careful to protect information they know is confidential, of course. They simply may be unaware that the need for safeguards is more important, not less, by virtue of the fact that they're running a Web server. The less technically savvy the operator, the less secure the server.

It's very much a question of whether the person who controls the server is simply running a Web server for fun, or is studying the technology to know how to do it right. It's fun to run a Web server, and it's very easy if you don't feel any need to find out how it might be compromised.

FINALLY! A REASON FOR A COMMITTEE!

Whether pages are being served internally or externally, policy issues like security and the eventual deployment of Web servers should be addressed. For the immediate future, most people aren't going to have the technical ability to prepare, let alone serve, their own Web pages. But running a Web server is deceptively easy, and there will be those who will attempt it—perhaps before you'd like.

The committee approach just won't work for many aspects of your Web site, but for policy decisions it's perfect. Stack your committee if you can with 55 percent Web-savvy staff—okay, as savvy as you can find—and 45 percent general-policy types. You need the second group; they're balance for the technology mavens. Have the Legal department represented, if possible. The Web is going to demand their skills before it's all over. You can be sure of that.

You accomplish more than just settling policy with the arrangement of this group. It's an opportunity to educate at a slightly elevated level, and quite possibly a chance to achieve buy-in from some who might not otherwise have been interested in your efforts. The more buy-in you accomplish at all levels, the more future your job as site manager achieves. Of course, you knew that. That's why you wanted a committee in the first place, isn't it? Fine, but put your committee where it belongs—setting broad policy so that your Web developers don't have to make more decisions than they care to. They don't need to be micromanaged by you, and your Web site will choke on micromanagement by committee.

Broad guidelines and general oversight will be welcomed by your developers. As the committee members gain expertise about the Web, they may be very helpful with any number of issues that will arise. It's the rare developer or manager who doesn't appreciate not being forced, by virtue of lack of Web-savvy veterans of management, to make decisions they'd rather not make autonomously. Oh, they'll make them, for better or worse. It's the Web—somebody's got to do it.

What's In It for the Developers?

At this point, though probably not for more than a few years, there's certainly a future for people who can work with the not-completely-reliable tools used to produce Web pages. Until standards for HTML and VRML are more firmly established, and that may be quite some time, coding will remain an imprecise and sometimes frustrating function that will be fully understood only by those who are willing to continue to study. The editors and converters can't be expected to perform according to rules that are constantly changing.

The standards will eventually reach a level of maturity that will allow editors and converters to be written so that they perform reliably. At that point, your present word processing package is likely to become obsolete. What will be the point in saving documents in some proprietary form that won't allow them to be shared across platforms?

Businesses have been caught in the middle of the software wars from the day the first computers were introduced. They attempted, with more or less success, to standardize on specific applications within the company, so that information could be shared. Of course, not everyone wanted to use those applications. Unless you have very strict control of software within your business environment, it's likely that there are some people who simply refuse to use whatever standard packages you've chosen.

In addition to those who chose not to use the standard applications, sharing information with business partners and customers has required that we jump through what are often formidable hoops. Web technology may very well make all our lives easier, at least in that regard. Until that time, though, the people in your company who really do understand how to code pages for the Web are valuable resources.

The same rationales apply to those who can produce graphics for the Web. The software packages that graphic artists presently use will be adapted to produce those graphics in Web-ready form. That's hardly going to mean that people who aren't artistically talented are going to become so. But it will mean that talented artists will be able to prepare artwork for your Web site more easily. More people will learn how to design graphics specifically for the Web. That's an art in itself, and not every artist has the talent necessary for it.

There will also continue to be a demand for quite some time for people who can write for a Web audience. That audience is going to continue to be a somewhat more literate, affluent group, for the foreseeable future. New technologies are daily being proposed, discussed, and tested that will make access to the Web easier and faster. Unless those technologies overcome the shortcomings of our existing wiring infrastructure—or that infrastructure is replaced—and unless the cost of those technologies is such that most people can afford them, the Web simply isn't going to be available to everyone.

The technology will mature, and is likely to become ubiquitous. It will be a long time before universal access is achieved, however. There are still people who can't afford telephones. They're rather unlikely to spend precious money for Internet access, aren't they?

Those of us who have experienced the rapid growth of computing technology laugh now about the bad old days of punch cards. We'd as soon not go back to that, though at the time it was pretty leading-edge stuff and pretty darned remarkable. The Web may be slightly beyond punch card stage, but it's still an infant technology. There will be remarkable changes that come about in the next few years.

You've got an opportunity to be part of an exciting time of change. If you like slightly wild rides, this job definitely has a future for you. Of course, that's only if you manage to keep your sanity in the process. You're on your own with that.

DOES THIS EVER END?

Does the book ever end, you mean? I certainly hope so, because I'm tired and I have to get back to work on our Web site, as soon as I figure out how I killed my PC and what to do about that.

Oh! You meant your work on your Web site! No, it never ends. A Web site is a hungry beast that requires continuous infusions of talent, technology, and energy.

A Web site has a future that's defined by change and growth. It doesn't end, but it does change.

Some in the popular press are now talking and writing about a "backlash." Only companies who develop Web sites with the express purpose of coining instant cash from them are likely to experience any backlash. That will be because they didn't take the time or make the effort to learn about the Web—its culture or its audience.

Real commerce on the Web will become a reality in our future, and for some few companies that future will be soon. For the vast majority of others, commerce will have to wait for tested security models and for time to learn to appeal to the audience. It's also going to wait for the technology to catch up to the needs of business on the Web.

Security Models

You'll see much about secure cash transactions in most books and articles about the Web. The standards for secure transactions don't yet exist, and that means one very simple thing for your business: Whatever form of transaction you choose will be unusable by many visitors to your site, because their browsers may not be able to transmit the information appropriately for your server. VISA and MasterCard have only recently announced their own (mutual) approach to commerce on the Web. They have the installed customer base to change the entire face of Web commerce. The odds are good that if they manage to maintain their coalition, those who produce browsers and servers will fall into line behind them.

Unsecured transactions are a different creature. You don't offer your customer any guarantee that you can safeguard the transaction. The customer chooses whether or not to transmit her credit card number to you. Some people will; some won't. It's truly that simple.

Other forms of payment are certainly possible. A purchase order is as acceptable over the Web as it is over a fax or a phone. You might consider putting your 800 number on your Web pages so that people can browse your catalog online, place orders, and receive order numbers that can then be used when they telephone their credit card numbers.

Those people who would prefer that business never heard of the Web are eventually going to accept business on the Web, however grudgingly. They'll accept it because business will force the technology to grow at a faster pace, and will ultimately fund wider access to that technology.

So no, it never ends. You have to keep listening, studying, and learning. That's the key to the future of your Web site and your future as its manager. As you apply yourself to the adventure, you'll acquire a base of knowledge that will grow. There are some amazingly bright people working on the Web.

You have a fine opportunity to learn from them if you're willing. If you are, remember that age doesn't mean much in this medium. That 20-year-old programmer may have quite a lot to teach you—about her programs and about your future Web audience. You may have a lot to teach her about life in the real world of business.

▶ **NOTE**   My mentors in matters of the Web, Dr. Marcus Speh and Dr. Joseph Wang, are both nearly young enough to be my children. They were kind enough to be very helpful to an old lady who quite literally dropped in on their technical conversations. Very little of what they said made sense to me in the beginning. They were patient enough to put up with my endless questions. Had I approached what they had to say with any obvious attitude that my age gave me advantage over them, I'd have been wrong entirely, and it's unlikely that they would have been quite so willing to share their vast knowledge. ◀

Approach this project as the most exciting learning opportunity that you're likely to have for a long time. It will indeed be a lot of work for you, but it will be a tremendous amount of fun. Equip yourself with as much patience and sense of humor as you can muster. They will be the only things that save you on those days when everything breaks and absolutely nothing goes right.

So, you've got a lot of work ahead of you. Have fun with it! It's a project that begs you to have fun. If you don't, you have no one but yourself to blame.

Now get busy! The Web isn't waiting for you. The seasonal redesign was installed this morning, there are 14 new accounts to set up on both the internal and external Web sites for people who want to start working on their own pages, the conferencing software needs some tweaking, and... are you still there? I'm just making my to-do list. You've got your own Web site to manage. Close this book and go have your own fun!

APPENDIX
USEFUL WEB SITES

There's a wealth of information on the Web to guide you in planning, designing, advertising, and updating your Web site. The following URLs are sites that I have found to be particularly useful. Several of them offer additional links to other sites that can also be very helpful. The electronic magazines at the end of the list are those that I have found particularly handy for keeping abreast of the current trends and latest technologies.

I've made a point of choosing sites that have been updated recently, and have contacted several of the site owners of these and other URLs listed in this book's text in order to offer information that's current and that I believe will be available to you when this book is published. However, sites do disappear or the names change. The fact that you may not be able to reach a site may mean that it's no longer available, or it may very well mean that it's simply very busy and unable to handle the number of people requesting it when you try it. Keep trying.

- *Writing Business Web Pages*
  http://www.iinet.net.au/~heath/

- *Mary E. S. Morris (former Sun Microsystems Webmaster) on Web sites*
  http://www.iinet.net.au/~heath/morris.html

- *Advertising Rules on the Web*
  http://www.procopio.com/resource/library/articles/ ad_rules.htm

- *CyberSmart Marketing*
  http://www.martinagency.com/CyberSmart Marketing

♦ *From Grass Roots to Corporate Image—The Maturation of the Web*
http://cast.stanford.edu/cast/www/paper.html

♦ *Free Range: The Builder Page*
http://www.freerange.com/home/howto/fr–builders/index.html

♦ *The WWW Consortium*
http://www.w3.org/

♦ *Bare Bones Guide to HTML*
http://werbach.com/barebones/barebone.html

♦ *Guides to Writing Style—HTML Documents*
**http://union.ncsa.uiuc.edu/HyperNews/get/www/html/
guides.html**

♦ *How Do They Do That with HTML?*
http://www.nashville.net/~carl/htmlguide/

♦ *How to Promote Your Business Web Page*
http://www.iinet.net.au/~heath/rhodes.html

♦ *HTML 3.2 Reference*
http://www.wvitcoe.wvnet.edu/~sbolt/html3/

♦ *HTML Writers Guild*
http://www.hwg.org/info.html

♦ *NCSA—A Beginner's Guide to HTML*
**http://www.ncsa.uiuc.edu/General/Internet/WWW/
HTMLPrimer.html**

♦ *The HTML Authors' Board*
http://www.tnet.de/~aw/hab/

♦ *The Toolbox (for graphics designers)*
http://member.aol.com/royalef/toolbox.htm

♦ *The Web Developer's Virtual Library*
http://www.stars.com/

Appendix

- *The WWW Security FAQ*
  http://www-genome.wi.mit.edu/WWW/faqs/www-security-faq.html

- *Tom's Tips for Web Designers*
  http://the-tech.mit.edu/KPT/Toms/ Tom's Tips for Web Designers

- *Yale C/AIM WWW Style Manual*
  http://info.med.yale.edu/caim/StyleManual_Top.HTML

- *VRML-o-Rama*
  http://www.well.com/user/spidaman/vrml.html

- *Macromedia—Shockwave*
  http://www.macromedia.com/

- *Progressive Networks—RealAudio*
  http://www.realaudio.com/

- *Sun Microsystems—Java*
  http://java.sun.com

- *Webmaster Magazine*
  http://www.cio.com/WebMaster/wmhome.html

- *InformationWeek*
  http://techweb.cmp.com/techweb/iw/current/

- *Ad Age—Interactive Media & Marketing—Internet Marketing*
  http://www.adage.com/IMM/Internet/

- *Internet World*
  http://www.iworld.net/

- *Ziff-Davis*
  http://www.zdnet.com/

GLOSSARY

Archie   A program used to search networks for files that can be retrieved via FTP.

ASCII (American Standard Code for Information Interchange)   The worldwide standard for text documents. E-mail and newsgroups use ASCII primarily.

bandwidth   Technically, the difference between the highest and lowest frequencies available for network signals. More commonly used to describe the capacity of the throughput for signals over a network connection.

browser   The software that allows you to "browse" the Web. Sometimes called a *client*. Netscape, Internet Explorer, and Mosaic are graphical browsers; Lynx is a text browser.

client   See *browser* and *client/server*.

client/server   One way information is distributed over a network. The server delivers the information and the client interprets it for viewing or use.

daemon   A UNIX program.

domain name   The Internet addressing system that allows a computer to be uniquely identified to other computers on the network.

download   To retrieve a file from the network and store it on your local computer.

e-mail   Electronic mail.

firewall   Hardware and/or software used to secure data networks from intrusion.

frames   A nonstandard way (at this time) to format information on a Web page, by segmenting the display into discrete sections and displaying more than one document or file simultaneously.

freeware   Software applications available on the Internet that are free.

FTP (File Transfer Protocol)   Protocol used to transfer files from one computer to another.

GIF (Graphics Interchange Format)   The most common graphic file type on the Web. Developed by CompuServe as a file format for graphical images.

Gopher   A menu-driven tool that allows access to various network files archived for use on the Internet. Gopher sites are disappearing quite rapidly since the development of the Web.

home page   The primary gateway to a Web site.

HTML (Hypertext Markup Language)   The standard set of commands that can be used to code Web pages.

HTML extensions   Nonstandard markup tags used by proprietary browsers to display files.

HTTP (Hypertext Transfer Protocol)   The standard rules for serving documents by Web servers.

Internet   The network of networks that's the "glue" for the World Wide Web.

IP address   The number assigned to a specific computer on a network to identify it uniquely.

ISDN (Integrated Services Digital Network)   Protocol used by telephone companies to carry data, voice, and other signals.

kbps   Kilobytes per second. Approximately 1000 bytes per second.

JPEG (Joint Photographic Experts Group)   Like GIF, a file format for graphical images.

Glossary

login   The act of accessing a computer by means of a user name and password.

Mbps   Megabytes per second. Approximately 1 million bytes per second.

modem   Modulator/demodulator. A modem translates digital signals (computer) to analog signals (telephone) so that the signal can be carried through telephone lines and equipment, and then translates them back to digital signals for the computer on the other end of the transmission.

netiquette   The etiquette of the Internet and the World Wide Web.

operating system   Often referred to as OS. The underlying software that drives the computer; UNIX, VMS, Windows 95, and Windows NT are operating systems. Other programs can be installed to work in conjunction with the operating system.

platform   Synonymous with *operating system*.

protocol   The rules governing the transmission of files across a network—the format, timing, error control processing, etc.

shareware   Software applications that are available on the Internet for a (generally nominal) fee.

T1   Telephone company terminology for connections that can carry signals at the rate of 1.544 Mbps.

T3   Telephone company terminology for connections that can carry signals at the rate of 45 Mbps.

tables   HTML tags that allow information to be viewed in discrete rows and columns.

TCP/IP (Transmission Control Protocol/Internet Protocol)   The standard protocol of the Internet.

Telnet (or *remote login*)   Interactive use of a remote computer, achieved by logging in.

UNIX   Operating system developed by AT&T Bell Laboratories, widely used on the Internet.

URL (Uniform Resource Locator)   The unique address of a Web page; a combination of its domain name and path/file location.

VMS   Operating system developed by Digital Equipment Corporation.

Veronica   Like Archie, a system developed to search for files on the Internet.

INDEX

D

daemons, 305

dead links, 151

dealing with site criticism, 240

dealing with site rejection, 140

delegation of responsibility in site development, 122

demographic overview of the Internet and WWW, 34-36

departmental needs from sites, 162-163

design and implementation planning for sites, 10

design skills needed by Webmasters, 87

designers, skills needed for site development team, 98

determining

corporate departmental needs of Web site, 162

what can and can't be done on Web site, 222

which types of new technology to include on site, 175

why work is not completed, 219

development

considerations for Web site planning, 6

requirements for Web sites, 8-10

staff

selection, 84

task assignments, 249-252

direct access to Internet via Internet backbone, 57

directories, determining file locations by URL, 209

displays (video), testing site viability, 155

distributing tasks to ease workload, 191

document converters, 103-104, 213-214, 238

documentation of page and site content guidelines, 259

documents

adding to Web sites, 214

legacy documents, 103

preparing for HTML coding, 146

site delivery and development considerations, 65

site inclusion considerations, 113

domain names, 51, 58-60, 305

downloading, 305

new software for trial use, 117

Web pages, 156

dumb terminals, 166

E

e-mail, 305

addresses

author of book, 180

confidentiality, 137

junk e-mail, 135

messages sent as a result of site, 30

proper and polite responses, 205

signature lines, advertising new sites, 132

e-mail lists as knowledge sources, 117

early site development efforts, viewing, 149

J-K

L

T

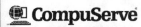

A · V I A C O M · S E R V I C · E

The Information SuperLibrary™

Bookstore

Search

What's New

Reference

Software

Newsletter

Company Overviews

Yellow Pages

Internet Starter Kit

HTML Workshop

Win a Free T-Shirt!

Macmillan Computer Publishing

Site Map

Talk to Us

CHECK OUT THE BOOKS IN THIS LIBRARY.

You'll find thousands of shareware files and over 1600 computer books designed for both technowizards and technophobes. You can browse through 700 sample chapters, get the latest news on the Net, and find just about anything using our massive search directories.

All Macmillan Computer Publishing books are available at your local bookstore.

We're open 24-hours a day, 365 days a year.

You don't need a card.

We don't charge fines.

And you can be as **LOUD** as you want.

The Information SuperLibrary

http://www.mcp.com/mcp/ ftp.mcp.com

Complete and Return this Card for a *FREE* Computer Book Catalog

Thank you for purchasing this book! You have purchased a superior computer book written expressly for your needs. To continue to provide the kind of up-to-date, pertinent coverage you've come to expect from us, we need to hear from you. Please take a minute to complete and return this self-addressed, postage-paid form. In return, we'll send you a free catalog of all our computer books on topics ranging from word processing to programming and the internet.

. ☐   Mrs. ☐   Ms. ☐   Dr. ☐

me (first) ☐☐☐☐☐☐☐☐☐☐☐   (M.I.) ☐   (last) ☐☐☐☐☐☐☐☐☐☐☐☐☐☐☐☐

ddress ☐☐☐☐☐☐☐☐☐☐☐☐☐☐☐☐☐☐☐☐☐☐☐☐☐☐☐☐☐☐

☐☐☐☐☐☐☐☐☐☐☐☐☐☐☐☐☐☐☐☐☐☐☐☐☐☐☐☐☐☐

ty ☐☐☐☐☐☐☐☐☐☐☐☐☐☐☐   State ☐☐   Zip ☐☐☐☐☐ ☐☐☐☐

one ☐☐☐ ☐☐☐ ☐☐☐☐   Fax ☐☐☐ ☐☐☐ ☐☐☐☐

mpany Name ☐☐☐☐☐☐☐☐☐☐☐☐☐☐☐☐☐☐☐☐☐☐☐☐☐☐☐

mail address ☐☐☐☐☐☐☐☐☐☐☐☐☐☐☐☐☐☐☐☐☐☐☐☐☐☐☐☐

Please check at least (3) influencing factors for purchasing this book.

ont or back cover information on book .... ☐
ecial approach to the content .... ☐
mpleteness of content .... ☐
thor's reputation .... ☐
blisher's reputation .... ☐
ok cover design or layout .... ☐
lex or table of contents of book .... ☐
ce of book .... ☐
ecial effects, graphics, illustrations .... ☐
her (Please specify): _____ ☐

How did you first learn about this book?

w in Macmillan Computer Publishing catalog .... ☐
commended by store personnel .... ☐
w the book on bookshelf at store .... ☐
commended by a friend .... ☐
ceived advertisement in the mail .... ☐
w an advertisement in: _____ ☐
ad book review in: _____ ☐
her (Please specify): _____ ☐

How many computer books have you purchased in the last six months?

is book only .... ☐   3 to 5 books .... ☐
ooks .... ☐   More than 5 .... ☐

4. Where did you purchase this book?

Bookstore .... ☐
Computer Store .... ☐
Consumer Electronics Store .... ☐
Department Store .... ☐
Office Club .... ☐
Warehouse Club .... ☐
Mail Order .... ☐
Direct from Publisher .... ☐
Internet site .... ☐
Other (Please specify): _____ ☐

5. How long have you been using a computer?

☐ Less than 6 months   ☐ 6 months to a year
☐ 1 to 3 years   ☐ More than 3 years

6. What is your level of experience with personal computers and with the subject of this book?

	With PCs	With subject of book
New	☐	☐
Casual	☐	☐
Accomplished	☐	☐
Expert	☐	☐

Source Code ISBN: 0-7897-0911-2

7. Which of the following best describes your job title?

Administrative Assistant ☐
Coordinator ☐
Manager/Supervisor ☐
Director ☐
Vice President ☐
President/CEO/COO ☐
Lawyer/Doctor/Medical Professional ☐
Teacher/Educator/Trainer ☐
Engineer/Technician ☐
Consultant ☐
Not employed/Student/Retired ☐
Other (Please specify): _____ ☐

8. Which of the following best describes the area of the company your job title falls under?

Accounting ☐
Engineering ☐
Manufacturing ☐
Operations ☐
Marketing ☐
Sales ☐
Other (Please specify): _____ ☐

9. What is your age?

Under 20 ....
21-29 ....
30-39 ....
40-49 ....
50-59 ....
60-over ....

10. Are you:

Male ....
Female ....

11. Which computer publications do you read regularly? (Please list)

_____
_____
_____
_____
_____
_____
_____
_____
_____
_____

Comments: _____
_____
_____

Fold here and scotch-tape to m